Stephenson Blake

The Last of the Old English Typefounders

Stephenson Blake and Company Limited
199 Upper Allen Street, Sheffield, 1924

Stephenson Blake

The Last of the Old English Typefounders

by

Roy Millington

OAK KNOLL PRESS

THE BRITISH LIBRARY

2002

First Edition,

Published by **Oak Knoll Press**,
310 Delaware Street, New Castle, Delaware, USA
Web:http://www.oakknoll.com
and **The British Library**
96 Euston Road, St. Pancras, London, NW1 2DB, UK

ISBN: 1-58456-086-X (USA)
ISBN: 0-7123-4795-X (UK)

Title: Stephenson-Blake
Author: Roy Millington
Typography: Spearhead Worldwide, Inc.
Publishing Director: J. Lewis von Hoelle

Library of Congress Cataloging-in-Publication Data

Millington, Roy.
   Stephenson Blake: the last of the Old English typefounders / by Roy Millington.-- 1st ed.
      p. cm.
   Includes bibliographical references and index.
   ISBN 1-58456-086-X (acid-free paper)
   1. Stephenson, Blake and Company--History. 2. Type and
   type-founding--England--History--19th century. 3. Type and
   type-founding--England--History--20th century. I. Title.

   Z250.A2 M654 2002
   686.2'21--dc21

                                                      2002072568

British Library Cataloguing-in-Publication Data
A CIP Record is available from The British Library

This work was printed in the United States of America on 60# archival,
acid-free paper meeting the requirements of the American Standard for
Permanence of Paper for Printed Library Materials.

Table of Contents

Chapter 1 A Historical Scenario: Sheffield Township, 1800   1
Chapter 2 The Caslons and the London Letter Founders   5
Chapter 3 Printers, Typefounders and the Sanspareil Matrix   13
Chapter 4 Partnerships and Associations   19
Chapter 5 Blake, Garnett and Company of Sheffield, 1819-29   27
Chapter 6 A Passing Partnership, 1830-1840   37
Chapter 7 Fashionable Types   47
Chapter 8 The Changing Scene, 1840-1870   59
Chapter 9 Mutual Friends and Competitors   67
Chapter 10 Techniques and Technicalities   77
Chapter 11 Types: Gentlemen and Players   83
Chapter 12 Owners in Waiting   89
Chapter 13 Making the Point   97
Chapter 14 The Broken Reed   103
Chapter 15 Social Nuances   111
Chapter 16 Punchcutters and Engravers   121
Chapter 17 Types of Influence   131
Chapter 18 The Call to Arms   139
Chapter 19 Ambiguous and Ambitious Strategies   145
Chapter 20 Humane Resource Management   157
Chapter 21 Cat and Mouse   165
Chapter 22 The Changing Face of Type   169
Chapter 23 Dynastic Succession   177
Chapter 24 Postwar Changes and Reorganisation   185
Chapter 25 The Ending of the Gutenberg Galaxy   195
Appendix   I References   211
Appendix II Index of Contents of *Printing Types*, 1924 Specimen Book   220
Appendix III A Checklist of Stephenson, Blake Typefaces.   225
Appendix IV Glossary   233
Appendix V Bibliography   241
Appendix VI The Ancestry of English Typefounding   245

List of Illustrations

Frontispiece: James Blake's croft, Upper Allen Street, 1819

fig 1 The tools of the craftsmen typefounder

fig 2 William Caslon I, brass letter for sand-cast type, 12-lines pica

fig 3 Blake and Garnett, 1826, sanspareil matrix and cast letter

fig 4 James Blake, 1785-1831

fig 5 Type specimen, Trafalgar No. 1, 1819

fig 6 Advertisement, Sheffield and Commercial Register, 10th December 1819

fig 7 Decorated types, Blake and Garnett specimen book, 1819

fig 8 Placard types, Blake and Stephenson, 1831

fig 9 Ornamented type, Blake and Stephenson, 1831

fig 10 Sans Surryph and Ornamented types, 1833

fig 11 Typefounders' Strike notice, Sheffield, 1843

fig 12 Polytyped ornaments, 1833

fig 13 Hairlines and Tuscan types, 1838

fig 14 Tuscan and Decorated types, Blake and Stephenson, 1834

fig 15 Specimens of Shaded and Decorated types, 1844

fig 16 Sheaf Works, Sheffield, 1840

fig 17 Advertisement, The Printers' Register, 1865

fig 18 London office and warehouse, 33 Aldersgate Street

fig 19 Railway polytypes, 1844

fig 20 Sir Henry Stephenson, KT, 1827-1904

fig 21 Stephenson, Blake, Woodworking Department, 1911

fig 22 Production activities, wood manufacturing, 1911

fig 23 Irish typefaces from Sir Charles Reed and Sons, 1904

fig 24 Fry's Ornamented specimen, 1907

fig 25 A displayed advertisement setting for Hogarth, 1906

fig 26 Across Marsden Lane, 1900

fig 27 Thomas White Smith, Chairman, H. W. Caslon and Sons Limited

fig 28 The typefoundry work in the late nineteenth century

fig 29 Baskerville Old Face type leaflet cover, 1909

fig 30 Art ornaments: Pomona series, 1924

fig 31 Sir Henry Stephenson, Bt. DSO, 1865-1947

fig 32 Specimen book, Printing Types, 1924

fig 33 Stephenson, Blake's 20th century Old Styles

fig 34 Artist drawing of Stephenson, Blake premises, 1924

fig 35 Modern No. 20 specimen sheet

fig 36 Robert Greaves Blake, DL, 1875-1947

fig 37 Granby Series, 1930

fig 38 Specimen setting of Bologna, 1946

fig 39 Specimen of scripts and rondes

fig 40 Sir Francis Stephenson, 1950s

fig 41 Managing Directors: Henry U. Stephenson and James Barbour Blake, 1969

fig 42 Charles Lyon Stephenson, 1984

fig 43 Fleet Street: re-equipping the national newspapers.

fig 44 Sorts service specimen sheet, 1980s

fig 45 Thomas James Blake, 1995

fig 46 Type casting department at Upper Allen Street, 1993

fig 47 The Consort Series

fig 48 The Foundry Bell

fig 49 Stephenson, Blake and Company Limited, 2002

fig 50 Tail Pieces, 1952

Acknowledgements

This history has been written as a result of some fifty years personal contact with Stephenson, Blake and Company Limited. Over this period of time, I became acquainted with almost every member of the staff from the Managing Directors down to the foundry labourers. So much of my time was spent on the premises that there were times when many thought that I was actually employed by the company. Although as honorary curator-archivist the work was interesting, there were times when the sheer volume of material spread around the company was daunting and what was really needed was a full-time, expert archivist. Much of the information and material gathered in order to write this history has been acquired over a very long period of time. A good deal of it has been used in lectures, talks and papers which I have produced on the history of typography in general and on the company in particular.

My thanks therefore relate not only to the present but also to the past. As a consequence, I owe a debt of gratitude to the former joint Managing Directors, James Barbour Blake and Henry Upton Stephenson for their kindness and indulgence over a period of fifty years. Equal thanks are also due to the former Managing Director, Charles L. Stephenson and to the current owner, Thomas James Blake.

Sadly, William Greaves Blake died in 2001, but not before his delightful monograph: *A South Yorkshire Family of Typefounders* was published. William Blake was not a typefounder but the principal partner in a leading Sheffield law practice. For many years he (and his lately-departed friend Dr. Stephen Bartolomé) suggested that I should complete and publish a history of the firm. We shared extensive correspondence over the years and I had access to his family history notes for which I am most grateful.

Thanks are due to Jack Baker, the former Sales Manager and to Geoff Hulett and Reg White formerly of the London Office for their advice. Thanks are also due to all the staff of Stephenson, Blake of yesteryears; all retired and many long dead. They were always most agreeably helpful and entered into the spirit of preserving the company's artefacts.

The research into the history of the company which Sydney Pollard undertook in the 1950s was of value. I can well appreciate the difficulties under which he laboured at that time and understand his disappointment in the fact that his work was never published. He went on to become Professor

Sydney Pollard and enjoyed a distinguished academic career in Economic History both at the University of Sheffield and at the University of Bielefeld in Germany.

Acknowledgement is due to Ian Spooner, Public Relations Office, the University of Sheffield for assistance with digital photography and imaging, and Mark Hutchinson, Trimac Services for retouching and digitising.

Thanks are due to the staff of that wonderful repository of printing knowledge: the St. Bride's Printing Library. Nigel Roche, the librarian and his assistants have been most helpful. The staff and support services of the Local History Department of the Sheffield City Libraries too are to be thanked for their most helpful assistance and for granting permission to reproduce from certain works. Thanks are also due to Keith Stubley, Chairman of J. W. Northend Limited for permission to use material from that company's history.

No account of the history of Stephenson, Blake can be allowed to pass without an acknowledgement of the work of Nicolas Barker, OBE, formerly of the British Library and now Chairman of the Trustees of the London Type Museum. As a result of his endeavours he not only ensured the Stephenson, Blake collection remained in Britain but also that the entire collection has been kept intact. Nicolas lent much personal support to the initial bid to keep the collection in Sheffield and when this failed to gain sufficient local support he ensured the collection was secured for the benefit of the London Type Museum.

A note of appreciation and thanks are also due to the British Library and the Oak Knoll Press, not only for presenting me with the opportunity of writing a history of the last English typefoundry—a business with which I have a remarkable series of life-time connections—but also for publishing the work. Thanks are also extended to John von Hoelle, Director of Publishing, the Oak Knoll Press for his help, encouragement and infinite patience.

Finally, the preparation of the work: the drafting of the manuscript, keyboarding, and preparation of the disks and initial editing would not have been possible without the dedicated and painstaking work of Mrs. Iris Harrison of Wakefield, my former PA and Secretary—the only person capable of deciphering my almost illegible handwriting.

Roy Millington

Introduction

T HIS is the story of an early nineteenth century provincial type-
foundry which rose, in its heyday, to become a national institution.
The history of Stephenson, Blake and Company Limited of
Sheffield is an account of five generations of two Sheffield families: the
Stephensons and the Blakes, whose business spans almost two hundred
years.

As the custodian, by acquisition, of the historical legacy of the Old
English typefoundries, it can trace its business ancestry to the very beginnings of printing in England. The company grew from very modest beginnings until it came to dominate the British typefounding industry. It is a
story of calculated successes, of battles with rivals and of diversification.

It is also a contemporary story of how the coming of the computer has
revolutionised the whole science and art of printing and has swept away the
five hundred years of letterpress tradition.

Histories of businesses all too often abound with facts, figures and
statistics, which, for the majority of readers, are boring and irrelevant.
Meanwhile, the examples of specimens and ornaments have been selected
to reflect design 'tastes' of yesteryears rather than examples of good
design. The inclusion of detail has been limited to that which is relevant to
the narrating of an intriguing story. Particular cognisance has been taken of
the changing technical and social milieu in which the company operated.

From the first, Stephenson, Blake has been a company which set its
products and its business dealings on the highest plain of quality and
integrity. Uniquely, its owners have also been its managers. For over five
generations the principals managed the business either as Chairmen and
Managing Directors or as Executive Directors when, all too frequently,
other businesses had come to rely on professionally qualified executives
recruited from outside their companies.

The principals have also been gentlemen and, as gentlemen, they
demanded the same standards of behaviour from their employees, their
associates and their customers. In the twenty-first century, the rules and
conventions of Victorian, Edwardian and pre-1939 Britain may seem
quaint and unacceptable when measured against today's stiflingly politi-
cally-correct mores. Whilst autocratic management at its best and at its
worst was the order of the day, Stephenson, Blake created and provided

regular work for local families and it cared for the welfare of the employees and for their families. The success and profitability of the venture also
enabled the principals to engage in civic, educational and charitable works
to the greater benefit of the local community.

That typefounding would eventually run its final course was a situation
well understood by the owners. In these times of intensive corporate investment, where shareholders' money is freely applied, sometimes to the disadvantage of the investor, it is important to remember that Stephenson, Blake
and Company was, and is, a private limited company. In any venture
whether commercial or charitable, the financing came from the resources
of the two families. Whilst over five generations the Stephensons and the
Blakes continued their involvement in the firm, they also invested their
profits in industries and ventures far removed from the narrow world of
typefounding.

Now, subsequent generations follow different mores and manners and
seek new horizons. The successors of the Stephenson and the Blake families are no longer typefounders; for commercial typefounding has become
a thing of the past.

Stephenson Blake

The Last of the Old English Typefounders

James Blake's croft Upper Allen Street, Sheffield, 1819

Chapter 1

A Historical Scenario: Sheffield Township, 1800

A T the turn of the eighteenth century, the township of Sheffield in the West Riding of Yorkshire was ill-regarded. It had grown round the site of a long-demolished Norman Castle at the point where the river Sheaf joined the waters of the Don. In succeeding centuries the town gradually extended along the valleys of five small fast-flowing Pennine rivulets which flowed into the river Don. Each of these rivulets had been progressively dammed since the sixteenth century to provide for the scores of water-powered workshops which lined the banks. There were abundant supplies of timber for charcoal production, varieties of local sandstone which were quarried for the cutting of grindstones and rich seams of coal for coke production but, the iron which was needed, came from Scandinavia as the local supplies of ore had been exhausted in the century before.

Although Sheffield as a centre of manufacture of knives and cutting tools had long been established, geographical isolation made the township and its population of approximately 46,000 (1801 census) singularly insular. By exploiting the natural resources, the local population had developed a variety of highly specialised skills producing knives, scythes, sickles and all manner of sharp-edged implements[1]. These were skills which were to be jealously guarded and in 1624, the Sheffield cutlers petitioned to establish a chartered company in order to obtain exclusive trading rights and privileges. But the business of the cutlers and the supporting trades was constantly fraught with difficulties. In dry or drought summers, the flow of water from the fast flowing rivulets was greatly reduced, limiting the operation of the water wheels. In the depth of winter the lack of daylight and the freezing of the mill ponds again imposed restrictions on production. The local economy was also all too frequently vulnerable to the uncertain state of trade both at home and abroad.

Up until the middle of the nineteenth century, industry comprised a complex of small specialised workshops. The masters, the craftsmen and their families coexisted in cottages and crofts—cottages and houses with gardens and smallholdings attached—which were sited near or alongside the workshops. It was a community which still, out of necessity, maintained an interest in cultivating smallholdings.

During the latter part of the eighteenth century the local industry had benefited by the introduction of two metallurgical innovations. In 1740, Benjamin Huntsman, a local iron master, developed a process for smelting crucible steel. This made it possible to produce a particular type of steel which could support finer, sharper and more durable cutting edges. It also provided a material which could be cast into shape, forged and rolled into bars for making dies, punches and machine parts which required durability.[2]

Although the cutlery industry primarily needed steel for the production of tableware—knives, penknives and pocket knives—it also needed nonferrous metals and a variety of other materials to provide for the making of handles. The making of foldout spring pocketknives and penknives for example required numerous small items: springs, side plates, wire, rivets and scales made of brass or of other materials. The supply chain of needs and the skills required to meet them became increasingly technical and diverse. Smelters rolled silver and nonferrous metals to form sheet-plate. Dies were cut in crucible steel to stamp out blank shapes for forks, spoons and tableware. Punches were cut by counter-punching and filing the ends of small fillets of crucible steel to make trademarks and raise or punch decoration on table and silverware.

Although by the 1800s steam power was being introduced, much of the local industry was still very dependent on water power and the particular and peculiar skills of the craftsmen. There were clear and distinct divisions of labour. There were cutlers who were blade forgers, others grinders. Some would specialise in forging larger tools such as scythes and sickles. There were tool-makers supplying implements for coopers, shipwrights, wheelwrights and the like. Others would work in the grinding hull with the sandstone wheels revolving in a trough of water—cooling the blade being ground and washing away the waste. It was dangerous and unhealthy work. Supporting the cutling of blades, were those who assembled the flatware;

dressing knives, forks, penknives and pocketknives with handles and scales in a variety of products: silver, bone, tortoiseshell, ivory and mother of pearl. There were also many other supporting trades: iron-founders, steel-makers, die-sinkers, mark-makers, silver-rollers, scale-makers all contributing to the manufacturing processes. As an apprentice, a craftsman cutler would have served an apprenticeship with one of the jobbing cutlers known as *little mesters*—probably a working owner of a family business which had for several generations been members of the Cutlers' Company of Hallamshire and would have subsequently become self-employed, renting a water-powered tilt-hammer, a forging shop or grinding-wheel facilities from the owner of a 'wheel'.

The second metallurgical innovation came in 1780 when a metalsmith, Thomas Boulsover, created a method of producing silver-plated copper by fusing fine silver on to the surface of copper plate. This fused metal which came to be known as *Sheffield Plate*, was the stimuli for the development of a whole new series of design and artistic metal-craft techniques.

Yet, even at the beginning of the nineteenth century, the fashioning of metal was still only achieved by a relatively limited range of manual or machine-assisted skills. Metal could be smelted by heating and shaped by casting in a mould. It could be forged under a hammer. It could be rolled, ground, stamped or engraved. However, one technique which was universally applied was that of filing. The craftsman filer was always regarded highly for his skill of hand and eye in accurately reducing, fitting and engineering a product. However, a skilled filer was only as good as his files. In consequence, the file-maker, known locally as a *nicker-pecker*, held the key to the final shaping of metal.[3] The filemaker's work entailed the 'cutting' of rows of teeth by striking a hardened chisel-like punch into a softened steel blank which was subsequently tempered and hardened. It was hard and laborious work in which women were frequently employed. Some were out-workers who cut the teeth of the files in their own cottage workshops.

However, by the beginning of the nineteenth century the social and economic scene was beginning to change. Under the pretext of improving agricultural methods, the Enclosure Acts had effectively transferred ownership of the common lands to a small but powerful group of local land owners, who quickly took the opportunity of leasing their land for industrial and urban development and, particularly in the case of the Sheffield township, of leasing rights for the mining of the rich coal seams which lay close to the surface.

Meanwhile, the inhabitants of the town appeared as complex as its cottage industries. Public behaviour ranged from diligent, industrious activity to excessive drunkenness and disorder. In contrast there were many followers of the various Nonconformist faiths, coupled with strongly argued liberal political views. Whether the issue of the day was the politics of the Corn Laws, anti-combination demonstrations or Free Trade issues, there was always a vociferous voice of contention. The weekly news sheets were publications which contained editorials with strong libertarian views which frequently resulted in their editors either fleeing the country or being imprisoned. In contrast, the cultural and political heart of the township and the government of it was vested in a relatively small group of *petit bourgeoisie:* land owners, medical men, clergy and lawyers whom the general population regarded with some disdain.

As the nineteenth century opened, Sheffield, in Hallamshire—lying amidst sylvan, rolling hills situated betwixt the West Riding of Yorkshire and the County of Derbyshire—was a filthy, ill-begotten industrial township; its five rivulets were stinking and polluted open sewers, its valleys seemingly eternally shrouded in smoke and the majority of its uncouth inhabitants accommodated in overcrowded hovels.[4]

Chapter 2

The Caslons and the London Letterfounders of the Eighteenth Century

MANUFACTURERS in Sheffield during the late eighteenth century were either producing utilitarian products such as agricultural implements and hand tools or, in contrast, high-value luxury items such as cutlery and roll-plated silverware. It was not a unique situation. Throughout Britain specialised manufacturing was developing rapidly. It brought with it times of prosperity and times of economic distress. In the developing urban centres, life was hard and there was little provision for the education of the working class and their children. Gaining employment, and the learning and acquiring of an industrial skill or even of being employed supporting such skills by labouring work, was of prime importance. The nature of the products and manufactures was such that the people who made them had little need either of literary skills or the printed word. It was a condition which existed throughout most of the Kingdom. Voluntary and charitable foundations and the Church struggled to provide rudimentary education and it was only in London, Edinburgh, Dublin, Oxford and Cambridge, and a handful of ancient cities that there was any semblance of literary enlightenment and culture or significant printing and publishing activity.

As a consequence, the quality of printed works produced in Britain can best be described as utilitarian. Typographical and press-work standards were, in general, poor when compared with the best of the European printers and publishers. Whilst a number of discerning typefounders and printers, conscious of a need to improve the quality of their output, purchased type, punches and matrices from continental sources, the general situation remained. Updike summed up the situation exactly . . . *the English printer* [was not] *very skilful or tasteful in the arrangement of types—good or bad; and thus English books did not equal those printed by good presses on the Continent—either in workmanship, beauty, or correctness.*[1]

The supporting art of typefounding was equally mediocre in terms of typeface design and the quality of the product. Until almost the middle of the eighteenth century, English punchcutters and typefounders made little contribution to the development of typography—printers and typefounders alike being influenced by the Dutch typefounding industry. Talbot Baines Reed in *A History of the Old English Letter Foundries* declared that as a result of . . . *the intimate relations which existed at that period between English printers and Dutch founders . . . There was probably more Dutch type in England between 1700 and 1720 than there was English. The Dutch artists appeared . . . to have the secret of the true shape of the Roman letter; their punches were more carefully finished, their matrices better justified, and their types of better metal, and better dressed, than any which our country could produce.*[2]

From the time of the cutting of the first humanistic Roman type form by Nicholas Jenson in 1470, the calligraphically originated Roman letter design had dominated Western Europe. For three hundred years individual lettercutters, influenced by cultural fashion and regional characteristics, had created variations which, although broadly known as Old Face, nevertheless reflected a unique historical development lineage: Venetian, Aldine, French, Dutch and English.

However, the eighteenth century marked the beginning of the end of the Old Face-derived tradition. The preparation of an exclusive typeface for the Imprimerie Royale du Louvre, designed by the *Academie Francaise* and the subsequent cutting and casting which began in the 1690s, of the *Romains du Roi* by Phillipe Grandjean and his successors, marked the beginning of a century of typeface design innovation. Although, the exclusivity of the royal types remained, due to the constraints which were imposed, there were Continental letter cutters and founders whose designs emulated the innovation and a significant stage was reached when the Parisian typefounder, Pierre Simon Fournier, began to cast, in 1740, letter forms which subsequently came to be identified as *transitionals*.

Meanwhile, two contrasting typeface design developments were taking place in England. William Caslon of Birmingham, an engraver of weaponry was persuaded to cut an alphabet of brass letters for gold-block finishing. It was a commission which proved to be highly successful. As a result Caslon turned his skill to punch-cutting and typefounding. Encouraged by early success he removed from Birmingham to London.

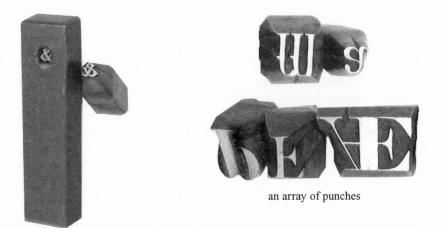

an array of punches

punch and struck, unjustified matrix

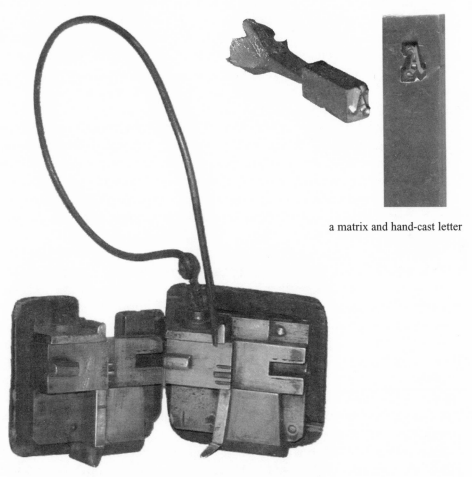

a matrix and hand-cast letter

a rat-tailed hand casting mould in open position

Fig 1 The tools of the craftsmen typefounder

Caslon's Roman—whilst derived from and influenced by the Dutch type-faces which dominated the English printing scene—projected a sharpness and idiosyncratic elegance reminiscent of the Aldine and French typefaces of the sixteenth and early seventeenth centuries—a characteristic which had tended to become lost by the latter day Dutch lettercutters. Caslon issued his first broadsheet of specimens in 1730 and for the first time in the annals of the English printing industry there emerged a letterfounder whose typefaces equalled, in quality and design, those of the Continental founders. Consequently, in the English-speaking world Caslon's Roman was successful and the design remained fashionable until the 1760s.

However, the design of the Caslon Roman was anachronistic, and, whilst the cutting of a traditional Roman form produced an essentially English variant, its appearance represented a step backwards in relation to the emerging Continental designs. By the 1760s, the popularity of Caslon's letter began to be challenged by the designs of John Baskerville of Birmingham, a non-traditional, private printer. Baskerville was a wealthy merchant; one-time writing master, designer and manufacturer of japanned goods, who had turned his interest towards printing. As an expert calligra-pher he had studied the emerging transitional alphabets of the Imprimerie Royale du Louvre, of Pierre Simon Fournier and other Continental founders whose designs were moving away from the Aldine model. The merits of Caslon's letter were weighed against Baskerville's and the issue was the subject of considerable debate amongst printers and the English literati.

Subsequently, the typographical and commercial influence of Caslon's and Baskerville's designs moved in different directions. Although Baskerville's adventure into printing was relatively short-lived, his work represented the first attempt by an English typefounder to emulate the increasingly dominant Continental trend and was to become a major influ-ence on later English typefounders such as Fry, Thorne and John Bell. Of even more significance, was the influence he brought to bear on the early nineteenth century generation of Continental type designers such as Bodoni and Didot.

Although in many respects Caslon's Roman from the outset might be considered to have been *fin de siecle*, it would probably not have had endur-ing success had it not been for the political situation in Europe and the coincidence of Britain's colonial expansion. The British Government's mercantilist policy ensured that British goods and manufactures went to the newly established colonies and to those countries with whom Britain had close trade links. Caslon's types were well-designed and well-cast but the success of the foundry lay primarily in the opportunities offered by being in business in the right place and at the right time.

Fig 2 William Caslon I, brass letter for sand-cast type, 12-lines pica

Meanwhile, the success of the Caslon letterfoundry continued. William Caslon I took his elder son, William Caslon II, into the business in 1742. The Caslons, father and son, not only became first-class typefounders but they also proved to be sound business men. With their business established in Chiswell Street in the heart of eighteenth century London they became affluent and were able to rise rapidly to some degree of social eminence.

On the death of William Caslon I, in 1766, the foundry passed to Caslon II, who in turn, brought his two sons into the business. Following the death of William Caslon II in 1778 the business came under the direction of his widow, Elizabeth Caslon and her two sons, William III and Henry. In the course of some fifty years the Caslon letter foundry enjoyed immeasurable success. However, by the 1780s, typographical fashions were changing. It was becoming increasingly difficult to profit from casting a typeface which was now unfashionable, even though it had successfully dominated the English-speaking world for so many years. The business was under threat, particularly from smaller foundries which were cutting exciting new faces, novelties and early versions of the new Continentally inspired modern face.

The Caslons began to disagree. Their business policy lacked direction. William Caslon III wished to innovate. He was forward-looking and could see business being lost to competitors. New designs of modern types and novelty letter faces were needed. William disagreed with his mother and his brother, widow Elizabeth and Henry Caslon, who were of the view that the original Caslon design had been, and continued to be, a success and that the trend towards the modern design was merely an ephemeral one. Finally, in 1792, it was agreed that William Caslon III should take his share out of the business. However, the situation was one of cause and occasion. Seemingly, the cause of William Caslon III's break from the family business was the inability of Henry and Elizabeth Caslon to accept the changing demands of typographical fashion. The occasion was the death of Joseph Jackson, a successful London typefounder, and with it the opportunity to acquire his foundry, which, at the time was one London's most respected. Historically, the situation was not without a touch of irony.

In earlier times, two London letterfounders, Thomas Cotterell and Joseph Jackson had both served an apprenticeship under William Caslon I, and during that time were allegedly employed in the more menial tasks of the typefounding operation—the Caslons keeping the techniques of punch-cutting secret by locking themselves in their workshop . . . *but the two apprentices . . . wishing to master the whole art in which they were engaged to perform only a minor part, bored a hole in the wainscot, and observing the Caslons at work, thereafter practised assiduously and qualified in the whole art.*[3]

After completing their apprenticeships, Jackson and Cotterell continued to work at the Caslon Foundry. However, in 1757, a dispute arose over working conditions and Jackson and Cotterell—now fully fledged craftsmen journeymen—became involved in an argument with William Caslon I and, as a result, were dismissed. This led to Cotterell and Jackson setting up together in partnership as lettercutters and typefounders. The arrangement lasted only two years. Jackson left the business and joined the Royal Navy. Thomas Cotterell now went his own way. Setting up as typefounder in premises in Nevil's Court, off Fleet Street, he was commissioned to cut and re-cut a number of distinguished founts and is said to have been the first letterfounder to produce poster-letter patterns in order to cast large, proscription letter in sand. When Thomas Cotterell died in 1785 the stock from his Nevil's Court foundry passed to Robert Thorne.

Meanwhile, Joseph Jackson having served four years in the Royal Navy as an armourer, initially rejoined Cotterell in 1763. A year later, in 1764, having received 'prize' money earned whilst at sea, he set himself up in business in Cock Lane. As his business grew more successful and increased in size, he removed the foundry to larger premises in Salisbury Square. In his time Jackson produced a whole stream of exotic and learned letter founts of considerable merit as well as several distinguished founts of English Roman. Much of the later success of Jackson's foundry can be attributed to his one-time apprentice-cum-manager, Vincent Figgins. By 1792, Joseph Jackson had been in business in his own right for 28 years, but at the age of 59 years he succumbed to a severe attack of scarlet fever and died. His death presented an immediate problem for Figgins who, although invited to purchase the foundry found himself unable to raise the money.

The prospective sale of the Jackson foundry in Salisbury Square presented William Caslon III, with a promising business opportunity. With the money received from his share of the family business, he purchased it and, almost immediately, relocated it from Salisbury Square to premises in Finsbury Square. Unfortunately in 1794, after two years' trading, he became insolvent whereupon he sold the Finsbury Square premises and restarted the business back in Salisbury Square.

There were now two Caslon letter foundries: 'William Caslon and Son' trading from Salisbury Square and 'William Caslon and Successors' located in Chiswell Street. Following the death of Caslon II in 1778, the name of the company had remained unchanged, trading from Chiswell Street as William Caslon and Son (1784). When Caslon III broke away from the original business he began preparing a specimen book entitled *A Specimen of Printing Types by William Caslon, Letter-Founder to the King* It was printed by Charles Whittington and was dated 1796—appearing as it did two years after the bankruptcy. Initially, the bulk of the stock of the Caslon III foundry was that of Joseph Jackson, supplemented by exotic and early English founts from the original Caslon Foundry which were cast from matrices which he appears to have acquired before he left the family business. Between 1795 and 1800, his specimen books were issued under the proprietorship of William Caslon, then in 1803 the business title changed to William Caslon and Son, as William Caslon IV joined the business.

However, these were parlous times. Economic conditions were uncertain. The French Revolution had encouraged fractious groups at home, whilst the oncoming Napoleonic Wars with France affected trade at home and overseas. The twenty or so years of war (1795-1815) created a watershed of change both economically and technically. British industry was changing from handcrafted output and moving towards machine and mechanically orientated production methods. Although mechanisation and innovation in the printing industry would be slower in comparison with other industries, the changes in typographical style and fashion were remarkable.

The gracious and gradual evolution of the transitional type faces gave way to the mechanistic Moderns only to be augmented by the appearance of Fat Blacks—typefaces with exaggerated thin and thick strokes, ornamented with hairline serifs, which began to appear in great abundance. The long out-of-fashion gothic reappeared in heavily redrawn grotesque forms. In the printing of text matter the sharp serifs and contrasting strokes of modern faces became the fashion of the day, whilst the classical Roman typefaces were, in the meantime, consigned to the melting pot. However, as the nineteenth century opened another significant change was taking place within the typefounding companies. The secrecy surrounding the techniques of letterfounding was beginning to pass and the organisation of the work pattern was changing. The distinguished English letterfounders of the eighteenth century, William Caslon I and II, Thomas Cotterell, Joseph Jackson and their contemporaries were at the heart of their enterprises—they were skilled punchcutters but, as Reed observed: . . . *when typefounders no longer cut their own letter-punches, the cutter became an anonymous mechanic.*[4]

Chapter 3

Printers, Typefounders and the Sanspareil Matrix

EVEN by the late eighteenth century, the casting of type in text sizes had changed little since the time of Gutenberg and Caxton. The quality of the printing surfaces and the density of the type body were frequently variable and the production of any type in sizes larger than 5-lines pica was technically difficult. An attempt to overcome this was made in the 1760s by Robert Cotterell who developed a means of casting large-sized characters, variously termed by typefounders and printers as 'placard', 'poster' or 'proscription letter'. Cotterell modelled and cut master patterns in brass. These patterns were subsequently used to mould the character in sand laid within a moulding box—the moulded sand providing a matrix form. Whilst the technique was practical, the quality of the resulting output was singularly indifferent owing to the bubbles and the air voids which occurred during the casting process. The resultant typographical characters needed to be dressed and the printing surface burnished. Nevertheless, the method was adopted and during the period 1766-1810, the principal English letterfounders cast or offered placard types ranging from 5-lines to 19-lines pica, but trading in these large-sized letters appears to have been somewhat desultory and specimen books make little of their availability.

About 1808, the William Caslon (Junior) Typefoundry, (Caslon IV) issued, quite randomly, two single specimen sheets showing large sized letter, which have been described as displaying 'Sanspareil 8-lines Pica and

Sanspareil 15-lines Pica'. These were large-sized types which were uniquely described as sanspareil. However, when Berry and Johnson[1] published their work in 1935, the location of these two specimen sheets was unknown, reference to their existence having been taken from the catalogue of the *Typothetae* of New York in 1896. As these specimens had not been seen since being catalogued in 1896, the veracity of the description must be left open to question. James Mosley advises that the date which is indicated as *circa 1808* may be purely conjectural as *sanspareil matrices seem to have been new in 1810*.[2]

More tangible evidence is to be found elsewhere. Slater, Bacon of Sheffield produced a specimen sheet of Improved Printing Types in 1809.[3] It seems likely that this is probably the same as that issued by the William Caslon Foundry (IV), dated by Berry and Johnson as circa 1808, the dating of which is dismissed by James Mosley. Although the making of sanspareil matrices was described in *Caslon's Circular* published in July 1877, it is claimed that there was a much earlier *Caslon Circular,* dated January 1810, which announced the introduction of types cast from sanspareil matrices.[4]

The phenomena of why, in a relatively isolated northern township, with a printing industry of little consequence, a typefounding business came into being is a mystery to be unravelled. It appears to have to have arisen in the following circumstances: about 1797, John Slater (1757-1831) a bookseller and printer in business at 56 Westbar, Sheffield, formed a partnership with another local bookseller-printer, William Bower (1765-1833) trading as Slater and Bower. In 1806, William Bower withdrew. Slater then formed a partnership with another local printer, Clay Bacon (1771-1836). Trading as Slater, Bacon and Company they began to diversify into typefounding and issued a specimen sheet of sanspareil types in 1809. However, towards the end of the year, Slater left the partnership to establish his own printing and bookselling business in George Street, whereupon William Bower and his son, George Bower, joined partnership with Clay Bacon, establishing Bower, Bacon and Bower, Printers and Typefounders. Although Clay Bacon's son, Henry Andrew Bacon (1794-1838) also joined the company in 1808 as an apprentice printer under the supervision of his father, the prime purpose of forming the partnership appears to have been directed towards establishing a typefoundry.

The products of the typefounding operation quickly became available. Trading as Bower, Bacon and Bower they produced a *Specimen Book of Improved Types* comprising 32 leaves which was published in 1810.[5] This specimen book carried 14 leaves of placard types, ranging in size from 5-lines to 22-lines pica. The existence of such a range of sizes of large-sized letter appears to indicate that a substantial amount of preparatory work must have been in progress some years prior to the date shown on the title page and the specimens displayed in the book could well represent the products of some four years' work. Its contents present a unique innovation for within the 28 specimen leaves there are two distinct categories of type. Analysed, there are:

(a) 14 leaves of modern-face body types ranging from pica to 4-lines pica;
(b) 14 leaves of sanspareil letter comprising:

        2 folios of 5-lines pica
        2 folios of 7-lines pica
        1 folio of 8-lines pica
        2 folios of 9-lines pica
        1 folio of 9/10-lines pica
        1 folio of 12-lines pica
        2 folios of 14-lines pica
        1 folio of 16-lines pica
        1 folio of 19-lines pica
        1 folio of 22 lines pica

The leaves of modern-face letter would have been produced by normal punch-matrix-mould casting, except that the striking of matrices above 2-lines pica was most likely effected by the use of a fly-press in order to force the punch, under considerable pressure, into the blank copper matrix. Beyond 6-lines pica this was physically impossible, hence the development of the sanspareil method. In the case of the 1810 specimen book, the production of the 5-, 6-, 7-, 8-, 9-lines pica, 9/10-lines, 12-lines, 14-lines, 16-lines, 19-lines and 22-lines of pica were all produced by the sanspareil method.

Bower, Bacon and Bower described these founts as 'Improved Types'. It is a description which is ambiguous. The term was first used by Robert Thorne as a description of the Modern typefaces he had cut for his specimen book which he issued in 1803. On first sight it may seem to refer to the early nineteenth century enthusiasm for the sharp featured modern type face. Alternatively it may be considered to be a description advertising the improved quality of larger-sized type cast by the sanspareil matrix method.

The sanspareil matrix technique involved fretting out the profile of a letter in stencil outline style. These profiles were cut out of brass plate, the thickness of which represented the height of the shoulder of the typeface. After the stencil profile was cut, the face of the matrix was formed by pinning (riveting) a back plate over the stencil. A specially designed mould

Fig 3 Blake and Garnett, 1826, 24-lines Pica Antique, sanspareil matrix and cast letter

was developed. This is described by latter-day usage as a barrow mould so termed by reason of the two short handles which were used to agitate the mould and matrix as the molten metal (an alloy of lead, tin and antimony) was poured into the casting aperture. The movement of the mould during the pouring and casting operation served to dissipate air trapping and bubbles in the metal. The quality of sanspareil cast type proved to be far superior to that which was sand-moulded.

Both Clay Bacon and William Bower were printers and as such it is highly unlikely that they had the skill and expertise to cut punches, strike matrices, or make moulds—particularly as they had ventured into type-founding quite late in their working lives. Whether, when they set up their foundry, they acquired punches, matrices and moulds for the production of their body types by purchase is an unknown factor.

However, within the township of Sheffield there were many craftsmen in the 'artistic' trades who could readily transfer and adapt their skills. Punch-and mark-making was a common enough practice as it was a requirement of the Cutlers' Company of Hallamshire that all cutlery and related manu-factures should be struck by a registered maker's mark. The finishing of flatware[6] also frequently involved shaping, engraving and decorating a range of materials to provide knife handles and, since Boulsover's invention of rolled-silver, there had been a considerable growth in the making of hollow ware in Sheffield Plate which had attracted into the town a growing number of silversmiths.

About 1805, a young silversmith, William Henry Garnett, lately out of his apprenticeship, undertook work as a lettercutter and engraver, firstly for Slater and Bacon and then for Bower, Bacon and Bower. Born on the 8th February 1782, he was the son of William and Frances Garnet, and christened as William Henry Garnet.[7] Superficial research appears to link his family to John Garnet (1736 to 1753) who is recorded as being the first printer in the township of Sheffield .

Whether Garnett was employed by Slater Bacon and subsequently by Bower, Bacon and Bower in a full-time capacity or whether he was engaged on a casual basis is not known. Hearsay sources of long-standing describe him as 'a good general mechanic who could turn his hand to anything'. Producing punches and matrices involved techniques much akin to the work of a silversmith. However, the making of moulds entailed a different set of skills. It was the work of a mechanic—the practical engineer-toolmaker. Principally, such craftsmen worked in iron or steel, the raw material being fashioned by casting molten metal, hammering, forging, grinding and filing.

The accuracy of their work depended on the use of callipers, depthgauges, squares and levels which craftsmen made for themselves. This was a starting point and the quality and accuracy of these artefacts determined the degree of precision which a mechanic could exercise. In the absence of accurate measuring instruments such as the micrometer, precision was a feature which could only be achieved as a result of meticulous and painstaking craftsmanship.

It was from amongst this early group of Sheffield printer-typefounders that the idea sprang of creating the sanspareil matrix. However, neither, Slater, the Bowers nor the Bacons were practical mechanics. Garnett was. He was also, an engraver and probably familiar with printing techniques—particularly as it is likely that one of his antecedents was John Garnet. This tribute to his skill is further endorsed by his subsequent work as a typefounder and stereotyper. It is not possible to know of Garnett's role, status, or of his ambitions at this time. In his later activities certain personal traits appear which seem to indicate a general lack of satisfaction with his lot in life.

However, credit for the invention of the sanspareil matrix method was assigned not to Garnett but to William Caslon IV. Thomas Hansard in his magisterial work, *Typographia,* published in 1825, is generous in his praise for the sanspareil matrix technique, citing it as . . . *the greatest improvement in the art of typefounding that has taken place in modern times.*[8] Caslon IV never refuted the credit ascribed by Hansard, nor made any known attempt to attribute it to Garnett. However, the idea was never patented and this is surprising in view of the fact that the Caslons (III and IV) patented several innovations, including a method of producing wedge-shaped types for cylindrical impression and took out several other patents unconnected with typefounding and printing.

William Caslon IV entered the family business in 1803 and, by 1807, had become the proprietor on the demise of his father. He had joined the business in difficult times. Trade was particularly bad due to the wars with France and this is reflected generally in the dearth of type specimen books issued by the English typefounders during this period. As for the direction of the Caslon Foundry under Caslon IV, apart from the two insubstantial and unsubstantiated specimen sheets issued about 1808-10, which displayed sanspareil type, the foundry only issued two full specimen books, one in 1796 and the final specimen book issued in 1816 which appeared under the trading name of William Caslon Junior (late William Caslon and Son).[9] Meanwhile, the two unique single specimen sheets of sanspareil, which remain unrelated to any other founts, appears to support a view that the invention of the sanspareil method cannot be ascribed to either William Caslon IV or his foundry.

Chapter 4

Partnerships and Associations

A LTHOUGH the social cohesion and economic interdependence of the *little mesters* and their workers in the township of Sheffield in the early nineteenth century appeared to be close, they were in reality, often very distant, mean and bitter. Many of the mesters and their like were clearly seeking to improve their lot in life and, all too often did so at the expense of their rivals, associates and their workers. On Sundays they upheld the moral and social virtues of the Christian doctrine in the churches, chapels and Sunday schools, on other days they were driven by a hard-bitten work-ethic philosophy of value for money, maximisation of profit from minimum outlay and a self-centred colloquial belief of: *if th'a ever does owt for nowt, all'ys do it for thi'sen.*[1]

Such attitudes and relationships must have existed in the Bower, Bacon and Bower partnership. By 1819, the principals claimed the foundry had been in existence for some thirteen years. The foundry premises were situated on the north bank of the river Don at White Rails, Bridgehouses, a hamlet about half a mile from the town centre. The three principals were William Bower, aged 37, George Bower, his brother, aged 33 and Clay Bacon aged 47. Also serving in the firm was Clay's son, Henry Andrew Bacon, aged 24, and William Henry Garnett, aged 36.

Whilst William Bower and Clay Bacon were the main partners, it was Garnett, who had been employed since about 1805, who was the key craftsman. His skill acquired as a silversmith and engraver had developed further and extended into the art of punch-cutting and matrix-making. Circumstantial evidence seems to point to the fact that the sanspareil matrix and mould was most likely his invention. Whilst Caslon IV had shown sanspareil types in the form of two specimen sheets, it is possible that the types which were used to print these were either supplied by Bower Bacon and Bower as cast letter or that Bower, Bacon and Bower supplied sanspareil matrices and moulds to the Caslon Foundry. It seems likely that Garnett as the workman-inventor, would not initially have been conscious of the value of his innovation, particularly if he was given little credit. If this was the case, the dissatisfaction which he is said to have felt, was probably well-founded—particularly as the two principals were not prepared to allow him into the partnership. There was another possible reason why all may not have been well within the partnership. In a business such as Bower, Bacon and Bower, which advertised its services as printers and typefounders, it is likely that there would be a constant clash of interests as to whether their efforts should be directed towards printing or typefounding—particularly as the latter was a specialisation which was very much London-customer based. It is not too difficult to imagine the problems also created by Clay Bacon's son, Henry Andrew Bacon who, at the age of 24 was not only an ambitious printer, but a politically inclined liberal reformer. In November 1819, he left the Foundry to set up a printing works in nearby Snig Hill in order to establish a weekly newspaper, *The Sheffield Independent and Commercial Register.*

Meanwhile, internal dissension within the company worsened and Garnett decided to make preparations to set himself up in business. By 1818, Garnett and his friend and working colleague John Stephenson, had begun making and assembling typefounding tools and equipment in secret. A workshop was set up in the attic of the Garnett family home in Bridgehouses—a hamlet quite close to the site of the Bower, Bacon and Bower foundry.

Whilst John Stephenson's trade was described as a fender maker, his craft skills like others in the family, were wide-ranging. His father, John Stephenson senior, his brother George and his cousin John, worked together in business as diesinkers, ornamental chasers and general mechanics. However, such was his own skill, that even by his early twenties, he had acquired the reputation of being *the best filer in Sheffield.*

Finally, Garnett and Stephenson revealed their intentions. They severed their connection with the Bower foundry and set up in business as typefounders. On first sight the decision appears to have been somewhat foolhardy. However, there may have been other factors which influenced them. Were the two encouraged to believe that by setting up independently they could with, Garnett's expertise, sell their services to the Bower foundry for a better reward? Had Caslon IV offered them work? If, as is contended, Garnett was the inventor of the sanspareil matrix method, then Caslon would certainly have known of Garnett's skill and maybe felt that he deserved to be offered some reward.

Having taken the decision, the two partners quickly found that they needed capital. John Stephenson's father suggested that an approach might be made to James Blake, a master filemaker, with whom he was well acquainted and who supplied his family with files. Maybe Blake would be prepared to advance money or join the partnership?

James Blake, at the age of 33, was a somewhat daunting character. He was tall and willowy but was blind in one eye. It is recounted that as a baby a spark which flew out of the kitchen fire had burned his right eyeball. This unfortunate handicap left him looking somewhat grim and forbidding in appearance. As a boy he had been apprenticed to the family filemaking business, Thomas and Joseph Blake and Company. The antecedents of the Blake family emerged in the south of the West Riding of Yorkshire during the eighteenth century. At first they were engaged in the mining of coal but later moved into Sheffield as merchants and then as cutlers and filemakers. As the nineteenth century opened they were seen to be amongst the more successful of the *little mester* families.

Meanwhile, on his coming of age, James Blake had received a legacy of £600 from the will of his mother's brother and this capital enabled him to become a partner in the family filemaking business. The factory was situated in Scotland Street, north of the old town and in the heart of the district known as the Crofts. Although James continued to work in the business as a partner, after about three years, he felt that there were too many in the family firm and decided he could do better on his own.

In 1810 he purchased a croft in nearby Allen Street and within it set up his own business. The premises comprised a dwellinghouse and several outbuildings in which he installed a furnace and a cutling shop.[2] However, part of the dwellinghouse was occupied by Josephus Swallow, a forgeman and his family—James himself occupied the front parlour and a bedroom. It so happened that Swallow had a daughter Mary who was reported as being *a handsome young woman, but ignorant, conceited and unreasonable to a degree that can scarcely be believed*.[3] This did not deter James Blake from having a liaison with his tenant's daughter and, as a result Mary Swallow gave birth to a girl, Sarah. He was urged by his half-sister to marry Mary Swallow and several times a marriage was almost arranged but Mary Swallow was reputed to have a violent temper. Finally, James Blake demurred and in the end Mary married another. However, James Blake provided well for his illegitimate daughter and on reaching womanhood, Sarah married James's cousin, Thomas Blake. Sadly, at the age of thirty-four she died of consumption.

Fig 4 James Blake, 1785–1831

Meanwhile, during the summer of 1818, John Stephenson senior's approach to James Blake on behalf of his son was successful and agreement was reached that Blake would help finance the typefounding venture. On the 1st July 1818, a partnership was formed to be known as Blake, Garnett and Company, Typefounders, John Stephenson at the age of 28 being regarded as a very junior partner.

Meanwhile, the master typefounders of London had been working together in association for many years. They had long been members of the Worshipful Company of Stationers' and Paper Makers but towards the end of the eighteenth century they had come together and were now a tightly knit and powerful trade group. Whilst externally they preserved a degree of unity, in practice they were envious and cautious of each other's activities. In one area of activity they were in complete accord; that of ensuring that the price of type remained profitable and typefounding remained a fairly exclusive business. They were equally vigilant to ensure that production costs were kept to a minimum. The threat that typefounders situated in the provinces may have been able to cast cheaper letter as a result of paying lower wages was a constant one—even though the transportation of such heavy goods over long distances was not easy.

In 1807, William Caslon III at the age of 53, retired from the type-founding business having suffered considerably from cataracts on both eyes and was succeeded by his son. By 1818, William Caslon IV at the age of 36, was the active owner of one of the premier type founding businesses in the City of London, and he had numerous other business interests. Following the natural bent of the family for practical mechanics (both he and his father had invented and patented a number of devices both within and without the field of printing and typefounding), the family had become prosperous and their business interests were now spread more widely. In 1818, Caslon IV decided to sell the typefoundry in order to raise capital for a different kind of venture. At face value it might have seemed appropriate to have offered the sale of the business to the other typefounding branch of the Caslon family?

However, Caslon's IV relationship with the other Caslon foundry was singularly distant. Since Caslon III had seceded from the family business in Chiswell Street, Mrs. Elizabeth Caslon, William Caslon's II wife had died. Henry Caslon was also dead and the declining foundry was being run by his widow, Mrs. Henry Caslon, and Nathaniel Catherwood. Mrs. Henry Caslon who suffered from a long-term pulmonary affliction died in 1809 and within six months Nathaniel Catherwood died from an attack of typhus fever. The Caslon Catherwood foundry struggled on under the ownership of Henry Caslon II and Nathaniel Catherwood's brother. Clearly there was no real desire on the part of Caslon IV to offer the sale of the foundry to the Caslon Catherwood partnership now that family ties were loosened and the financial resources of the partnership limited.

Whilst the rivalry amongst the London founders was intense and competitive there was, in Sheffield, the reasonably well-established type-foundry of Bower, Bacon and Bower, with whom the Caslons appear to have had business dealings. Gossip travelled fast within the trade and there would be much speculation when news broke that William Henry Garnett, the highly skilled mechanic who had developed the sanspareil method, was now setting up in business. It seems likely that if Garnett had been the inventor of Caslon's sanspareil equipment or supplied sanspareil type

stock—even though it may have been through Bower, Bacon and Bower—
that personal contact could well have been made and possibly maintained
and if, as historical hearsay is to be believed, Garnett's great dissatisfaction
with his lot as an employee of Bower, Bacon and Bower had been noised
abroad, it may well have reached the ears of Caslon IV who, on hearing that
Garnett had set up in business, prompted the offer to sell his foundry to the
fledgling Blake, Garnett Company. Clearly, in the preliminary negotiations
the name Blake would have been of little consequence, whereas Garnett
would be known as an engraver and typefounder.

The background to the offer has long been a matter of some conjecture.
Why would one of London's leading typefounders sell to an unknown,
newly launched, untried typefounding partnership situated in a northern
township? One source considers that there was possibly a social connection
between an uncle of James Blake, Barnabas Blake,[4] who owned an hotel in
Jermyn Street, London and the Caslon family. However, there is much
more likely substance in the technical aspects of the situation.

The offer from Caslon to sell his foundry to the newly created partnership came not merely as a surprise; it represented a challenge. James Blake
and William Garnett journeyed to London. Staying for a month at the
Jermyn Street hotel owned by Barnabas Blake, they visited the foundry
daily. Garnett examined the equipment, took stock and made an inventory
of the contents, whilst the shrewd businessman, James Blake negotiated a
purchase price with Caslon, Finally, Caslon and Blake agreed on a
purchase price of £2,100 and further agreed that this could be paid in four
instalments.

Technically and commercially, Blake and Garnett considered that
Caslon's stock of punches, matrices and cast letter was in good order and
the asking price was fair value—having reckoned that to have made or
acquired such tools and stock would have cost them at least another £500.
Their main worry was that of raising capital to purchase the foundry.
Whilst James Blake lacked the immediate financial resources with which
to make the purchase possible, the other two partners were in an even less
favourable position. James turned to his father for assistance and, in the
end, Caslon agreed to accept a bond guaranteed by Thomas Blake, James
Blake senior, James Blake, Garnett and Stephenson.

With the purchase settled, plans and preparations were made ready to
receive the equipment and stock which was in the process of being transported in horse-drawn wagons from London to Sheffield. The business was
to be installed in James Blake's Allen Street premises. He relinquished his
filemaking business and its stock of files and equipment was transferred to
his father's factory in Scotland Street. James then moved out of Allen Street

and took up residence in nearby Solly Street. It was agreed that the junior partner, John Stephenson and his wife would move into Allen Street so that he could superintend the working of the foundry. Shortly before Christmas 1818, the equipment, punches, matrices and moulds arrived from London along with several former Caslon employees and their families. Early in 1819 typecasting operations began in earnest.

TRAFALGAR, No. 1.

Two lines Double Pica;   Or a regular size between Canon and Two lines Great Primer.

Quousque tandem abutere,

NORTHUMBERLAND

Quousque tandem abutere,

BEACONSFIELD.

£123456789

Fig 5 Trafalgar No1, from the Blake and Garnett Specimen book, 1819

Chapter 5

Blake, Garnett and Company of Sheffield, 1819-29

IMMEDIATELY the contents of the Caslon foundry were installed in Sheffield, the partners set about the task of producing their first specimen book of types under their own imprint: Blake, Garnett and Company of Sheffield. This was most necessary, for as successors of one of the most esteemed London typefoundries, they needed to establish quickly its new ownership and provincial location. It appeared late in 1819, and in many respects it was almost wholly made up of founts which had formed the major part of the 1816 Caslon Specimen book—many pages were either already available as printed stock or were in typeset page-form ready for printing. In reality it represented a credit not so much for the new owners but that of a final testimony to the foundry of William Caslon IV. It was clearly an omnibus version, not only did it display almost all the stock which had been acquired from Caslon—including the ancients, blacks and exotic text types which the foundry had not displayed for a number of years but also a number of sanspareil founts and text founts cut by Garnett. It was as if, after twenty years of war, the peace had brought the Caslon foundry into life once more. There were a number of founts which were distinctly innovative and unique and which reflected the variety of output from a foundry which had responded, in the immediate post-Napoleonic era, to the rapidly growing fashion for display faces and large-sized letter for poster and public advertising

The transfer of the Caslon Letterfoundry from London to Sheffield did not pass without criticism. The contemporary gossip, author and expert on typographical matters of the time, Thomas C. Hansard observed: . . . *in 1819 Mr. William Caslon, Jun., disposed of his foundry to Messrs. Blake, Garnett and Co., of Sheffield whither the whole stock has been removed. Mr., Caslon relinquished his profession to enter into a gaslight concern on the north side of the metropolis, transferring to the Sheffield founders such a specimen of type and flowers as will ever cause printers to regret the loss of such a competitor for fame in this difficult business.*[1]

The Sheffield partners were to find very quickly the essence of *this difficult business*. Printers had long enjoyed extended credit from their type-founder suppliers and although established customers were suitably addressed, and entreated to continue their patronage, the partners . . . *begged leave respectfully to inform the trade, that they have purchased the whole of Mr. W. CASLON's Foundry, which in addition to the specimen here for inspection, contains Founts of Greek, etc., etc.*[2]

However, the partners' working capital was severely limited and extending credit was almost unknown in a provincial town where traders *paid cash on the nail.*[3] James Blake, faced with the prospect of over extending credit, had little alternative other than to ask his father for his share of the family patrimony—a sum which proved to be in excess of £2000. This was additional to that which his father had already stood security for when the Caslon bond had been contracted. If the partners in the new company had some misgivings as to the future success of their venture, anxieties were matched in another way by the now somewhat bereft Bower, Bacon and Bower Company. On the 12th December 1819, the first issue of the *Sheffield Independent and Commercial Register*[4] established by Andrew Bacon, was published and an advertisement appeared high on its front page reminding readers that the Sheffield Type Foundry was still in business and customers could expect better service now the partners had established a Central Type Foundry. Obviously, there had been some disruption in the wake of Garnett's and Stephenson's departure.

The day to day activity of Garnett and Stephenson was now directed towards production. Garnett's twelve or more years' experience of producing punches, matrices and casting type, in a foundry which was owned by two practising printers who well knew the value of producing accurately cast letter, was invaluable. Now, as an experienced engraver and lettercutter, he was engaged primarily in punch cutting and matrix making whilst Stephenson's skill as a filer, diesinker and fender maker was applied to the making of moulds assisted by Joseph Benson, a mould maker from London who had been formerly employed by Caslon. The casting, dressing and finishing of letter was in the hands of Thomas Hughes, the former foreman type dresser who had also been a member of the Caslon foundry. John

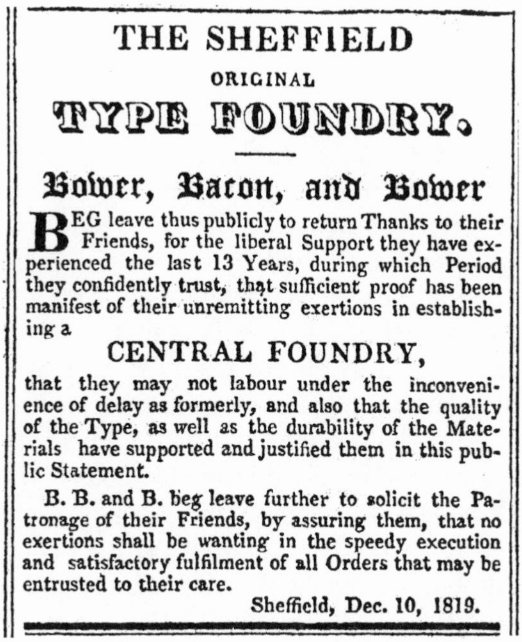

THE SHEFFIELD

ORIGINAL

TYPE FOUNDRY.

Bower, Bacon, and Bower

BEG leave thus publicly to return Thanks to their Friends, for the liberal Support they have experienced the last 13 Years, during which Period they confidently trust, that sufficient proof has been manifest of their unremitting exertions in establishing a

CENTRAL FOUNDRY,

that they may not labour under the inconvenience of delay as formerly, and also that the quality of the Type, as well as the durability of the Materials have supported and justified them in this public Statement.

B. B. and B. beg leave further to solicit the Patronage of their Friends, by assuring them, that no exertions shall be wanting in the speedy execution and satisfactory fulfilment of all Orders that may be entrusted to their care.

Sheffield, Dec. 10, 1819.

Fig 6 Advertisement, Sheffield Independent and Commercial Register, 10th December 1819

Stephenson, who had moved with his wife into residence in the house in Allen Street adjoining the foundry, maintained oversight of the production. The latter day expertise he had acquired in the art of typefounding he had gained from his friend, mentor and co-partner, William Garnett. Stephenson was now acutely aware of the need for accuracy and precision. The regularity of the fit of the matrices with the mould was of paramount importance if quality type was to be cast.

The workmen in the newly established company had to be organised and overseen. Production standards had to be set and, in the absence of precision measuring instruments, Stephenson began to devise, develop and make specialised tools to ensure a consistency of standards: callipers, depth gauges, profiles and lining markers and the like. In order to establish precise measurement and uniformity, he adopted a scale of measure which had been used by mechanics since the early eighteenth century, that of dividing the English inch into 5000 parts, each 1/5000th part being expressed as a degree. It was thus that John Stephenson established exacting standards, monitored the production and laid the foundation for producing printing types of superior quality.

Although the production and output of the foundry depended entirely on the two lesser partners, their financial stake in the business was minimal. In contrast, James Blake had not only raised money to start the venture by selling his own filemaking business; he had taken out a loan and had, out of necessity, also taken his patrimony. When the partnership agreement was signed on the 24th February, 1819, the venture had a nominal capital of £904 and it was agreed that the company would pay an annual rent to Blake for the house and premises in Allen Street which he owned. However, within two years there was a need to extend the premises in order to improve production facilities. A secure boundary wall was built, the court-yard was paved and workshops were built round it. By 1823, the partners were paying an annual rent of 10 guineas (Ten pounds ten shillings)—at that time a relatively large sum of money for a factory rental. Meanwhile, James Blake kept a tight hold on the company's purse strings. He ensured that any surpluses remained invested in the Company. The partners' remuneration remained modest even though the profits were relatively high. It was agreed that profits would be divided in proportion to the nominal capital of £904. Although this may have appeared to have been a reasonable basis, in cash terms, it meant that Garnett, as a lesser partner and Stephenson, as a mere junior partner were to receive very little. It is not difficult to appreciate the situation. Garnett and Stephenson were working long hours in the foundry whilst Blake was in the counting house keeping an ever watchful eye on the finances. There would be inevitable divisions of opinion regarding rewards and values. Garnett and Stephenson needed Blake's capital; Blake needed his partners' expertise and industry to ensure success. Clearly Garnett and Stephenson were less than satisfied with the prospects of their share of the profits. However, Blake could not afford at this crucial point in time to lose his fellow partners—particularly as their services would probably have been gladly taken up by the Bower, Bacon and Bower foundry. Finally the situation was eased by Blake lending Garnett and Stephenson £200 each of the nominal capital, interest free.

Even in the face of an increasingly competitive market, it soon became clear that the risk which Blake, Garnett and Stephenson had taken in starting their business and of purchasing the Caslon foundry had been worth-while. The stock which they had acquired from Caslon was sound in terms of saleable products which could be produced from it and the collection of jobbing matrices which Caslon had built up was useful in meeting the ever growing demand for fancy letter.

However, as a provinicial typefoundry, the partners quickly realised the disadvantage of their geographical situation. Sheffield was a long way from London, the centre of the English printing industry. The 1819 specimen

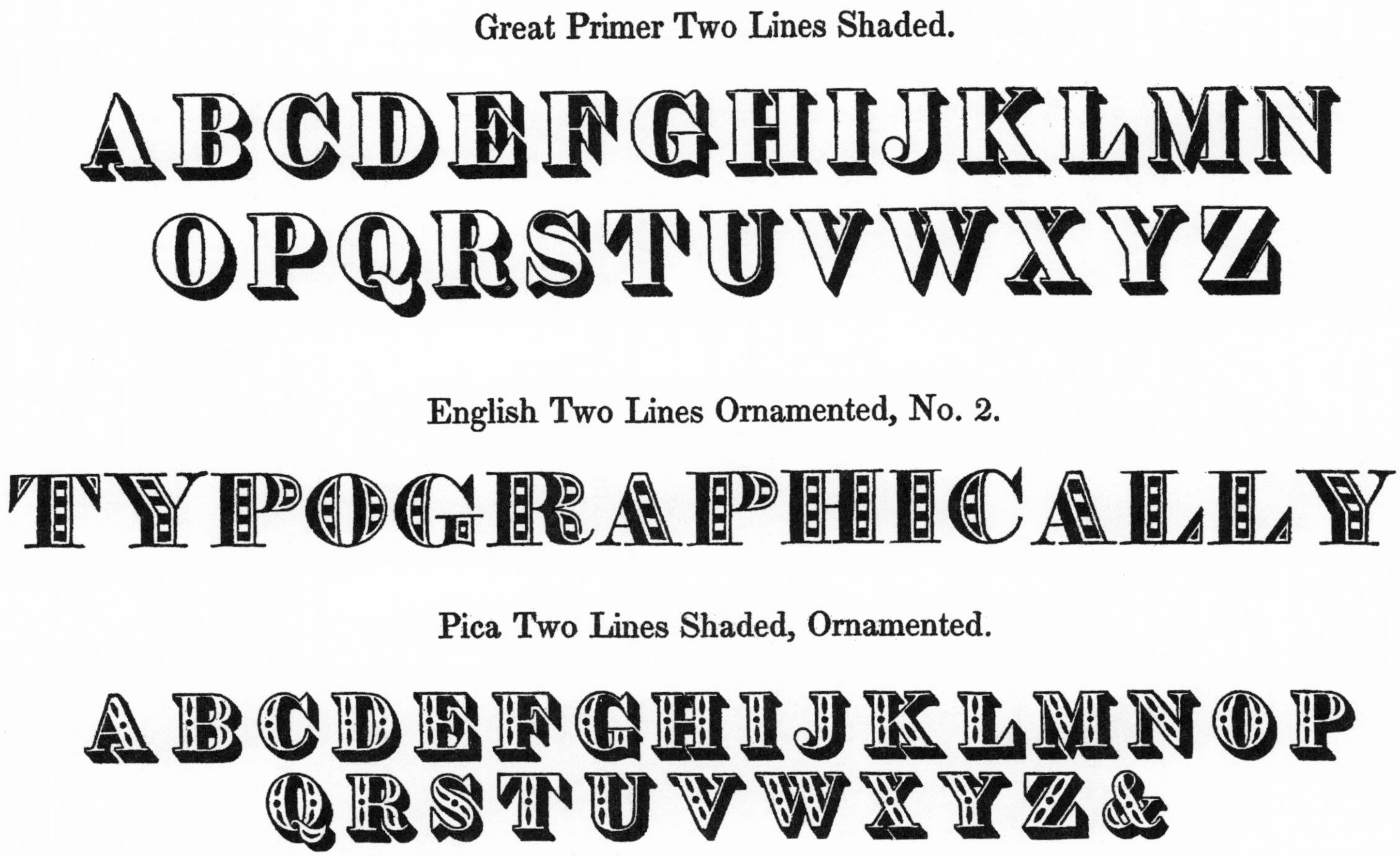

Great Primer Two Lines Shaded.

ABCDEFGHIJKLMN
OPQRSTUVWXYZ

English Two Lines Ornamented, No. 2.

TYPOGRAPHICALLY

Pica Two Lines Shaded, Ornamented.

ABCDEFGHIJKLMNOP
QRSTUVWXYZ&

Fig 7 Specimen of types from the Blake Garnett specimen book, 1819 (ex William Caslon, Salusbury Square)

book had been favourably received and many of the Caslon customers had kept their trade with the new owners in the North. A further specimen book was issued in 1821, another in 1826 and revisions followed in the years 1827, 1828 and 1830. The partners set great store by introducing their new type faces, additional sizes and a wider variety of decorated and novelty faces. Between 1819 and 1830, the Blake, Garnett Company issued six specimen books and the decade represents a gradual turnover of the Caslon stock and the progressive introduction of Blake, Garnett material indicative of the changes in typographical fashion and the demand for new typefaces.

Throughout the decade, the range and sizes of sanspareil letter was enlarged and the designs offered increasingly reflected a shift in letterform design from Moderns to Fat Blacks. The sanspareil matrix cutting method lent itself to the production of extremes in the weight of body strokes and hair line serifs. Variations in the form of shadow, inline and outline were offered. The larger sized types between Double Canon and Five-lines reflected the sanspareil variations with additional ornamentation set on the matrix face. The Antiques, an extra bold, slab-serifed range of letters (1826), a 6-lines Antique Ornamented, (1827) and the 12-lines Ornamented (1831) are representative of the highest level both of sanspareil and engraved matrix and patrix making skills. These founts probably represent the real forte of William Garnett—evidence of the artistic and engraving skills he had acquired as a silversmith.

In contrast with the variety of founts of sanspareil and jobbing letter, the range and design of Blake, Garnett types for the composition of text matter was singularly mundane. Nevertheless, the specimen books reflected the growing demand for a variety of intermediate sizes and set-widths. However, it cannot be said that the foundry produced any original typefaces except maybe for a single cleanly cut, but irregular, bracketed-serif Modern, in a size described as Trafalgar No 1.

Whatever shortfalls there might have been in the design quality of the Blake, Garnett types, their specimen books offered a wide variety of typographical style which met the needs of a growing number of customers. Within a short space of time the business was thriving and profitable.

In the foundry, the working of the partnership must have functioned in a very peculiar way. When an annual valuation was made of John Stephenson's workroom in the early 1820s, it was assessed at £7. By the 1840s the value had risen to £35. In 1827 the valuation of tools in Mr. Garnett's two rooms was £14 and contained goods valued at £350. It seems evident from records that the partners, particularly Garnett and Stephenson, worked independently and still regarded themselves as specialists, maintaining as they did their own workrooms. Whatever the

SIX LINES PICA ANTIQUE,

MASBRO

£1570,

ORNAMENTED.

Fig 8 A page of placard types, Blake and Stephenson, 1831

detailed working arrangements were, the success of the venture was undoubted when, after ten years' of trading, the nominal capital stood at £11,217—although the partners were always faced with the problem that almost 40% of the capital was permanently tied up in outstanding debts.

The end of the first decade was marked by a surprising accolade. The remarks which Thomas Hansard had made in *Typographia* in the 1820s berating the sale and transfer of the Caslon Letter Foundry to Sheffield must have stung the partners—particularly as they were not only struggling to compete with the London-based typefounders but embarrassed by the fact that Hansard had erroneously reported that the Caslon Foundry had been acquired by Bower, Bacon and Bower.[5] Thereafter the partners must have been very keen to ensure Thomas Hansard received copies of their current specimen book. However, the practice was not without benefit. In a copy of the 1831 Specimen book which belonged to Hansard the following handwritten commentary appears: *Presented to me Nov. 17 1831. In my Typographia, p.335 1st ed, I have mentioned this foundry 'in 1819 Mr. William Caslon junr. disposed of his foundry to Messrs. Blake, Garnett & Company of Sheffield, whither the whole stock has been removed, transferring to the Sheffield founders such a specimen of type and flowers as will ever caused us printers to regret the loss of such a competitor for fame in this difficult business.' This specimen shows that the removal of the stock and material alluded to has tended nothing towards lessening the credit of the original; and the improvements by addition to the variety in order to compete with every later founder, has altogether formed a specimen yielding in none to variety, excellence and perfection: the new size, or Emerald, perfects in the most happy manner the gradation of founts. Paternoster Row, 18 Nov 1831. TCH[7]*

By 1830, the original eleven-year partnership agreement was coming to a close. The future should have augured well. Unfortunately there was discord amongst the partners. The very minor partner, John Stephenson, had little room to manoeuvre. He was locked into the partnership. His wife, and young son still lived in the house situated across the foundry courtyard. James Blake was no doubt satisfied that his investment was now most profitable and the foundry well-esteemed—even by the London printers. However, Garnett appears to have resented the financial arrangements. Garnett and Stephenson had been the technical creators of the success. Blake had kept the accounts and finances under tight control, whilst Garnett possibly reflected that his rewards after ten years spent in the partnership had been little better than the ten or more years he had spent working for Bacon and the Bowers—he had exchanged one grudging taskmaster for another. One can well imagine Garnett and Blake in a

Twelve Lines PICA, Ornamented

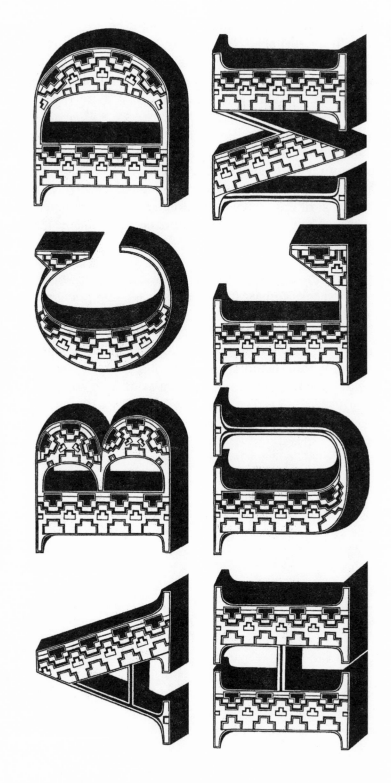

Fig 9 Placard types from Blake and Stephenson specimen book, 1831

situation of constant dispute. James Blake was now a very successful entre-
preneur with a profitable business, the financial resources of which he
controlled. He was in a strong position—one where even Garnett, the original innovator of the company, was no longer indispensable. The partnership came to an end. On valuation of his share, William Garnett was paid
£1550 and left the company. The real reasons for his break with the partners are lost in time. Clearly, Garnett was an innovator and remnants of his
work and artefacts which long-remained in the foundry indicate that he
continued, throughout the period, to experiment with new ideas and varied
techniques. The later examples of his letter cutting and matrix making work
are to be found in the ornamented large letters which appeared in the late
1820s—particularly the remarkably intricate 12-lines Pica Ornamented. He
was experimenting with a technique known as dab-casting, a method of
replicating in type metal, brass and woodcut originals; developing sweating
techniques for fusing type-shoulder-high brass originals and type-metal
stereotypes on to lead bases, as well as practising polytyping and stereotyping methods.

   After Garnett's withdrawal it became hearsay that he had retired to
become a gentleman farmer in nearby Dronfield, Derbyshire and all references to him within the company were obscured—his contribution to the
founding of the company being regarded as of little consequence.

Chapter 6

A Passing Partnership 1830-1840

W ITH the departure of William Garnett, at the end of 1829 it might have seemed that James Blake's position was paramount. At the age of 45, he held almost all the shareholding. In contrast, John Stephenson, aged 40, was still little more than a paid working manager even though his skill as a mechanic and as the manager of the production standards was crucial to the business. Garnett had made an immense contribution in the area of matrix making and lettercutting but Stephenson had made a longer-term contribution by establishing exacting production standards which made his technical control of the business unassailable. Some months passed before the terms of partnership were renegotiated. In the wake of Garnett's departure, did Stephenson achieve a personal stature which had hitherto eluded him? Whether, following the withdrawal of Garnett, there was a period of relief at Garnett's departure or apprehension regarding the future is an unknown factor. Clearly each of the partners, in different ways, was vulnerable. If Stephenson had decided to follow Garnett, Blake would have been in considerable difficulties.

Finally, a new partnership was negotiated and signed on the 25th September 1830 and would be for a period of eleven years, beginning retrospectively from 1st July 1829 and continuing until 31st December 1840. The company would in future be known as Blake and Stephenson. Within the contract there was a binding clause of some import '. . . *neither of the said parties shall or will during . . . this Co-partnership . . . carry on or be concerned in any trade or business . . . other than the trade or business agreed upon'*. Whilst the clause is understandable enough, it cannot but be mused: had William Garnett been undertaking outside work and was this proscriptive clause written in the agreement to bind Stephenson into the partnership? Some evidence appears to suggest that Garnett had possibly undertaken work outside the partnership—particularly as a number of decorative founts shown in the Bower, Bacon Bower specimen book dated 1826 and onwards are indicative of Garnett's work. Whether, during the ensuing interregnum, Stephenson pressed Blake for a better financial reward or not, Blake clearly realised that by offering Stephenson a more significant share and role in the business his loyalty and tenure would be maintained. During the earlier partnership Stephenson's share stood at a little over £1000. Blake now loaned Stephenson £1924 interest free. Blake's share approximated £6000 so that Stephenson, holding a share of £3000, represented a third of the capital.

The detailed partnership agreement contained fourteen sections and of all these, the final section was to have significant implications: If . . . *one of the said parties shall die before the expiration of the said term . . .* [the partnership shall be] *carried on by the survivor during the remainder of the said term . . . the Executors . . . of the deceased partner shall be entitled to the same interest and benefits . . . of the said partner . . . but such Executors . . . shall not be partners in their own right.*[1]

The new arrangements augured well. The two principals looked forward to developing their business yet further. Then, early in 1830 James Blake began to suffer from a series of recurring fits. Writing an account from family records, William Blake relates that James Blake *'went to Matlock for a fortnight to recuperate and came back home feeling much better. After a week at home he and his brother John, took their horse and gig to Buxton. During the night* [22nd June 1830] *Thomas Blake and William Thompson* [in Sheffield] *were called by messenger with a letter from John informing them that James had died of a 'spasm in the stomach'.*[2]

In an obituary which appeared in the *Sheffield Mercury* the writer extolled James Blake's virtues acclaiming his *high sense of honour and integrity . . .* [one who] *had the esteem of all who knew him. He was strictly punctual as a tradesman, sincere and warm-hearted as a friend.*[3]

Even before the new partnership had been agreed, Blake and Stephenson had begun work on an extended specimen book which was issued in 1831. It included founts which were intended to extend the range of sizes in the Fat Black series in Roman and Italic, a range of fairly heavy Modern text sizes in Roman and Italic and additional sizes and variations of the slab-serifed Antique and, obviously to meet popular demand, a range of Blacks (Old English) in the style of the Fat Blacks which were available in Roman and Roman Open from 5-lines Pica, 2-lines Great Primer, 2-lines English, 2-lines English Open, and Great Primer Open.

Under the direction of John Stephenson the format of the specimen books began to change. The previous style was found to be restrictive and unfashionable now that typefounders were beginning to display their founts in styles suited to their commercial usage. There was also technical innovation marked by the first showing of two sizes (2-lines Double Pica and Great Primer) of a script set on a square body and the new format of the specimen book allowed the displaying of the designs in the form of items of business correspondence. The design and production of types to replicate *copperplate* handwriting with its continuous pen stroke had long been a challenge for typefounders. The invention of a mould which enabled the casting of angular bodies appeared in the early nineteenth century. Caslon displayed a version Two-lines Pica Script No 2 in his 1816 specimen, whilst Blake and Stephenson displayed a more calligraphically refined version in their Great Primer Script No. 8. The introduction of types which recreated formal cursive were in considerable demand. Their limited use in a social and cultural sense was more than compensated for by the use of such types for the printing of formal business documents. However, the typesetting of script types was not exactly straightforward and founders sought to develop a script type cast on a square body—as exemplified in the Great Primer and Two-lines Double Pica shown in the 1834 specimen book. A further innovation was the beginning of large-sized letters in condensed forms—plain letter and decorated—whilst the basic sans serifed roman which first appeared in Caslon's 1796 specimen book as Two-lines English Egyptian had been used as a model for the design of a series of sans serifed letters which were cut in outline.

For the greater part of the second Blake-Stephenson period of partnership, John Stephenson was in sole charge. Although James Blake's relatives were non-executive partners taking their share of the profits, as time passed, Blake's direct legatees died and were thus reduced in number. The freehold land and the premises in Allen Street which had belonged to James Blake were bought by the company and the premises extended. During the early 1840s, John Stephenson made payments of £11,000 to buy off a number of them until, by 1841, the remaining heirs of Thomas Blake and William Thompson came together with Stephenson to form a new partnership known as Stephenson, Blake and Company. These were to be the years when John Stephenson gradually acquired the major shareholding which now stood at £6000, whilst Thomas Blake and William Thompson each had a holding valued at £3000.

John Stephenson, his wife and his son, Henry, born in 1827, had remained in residence in the foundry house in Allen Street. In 1840, they removed, first to a house in nearby Gell Street and then to St. George's

TEN LINES SANS SURRYPHS OPEN, No. 1. ¹/₆

EIGHT LINES ORNAMENTED, No. 2. ²/₄

Fig 10 Blake and Stephenson, 1833 Surryphs and Ornamented

Terrace—a fashionable, late Georgian development—a half-mile from the typefoundry, whilst Henry became a day-pupil at the Sheffield Collegiate School, situated in nearby Broom Park on the Sheffield Castleton Turnpike.

After severing his connection with Blake and Stephenson, William Garnett set himself up in business as a lettercutter, stereotyper and printers' joiner first in premises in Pinstone Street and then in Rockingham Street, Sheffield. One could well image his frustrated bemusement on hearing, within two years of his leaving the partnership, of the death of James Blake and of thinking ruefully of what might have been. Within the same year, his former employer, George Bower, whom he probably felt had cheated him, died and left an estate in excess of £5000—his interest in the Bower and Bacon Typefoundry passing to his grandson, George William Bower.

Meanwhile, whatever Garnett's feelings were towards Clay Bacon these must have been somewhat ameliorated by the misfortunes which followed: Clay Bacon died aged 64 in 1836, after a long illness, and his grandson, Clay Bacon junior, died in 1837 at the age of 24, whilst Henry Andrew Bacon, the founder of the *Sheffield and Rotherham Independent*, died in 1838 at the age of 44. Father, son and grandson—all dead within three years.

Garnett's modest business continued until his death at the age of 70. He had the satisfaction of outliving George William Bower, and his brother, Henry, and witnessed the decline and closing down auction of the Bower Typefoundry in 1852. Nevertheless, it must have been with a good deal of rancour and disappointment that he also witnessed the rise of the flourishing enterprise of his one-time friend and partner, John Stephenson, and his son Henry—a business of which he had once been one of the founding fathers.

Meanwhile, the third Stephenson, Blake Company partnership agreement made in 1841 saw John Stephenson firmly in the seat of power. The two Blake heirs, Thomas Blake and William Thompson, must have found the arrangement more than satisfactory. The company was profitable and well-managed. In a non-executive role they each held a quarter of the lucrative shareholding whilst in the meantime they pursued the long-established Blake family business of file manufacture in nearby Scotland Street.

By the 1840s John Stephenson could look back over the previous twenty-five years with a good deal of satisfaction. From acquiring skills as a typefounder from his one-time friend William Garnett, he now owned a major typefoundry, which was rapidly acquiring a national reputation.

However, commercial success as a typefounder, or otherwise, was pivoted on the London printing and publishing scene. The London typefounders were a tightly-knit group and had been in association in one form or another since 1793. In the past, the London scene had attracted to it letterfounders who, having commenced business in the provinces, found that transferring to London appeared to be the key to commercial success. Joseph Fry and partners had relocated from Bristol, William Caslon from Birmingham. As a consequence there were no typefounders of any import in the provinces, and as Musson observed: *almost all provincial printers appear to have got their type from London*.[4]

John Stephenson realised that he needed to establish a presence in the lucrative London market. In this endeavour he was fortunate in securing the services of Henry Bannister Smith who lived in Aldersgate Street. Smith not only ensured that long-established customers were carefully monitored but was at heart a particularly successful and aggressive sales representative. However, amongst the closed circle of the conservative London type-founders and printers, his selling techniques and trading methods were to cause considerable annoyance.

The making and selling of printing types for profit depended on keeping the cost of production low and the market value of the product as high as the market would stand. Whilst the London typefounders competed amongst themselves, collectively they jealously guarded their prices. The near monopoly enjoyed by the London Society of Master Letter Founders had lasted for some thirty years but, by the late 1820s, the scene was changing.

Since the ending of the Napoleonic Wars typeface design innovation had abounded and the demand for new typefaces had boosted profits. In foundries, the basic techniques of typefounding had changed little since the sixteenth century. Although the volume of output continued to rise year by year, punches were still being cut by hand, matrices struck in copper and justified to make them compatible within a fount. The casting of the type was made in a hand mould, whilst the cast letter needed finishing: the tail-pieces of the characters had to be removed, the foot of the letter needed dressing and all too often the face of the characters needed to be rubbed down. The art of typefounding also required a knowledge and a skill of smelting the typecasting alloy. Since the very beginnings, founders had, through experience, used alloys containing varying proportions of lead, tin, regulus (antimony), bismuth and copper. In the hand casting operation, it was essential that the molten metal was sufficiently fluid to fill all the corners and interstices of the mould and the matrix. The main constituent of type metal was lead—a relatively cheap and easily reduced material, but lead alone when molten was not sufficiently fluid to effect clean sharp cast-ings and too soft to withstand wear. Tin, in contrast, had a low melting temperature and ran into the mould freely, but it was expensive and in short supply. However, an alloy comprising 90% lead and 10% tin had a remarkable quality—an exceedingly low eutectic range. When heated it changed from solid metal into a fluid state within a few degrees of heat and vice versa it solidified rapidly after casting. The use of tin within the alloy not only made the casting of a usable type possible, it also gave strength and ductability to the cast letter. However typefounders soon discovered that on solidifying, there was shrinkage. In an attempt to reduce this, antimony was added to the alloy and later small amounts of copper. In smelting the type alloy, the temperature of the melting pot had to be increased, the constituent metals passed through their individual solid-to-molten stages. The alloying of lead with tin had a low eutectic temperature but, with antimony added, a greater temperature was required and where copper was added, the heat required to make and keep the metal molten was even higher. The testing and maintenance of the temperature was to some extent arbitrary, varying from listening for the actual molten metal boiling to plunging a rolled plug of paper into the pot and discerning the rate and speed of it being scorched or burned. The typecasting process was hot, uncomfortable and unhealthy. Even Moxon, writing in the seventeenth century recommended that; *Half a pint of Sack mingled with Sallad Oyl,* [be] *provided for each Workman to Drink; intended for an Antidote against the poysonous Fumes of the Antimony, and to restore the Spirits that so violent a Fire and Hard Labour may have exhausted.*[5] By the nineteenth century, working conditions were still less than satisfactory. Illness and early death frequently arose as a result of lead poisoning.

For the master typefounders, commercial success in the art of typefounding increasingly depended on the general state of the economy and the state of the printing industry in particular. As cyclical periods of nineteenth century boom and depression manifested, so the profits of typefounders and printers waxed and waned and competition became acute. By the 1830s, employees were becoming increasingly less compliant. Although legislation was in place to deter the growth of trade unions and combinations, workers in many trades were becoming militant and vociferous.

During the 1840s there was considerable economic distress throughout Britain and this condition had its effect on printers and typefounders alike—particularly those based in London. The London founders, in the wake of the improvement in the means of carrying goods which could be brought into the City by the newly opened railways, realised that they now faced strong competition from the typefounders based in the provinces. They also complained bitterly that the Sheffield and Scottish typefounders placed them at a considerable disadvantage as they were able to undercut their prices because of the lower wages paid in the provinces.

TYPEFOUNDERS' STRIKE.

W<small>E</small>, the Typefounders of Sheffield, having been eight weeks out of work, and all our efforts having failed to convince our employers of the gross injustice which they wish to impose upon us, have resolved again to appeal to your sympathy and your sense of justice. And we do assure you, Fellow Townsmen, that nothing has been left undone. that it has been in our power to do, to bring our protracted struggle to an equitable termination.

We would ask, Fellow Townsmen, what is to be done with such men as Messrs. STEVENSON, BLAKE, and Co., for they have told us in their letter (which appeared in the *Sheffield Iris*) that they declined from any controversy; they refuse to meet a deputation from our body, and well may they refuse to meet their old and faithful servants, in the field of argument, to discuss the eternal principles of justice and the rights of labour : for labour has its rights as well as capital, and we tell Messrs. S., B., and Co. that we will not allow them to wring from us the fruits of our industry under any pretence whatever. We now call upon the Master Typefounders of Sheffield to come forward and meet us before the Public, to discuss the merits or demerits of the monstrous system of rapine which they wish to carry out. If they will do this, our strike might soon have an end. We will submit to the decision of our Fellow Townsmen. But we believe they dare not meet us ; no, they dare not meet the men on whom they have formerly lavished their praises for being " Intelligent and industrious.' They dare not meet the men who have raised them to the exalted position in society which they now occupy, and to whom, they (the masters) have expressed the deepest sympathy and regard. They have told us that their interests were bound up with our interests, and that they were ever solicitous for our welfare. Nay, further, they have expressed an unbounded solicitude for the happiness of ' *our wives and our little ones.*' Yet strange to say, those very men who have expressed so much anxiety for the welfare of ourselves, our wives and our children, have for the last eight weeks past been trying, by all the means in their power, to starve both ourselves and our families. But their power is not equal to their wickedness, otherwise they would have done it. O ! HYPOCRISY, WHERE IS THY BLUSH !

Fellow Townsmen !---We wish now to draw your attention more directly to the objects of this appeal to you, which objects are the following :---First, to thank you sincerely for the very deep sympathy and generous support we have received at your hands ; and secondly, to solicit a continuance of that support to the end of our struggle with the rapacious capitalists ; and likewise to shew the pernicious nature of our business, the comparatively small remuneration we have received, and also the ability of our late employers to pay the prices they have formerly paid. We likewise wish to state the enormous reductions which the masters wished to enforce, with several other important matters to be hereafter mentioned.

The trade of a Typefounder is unhealthy in the extreme, and very destructive to life. The heat is so intense in the apartments allotted for casting, occasioned by such a multiplicity of furnaces being crowded together, that but few individuals can withstand its baneful influence for any length of time, without experiencing very serious injury arising therefrom. Moreover, the atmosphere which the Typefounder has to breathe is so oppressive, that it would be inconvenient to a person who had been brought up in a Tropical country---an atmosphere, heate to such a degree, that the Thermometer will range from 70 to 90 degrees in Winter time. Not only has the Typefounder to endure such an oppressive atmosphere, but he has to stand in one position for 12 or 14 hours per day, with his head very near to a pan of metal, which for casting small types, must be red hot. The composition of this metal is regulus of antimony, tin and lead, with a portion of copper, the fumes of which are rank poison. Nor is this all, for the particles of metallic dust which fly off in the process of dressing and other departments of our trade, are constantly being inhaled by those who are employed in the manufacture of type. The above causes bring on many painful diseases, premature old age, and untimely death.

Now for the very extravagant wages we have received for so much toil and misery. So very extravagant have our wages been, that the London and Sheffield Master Typefounders have formed a coalition league to take from us 3d. out of every shilling in several kinds of work. In others 6d. out of the shilling, and in some cases the very moderate sum of 9d. out of the shilling.

Here, perhaps, it may be said, that our wages must have been very great, otherwise the very serious reductions which have been proposed would reduce us to the very verge of pauperism. To all such enquiries, we boldly assert, that the remuneration which a type-castor has received, at the old prices, has not been more than 20s. per week, taking every foundry throughout the kingdom. Some have got rather more, others less than 20s. per week ; but we contend that what we have stated is a fair average of the earnings of castors. We now ask all the Master Typefounders of the United Kingdom to publish a list of the wages of their castors for the last twelve months, or any other given period ? If they will do this, we dare pledge ourselves to the assertion we have made, namely, that a Type Castor does not average more than 20 shillings per week.

You will now, Fellow Townsmen, be enabled to judge what would be our condition, if the Masters are allowed to take from our small pittance, 25, 50, and 75 per cent. They are at this time moving heaven and earth to effect their wicked purpose. A short time ago, they threatened that if we did not come in and work at their terms, our places would be filled up with men from London. They accordingly packed off, with the avowed intention of bringing a cargo down to Sheffield ; but mark the result — not a single individual could they bring with them.— Finding themselves *non-plussed* in this instance, as they were in the case of the POOR PARISH MEN, they turn round and say, well, if we cannot bring men to Sheffield, we will have our establishment in London ; for say they, there are plenty of poor ragged wretches in the Metropolis who will work for us there, at any price. Thus you see, Fellow Townsmen, these very gentlemanly Masters add insult to injury. This by the way argues very poorly for the high wages of the London Typefounders. However, if the London Typefounders are poor and ragged wretches now, what would they be at the villanous prices which have been offered by the London and Sheffield *Starvation League.* Our Sheffield worthies have again packed off, to use every artifice which malice can invent, or bribery accomplish ; but as yet with very little success in their *laudable* undertaking. It is indeed true, that they have tried a miserable dog-hole, resembling a potatoe cellar, to give a specious colouring to the ridiculous bugbear. They have also expressed their intention of engaging a few of those poor ragged wretches, as they have insultingly termed the London Typefounders. But in our opinion, the Operative Typefounders of the Metropolis, are far more honourable than the Masters.

Fellow Townsmen, it is our opinion, that the London Establishment is a miserable subterfuge, got up to intimidate the Workmen of Messrs. Stephenson, Blake, & Co. If Messrs. S., B., & Co. seriously intend to transplant their business to London, why do they not at once remove and make room for more honourable men. We can assure the Public, that if Messrs. S., B., & Co. should ever be so mad as to entirely remove, it would take at least 12 months to fit up an Establishment equal to the one they now have in Sheffield, and in that time their trade would be entirely ruined,

In our next address, we shall shew the enormous profits which the Masters have realised, and their ability to pay a remunerating price.

We remain, yours,

The Committee of the Journeymen Typefounders.

N.B.—Any pecuniary assistance will be most thankfully received by the Committee, who sit daily at the Three Cranes, Queen-street, from Twelve to Two in the Afternoon, and from Seven to Nine in the Evening, to give all necessary information.—Copies of this address may be had. gratis, on application at the Committee Room.

Committee Room, October 21, 1843.

PRINTED BY A. WHITAKER AND CO., IRIS OFFICE, SHEFFIELD.

Fig 11 Typefounders Strike notice, Sheffield. 1843

In June 1843, the London Master Letterfounders took action. The wages of the typecasters and type-dressers were to be cut. The London Committee of Journeymen Typefounders claimed these were wage cuts of between 25% and 75% whilst the employers claimed that they were a mere 15%. The workmen of four London foundries came out on strike. The Sheffield typefounder-workmen from Bower and Bacon and Stephenson, Blake Company worked on a month by month contract and gave notice of strike and placed themselves under the direction of the London Committee. The Sheffield Committee met at the Three Cranes tavern in Queen Street. By issuing strike notices describing the unhealthy conditions under which they worked, they lobbied their counterparts in other Sheffield trades for support and voiced their complaints in the local press. The strikers were well supported and their cause was greeted with some sympathy. After ten weeks of strike, they succeeded and their wage-rates were restored. Fourteen weeks later, the London Master Letterfounders gave way and their typecasters wage-rates were also restored.

Fig 12 Ornaments, polytyped and metal mounted, Blake and Stephenson, 1833

Chapter 7
Fashionable Types

T HE issue of typefounders' specimen books to some extent reflects the general rate of growth of the printing industry and of type-founding in particular. During the period of the Napoleonic Wars, 1793-1815, records show that there were some 60 different specimen books produced, half of these being issued by the six leading typefounders: Caslon, Caslon-Catherwood, Fry and Steele, Thorne, Figgins, and Miller. In the period, 1815-1830, 82 were issued by 20 typefounders of whom Caslon-Blake-Garnett, Fry and Steele and successors, Caslon-Catherwood-Livermore, Figgins, and Thorowgood were the main suppliers.[1]

The Napoleonic Wars marked a watershed of change in typographic fashion and design. The significance of this change was tortuously summed up by Berry and Johnson: *The rivalry between William Caslon's completely orthodox cutting of the Aldus-Garamond-Grandjean-Van Dyke-Moxon pattern; Fry's and Wilson's cutting of Baskerville's somewhat more open and wider variations of the same design, against the Bell-Austin pattern which was taken up by Figgins, Thorne and Thorowgood combined with later Continental practices, quickly developed in the last decade of the eighteenth century. Caslon's lost ground to Fry and Wilson; and finally, Thorne and Thorowgood as inheritors of the Bell inspiration, found their competitors imitating them. By 1790 the Caslon Foundry had completely changed its patterns, and at the end of the century the Aldine design of 1495 was practically extinct, not merely in England, but in Europe.*[2]

As the Transitional designs became more sharply delineated and finally emerged as Modern, many came to regard Robert Thorne's letter as marking a final definitive form. These design developments did not pass without considerable criticism. Dr. Edmund Fry in 1828, at the time of the sale of his foundry, wrote: *The Baskerville and Caslon imitations . . . were laid to rest for ever and many thousands of pounds worth of new letters in Founts . . . were recast into* [new] *Types . . .* [but they are not] *so agreeable to the reader, as the true Caslon-shaped Elzevir types.*[3]

In 1841, William Savage was led to reflect: *We had types of beautiful shapes and symmetrical proportions, but our typefounders have diverged, for the sake of variety, gradually to a fatter face until the lines have become so thick that the latter has hardly any white in its interior, and when printed it is nearly all black, with the outline only to guide us in knowing what it is; and on the contrary they have gone gradually to the other extreme, and produced what are called skeleton letters, which are formed of a fine uniform line; we have antiques, the line being also of uniform thickness, but strong and heavy; we have letters with the strong lines and the fine lines reversed; we have tall narrow letters, and we have letters which look as though they have been pressed down, till they were considerably broader than their height; we have letters drawing towards us, as if they were marching away; and as for italics, we have it now inclining to the left as well as to the right. The modern Gothic or black letter has not escaped this rage for change and variety, and we have forms introduced into it which would have puzzled our ancestors to know what they meant for then the modern Gothic was the standard character. These changes and varieties have not been introduced as improvements either in the forms or propor-tions of the letters, but to produce variety on what is called styled effect.*[4]

However, there were supporters for the new fashion. A contemporary view was put by Caleb Stower who, writing in 1808, considered that: *The great improvement which has taken place of late years in the form of print-ing types, has completely superseded the Elzevir shape introduced from Holland by the celebrated Caslon nearly ninety years ago. Everyone must observe with increasing admiration the numerous elegant founts of every size, which have with rapid succession been lately presented to the public.*[5]

From the 1820s onwards, the number of typefounding businesses increased—particularly in London—and Blake and Stephenson, as rela-tively newcomers to the trade, were anxious to secure a share of that partic-ularly lucrative market. Even though the company had engaged the services of Henry Bannister Smith in order to attract customers, John Stephenson considered, the best means of advertising the company's range of letter, in the absence of having an office and warehouse based in London, was by regularly issuing a specimen book containing typefaces which reflected the current typographical fashion. Whilst Sanspareil letter, Fat-faces and Antiques continued to dominate the Blake and Stephenson specimen books, the foundry was, nevertheless, offering a fairly extensive range of founts in both roman, and italic. By 1831, the changes in fashion had been reflected by the withdrawal of many of the 1816 (Caslon) and 1819 (Blake and Garnett) decorated types and these were replaced by the inclusion of many new typefaces including Tuscans and Fat-Blacks.

The fundamental changes in the design of text typefaces which had begun prior to the Napoleonic Wars had, by the 1830s, seemingly run their course. The use of the Modern face for book and text printing had well and truly superseded the Aldine model. In the decades which followed, the literati, printers and the observers of the publishing world began to view the changes in letter design critically. In 1875, William Blades observed that: *The year 1820 was a boundary line between the old and new style of punch cutting.* [Type design RM] *About that time great changes were initiated in the faces of types of all kinds. The thick strokes were made much thicker and the fine strokes much finer, the old ligatures were abolished and a mechanical primness given to the page, which artistically, could scarcely be called improvement. At the same time, printers began to crowd their racks with fancy founts of all degree of grotesqueness, many painfully bad to the eye and unprofitable alike to the founder and printer.*[6]

The problem with the majority of observers of the Victorian typographic scene was their general unwillingness or inability to differentiate between commenting on the quality of design of text types, and their views on the typefaces designed and used for jobbing work. Updike at least accepted the difference: *Robert Thorne [was] . . . responsible for the vilest form of type invented—up to that time. Thorne's specimen book of 'Improved Types' 1803 should be looked at as a warning of what fashion can make men do. His 'Jobbing Types' look as their name suggest! His black letter is perhaps the worst that ever appeared in England.*[7] However, Berry and Johnson viewed the development much more objectively: *Extra bold types which we sometimes call fat faces appeared in English typography about 1810. Bower, Bacon and Bower of Sheffield showed them in that year though it is probable that some London founder was the first to design them.*[8] *When the thickness of the main strokes as compared with their height reaches the proportion of one to two-and-a-half it may be said that we have reached the fat face.*[9]

Nicolette Gray was more aware of the differentiation; putting forward a view that, as a description, the term 'Modern' was applicable to text type and was based to a large extent on the characteristics of the lower-case alphabet, whereas the larger sizes of Modern issued by English type-founders of the time still maintained some bracketing. Gray went on to contend that it was Bodoni's latterly created designs and those of Didot

which were unbracketed[10] The differentiation between body-types and
jobbing-types is probably finally sealed by Updike's comment on the state
of mid-nineteenth century book production: *I have said that Grandjean,
Baskerville, Bodoni and the Didots had a mischievous influence on type-
forms; for the derivations from types that made their work more popular
culminated in a kind of letter which was capable of greater vulgarity and
degradation than was ever the case with older founts. The ordinary
English, French, or Italian book printed between 1830 and 1850 was very
often a cheap and mean looking production. Perhaps Bodoni and other
great persons were not wrong in their own day; but they put type-forms on
the wrong track.*[11]

By the 1850s, the general printing and newspaper publishing industry
was expanding and there appeared to be an ever increasing demand for
both text type and decorated novelties. Consequently, typefounding in the
mid-nineteenth century was profitable. Whilst the critics berated the typefounders and their designs, their opinions carried little weight. In the period
from the 1820s to the 1870s there were innovations but all too frequently
they were of the worst kind. The range of Fat Blacks and the over ornamentation of nondescript basic designs of Roman continued, but after the
1830s, these contrasted greatly with the delicacy of the Copperplate Scripts
and Plate Gothic designs which were being introduced. However, although
the principal typefounding companies who were members of the
Typefounders Association were facing competition from the small non-
member firms, they realised they were operating in a seller's market and
trade was good. There were lucrative profits to be made casting and selling
printing types—even if the designs were both tasteless and vulgar.

Meanwhile, English book typography remained singularly monotonous
and uninspired and there was little change in the general quality of book
printing for almost fifty years. The Modern face used for text setting
reigned supreme and in keeping with their competitors, Stephenson, Blake
produced innumerable versions of body-letter, identifying each by suffix-
ing a given number after stating its body size. The means of identifying
such types was unsystematic and apparently inconsistent. What is
described in one specimen as *Pica No 1* becomes *Pica No 2* in a subsequent
specimen book—importance of place being given to the newly cut or newly
acquired fount. Over the years No.1 became No. 2 or No. 3. At other times
new founts were given higher numbers marking a newly issued fount's first
appearance in the specimen book. Of the nature of such letter, little can be
said. Some founts were reasonably well-cut, printed cleanly, and had
balanced characters. Others possessed production idiosyncrasies; indifferent cuttings with weaknesses in individual letters which intruded in the

printed pages of text. Founts of capitals were especially weak and often capitals appeared to be at odds with the lower case alphabet they were intended to accompany. There was the makeshift expedient of utilising a fount of capitals and combining it with a number of different lower case alphabets, each with differing set-width dimensions. This practice was intended to create a variety of body-letter alternatives. Another expedient was that of utilising an alphabet of small capitals from the larger sized body founts as capitals for smaller sized founts.

However, if the design of body letter and the state of English book production had settled into unprecedented dullness, the same could not be said regarding the design innovations in jobbing types. As if for sheer perversity, the issue of widely contrasting designs continued. What appeared to be a further development of the Egyptian form came in 1845. In that year, Robert Besley of the Fann Street Foundry registered the Clarendon design, which had been engraved by Benjamin Fox. Whilst it was asserted that it was derived from the ubiquitous Egyptian design, it was in essence a basic roman, extended to accommodate the weight of a bold stroke, trimmed with bracketed slab-serifs and subsequently slightly condensed. The result was a bold type, which, although it appeared some-what characterless in the jobbing sizes, had distinct merit in body sizes. Clarendon was an undoubted success and was quickly adopted for it proved to be useful for use as a generic related-bold letter which, whilst compatible with the Modern romans, possessed sufficient differentiation and weight to give emphasis. Besley is said to have complained bitterly that, as soon as the registered design had run its three-year course, other founders were copying it—and so they did. The protection of type designs was an issue which the Typefounders Association tried hard to influence—even as late as 1916, Stephenson, Blake were pursuing the issue through the Courts, but the outcome of a test case against Legros and Grant resulted in a less than definitive ruling.

However, Besley's 1845 Clarendon was not new. The first appearance of a Clarendon style design was in the Blake and Stephenson specimen book of 1833, which, although in outline form was a Clarendon, was without the characteristic compression. But even the slightly anachronistic Clarendon was contrary to the incoming trend of lighter and more delicate typefaces. This had been anticipated. In the Blake and Stephenson specimen book of 1834, an example of Pearl Hairline appeared and the design was also displayed in a setting of Byron's poem *Address to the Ocean*. The design is characteristic of the lettering used on steel engravings of the time—a very delicate letter with monotone strokes and serifs. The classification can hardly be reckoned as light Egyptian, because the serifs are extended and

TWO LINES PEARL OUTLINE.

FOR THE
INSTRUCTION OF YOUTH
IN THE VARIOUS
BRANCHES OF MATHEMATICAL,
COMMERCIAL & CLASSICAL
EDUCATION.

ABCDEFGHIJKLMNOPQRSTUV
WXYZ, &c. Co. No.

BREVIER TUSCAN.

BLAKE & STEPHENSON,
LETTER FOUNDERS,
SHEFFIELD.

ABCDEFGHIJKLMNOPQRSTUVWX
YZŒÆ&

TWO LINES NONPARIEL SANS-SURRYPH.

SOCIETY OF ARTS.
NOTICE TO STUDENTS.
THE LECTURES AT THE ANTIQUE
ACADEMY,
WILL COMMENCE ON
MONDAY NEXT.

ABCDEFGHIJKLMNOPQRSTUVWX

Fig 13 Stephenson, Blake, Hairlines and Tuscans, 1844

there is a complete absence of stress; by current description it would be categorised as an Ionic, whilst further evidence of the influence of the art of the engraver is to be found in the delightful outline version of Fat-face which also made its first appearance in 1834 and which by 1838 was offered in several sizes under the name of Skeleton.

The mid-century development of Clarendons, Hairlines and Ionics was not entirely unrelated. Clarendons took the Egyptian design in one direction, whilst Hairlines took it in another; the classification of Ionics being doubtful. Nicolette Gray identified Ionic with Clarendon and probably, in nineteenth century terms, this was acceptable but, Ionic became a distinct design in its own right and its origins are to be found in the Hairline typefaces of the period. In practical terms, the characteristic of the Ionic design was its evenness of strokes and long unbracketed serifs which, when combined with a large x-height, short ascenders and descenders, and open counters, made the design particularly useful, in the late nineteenth-century, for replication by the stereotyping process for rotary press printing of newspapers.

Among the distinctive innovations in jobbing type design of the mid-nineteenth century was the development of the Tuscan character. Its first appearance is to be found in a highly decorated version cast by Figgins in 1815. However, the innovation was more than a passing typographical whim. It was the dictates of fashion and novelty which dominated mid-nineteenth-century trade in jobbing typefaces, and typefounders, with an ever ready wish to profit by making new designs available. Excessive decoration and ornamentation continued to be applied to such an extent as to almost transform both the original Tuscan form and its early variations.

Nicolette Gray's description of the Tuscan form is well reasoned: *I should define Victorian Tuscan as a letter the face of which may be plain or decorated. The form . . . bifurcated or curled at the terminals, and in the centre of the stem it may be enlarged or broken.*[12] From its introduction in 1815 until the mid-1850s, the design tended to be characterised either by swollen stems, which carried excrescences, or stems which were excessively waisted, the waisting often being compensated by pearls or 'blobs'. Sometimes the waisting was carried to the extreme—the line of the stem being broken or interrupted.

Once the fashion was set, typefounders began to introduce a great variety of Tuscan designs. These frequently carried heavily decorated interiors with the serifs formed from bifurcated stems which were either rolled or curled to form blobs; or were subjected to double forking. Surprisingly, Blake and Stephenson did not issue a version of Tuscan until 1834, when a shaded outline letter known as Brevier Tuscan appeared. The relatively late

FIVE LINES TUSCAN. 2/3.

HEMINGBOROUGH. 6318.

NORTHAMPTONSHIRE.

Brevier Two Line Tuscan. 4/6.

GALLERY OF BRITISH ARTISTS.

LANDSCAPES AFTER

BERGHEM, POUSSIN & CLAUDE.

NORTHAMPTONSHIRE.

CANTERBURY

Brevier Two Line Relief. 4/6

MANCHESTER MECHANICS' INSTITUTION

SPLENDID EXHIBITION OF

Fig 14 Stephenson, Blake, Tuscans and Decorated types, 1844

introduction of Tuscan types by Blake and Stephenson bears unfavourable comparison with some of the richly ornamented designs produced by other foundries at this time, many of which were lively and original. Conscious of the shortfall, the 1838-39 specimen book carried two further designs of which the Brevier Two-lines Ornamented Tuscan representes a crude example; decorated with dots in the centre of the main stems and with chevrons filling in the remaining open areas. The fount also possessed an incredible irregularity. The letters C S G in the specimen are incompatible to such an extent that they appear almost as wrong founts. In contrast, the Great Primer Two-lines Ornamented Tuscan bears characteristics which really belong to a later period of development. Its swelling stems give an appearance of being developed from a lozenge, whilst the bifurcated serifs seem as if they were formed through a series of 'bites' having been made at the end of the stems.

Whilst, in the typefoundry in Sheffield, John Stephenson was emphatic in his endeavour to produce type which possessed a high physical quality, the standard of the typeface designs left a great deal to be desired. After he had become the managing partner, his influence on the course of the business is marked by the much improved appearance of the specimen books. The character of the 1844 specimen book is markedly different from the preceding issues. Comparison shows that gradually from 1831 until 1838 the actual paper used in each was becoming smoother and the 1844 version possessed a very different feel, having been printed on a calendered paper. Whilst the letterpress impression remained, it was by no means as heavy as previous printings. There are a number of open spreads for displaying types which were becoming increasingly delicate and light—almost indicating that change was afoot, and the early leaves were given over to typographically tasteful specimen settings. Generous margins and border rules set off the type matter and some thought and skill had been applied to show off the types to best advantage. The Pica No 1 series which first began to appear in 1826 was now named Elephant whilst the fashion for delicate, condensed Modern titlings in the smaller display sizes continued. There was also condensation and elongation of the Antiques and Sans-serifs. From the literature of the specimen settings there also appears to have been a demand for jobbing types of about the size of double pica for the purpose of printing business notices. By 1844 the foundry had issued no fewer than twelve designs of Tuscan in twenty-one sizes, all of which bore the customary description of the time:

Brevier Tuscan 1834
Brevier Two-lines Ornamented 1838- 39

Great Primer Two-lines Ornamented 1838-39
Pearl Two-lines Tuscan 1844 (4 sizes outline)
Bourgeois Two-lines Tuscan 1844 (2 sizes)
English Tuscan 1844 (3 sizes) (outline with rosettes)
Great Primer Two-lines Tuscan 1844
Double Pica Two-lines Tuscan 1844 (4 sizes) (decorated shadow)
Pearl Two-lines relief 1844
Pica Two-lines in Ornament 1844
Great Primer Two-lines relief 1844 (open shadow)
Great Primer Two-lines relief No 2 1844 (open)

By the close of the 1850s, Tuscans had almost run the full course. The final stages of the development of the form was marked by simplification. The designs became blacker and plainer. The terminals on some versions bore fishtail characteristics and from this device developed rocker-shaped and star-shaped terminals which were often accompanied by a feathering of the mid-stem. This phenomena led Nicolette Gray to comment: *presumably the idea is developed from the feet of Gothic letters.*[13] [meaning Black letter]—a reference to the development of rocker and star shaped terminals. This observation of an affinity between the simplified Tuscans and Black-letter is particularly noticeable in a number of the later designs, many of which possess characteristics not only common to early uncial characters but also to the rising fashion of Victorian neo-Gothic plain and decorated Black Letter.

Between the 1820s and the mid-1860s, Stephenson, Blake's range of jobbing types had passed through four distinct design styles: Fat-faces, Antiques (Egyptians), Fat-blacks and Sans-serifs. As the 1860s approached, the decorative letter gradually became blacker and less ornate. The market for condensed typefaces continued and the foundry met the current demand by supplementing their range, by adding additional sizes and geometric versions (inline, outline, shadow, shaded reversed, etcetera). In contrast, the range of tasteful and discreet, engraver's-style titlings of card letter, in the smaller display sizes, was being extended.

Meanwhile, throughout the period, 1830 to 1860, there had been a most profitable and expanding trade in body types for book and newspaper printers. It was straightforward work which kept the foundry busy and required little effort except that of maintaining a close eye on the physical quality of the type produced. It was a keystone on which Stephenson and his son Henry had founded and was maintaining the business. In contrast, the cost of commissioning fancy new jobbing types was high in relation to the profit which they generated. Punchcutters' time and creativity were a

NONPAREIL-BREVIER SHADED.

LIVERPOOL

MEDICAL, PHILOSOPHICAL, AND LITERARY

SOCIETY.

HORTICULTURAL BEAUTIES.

BREVIER TUSCAN.

BLAKE & STEPHENSON,

LETTER FOUNDERS,

SHEFFIELD.

LITHOGRAPHIC PICTURESQUE VIEWS.

BREVIER ITALIC ANTIQUE SHADED.

NORWICH.

MANCHESTER. NEWCASTLE.

CHELTENHAM.

LEXICOGRAPHIC ILLUSTRATIONS.

BREVIER SHADED.

MEDALLION VIGNETTES.

CAMBRIDGE.

BIRMINGHAM. YORK. PETERBOROUGH.

OXFORD.

BREVIER ITALIC SHADED.

LANDSCAPE AND LAKE SCENERY.

MACCLESFIELD.

HUNTINGDON. DARLINGTON.

LINCOLN.

Fig 15 Specimens of Shaded and Decorated, 1844

limited resource and when time and money had been spent on developing a typeface which subsequently had a limited appeal, father and son often considered how much better their resources could have been used—particularly when there seemed to be a case for expanding body-type production facilities.

Although John Stephenson viewed the progress of the business with a considerable degree of pride, he was singularly aware that his company remained a provincial enterprise and that it lacked a real presence in the City of London—the heart of the English printing and publishing scene. He was at heart a cautious man and whilst he ensured that Stephenson, Blake and Company followed fashion for the sake of profitability, there were times, when he considered the company's response was not as focused on the needs of the printing trade as it should have been and the establishing of a direct link with the London trade would be to the company's advantage.

Chapter 8

The Changing Scene, 1840-1870

THE removal, in 1832, of John Stephenson, his wife and only child, Henry, from the foundry house in Allen Street, first to a house in nearby Gell Street and then to a house in the fashionable St. George's Terrace, marked the beginning of the upward social mobility of the family. St. George's Church, built in 1825, was one of the churches established as a result of Parliament passing The One Million Pound Act, in 1818, which was designed to provide for new Anglican churches in urban areas which had developed in the wake of the Industrial Revolution. When the Stephensons took up residence in the Terrace in 1840, they were already members of the Anglican faith and worshipped at St. George's Church which now faced their new residence from across the churchyard.

The building of four new churches in the town within the decade 1820-1930 had proceeded not so much as a means of bringing the Established Church to the working population but as an exercise in attempting to stem the rising tide of Nonconformity in general and of Methodism in particular. Throughout the latter half of the eighteenth century, radical Nonconformity had grown virtually hand-in-hand with the libertarian politics of the town's working class. Nonconformist chapels offered benefits in addition to religion; their Sunday schools flourished and they supported non-secular education for the children of the poor. The Anglican church also attempted to provide for the poor but there was a considerable long-held resentment by a large proportion of the local population against the Church of England and its institutions which was not without cause. For fifty years, the Vicar of the Parish Church, James Wilkinson, had not only been the resident Magistrate of the County but a Squire who lived not in his vicarage, but in a Georgian residence set in extensive grounds on the outskirts of the town, and whose family had been one of the main beneficiaries as a result of the Enclosure Acts. For fifty years he had virtually ruled the town, had little sympathy with the Nonconformists and their radical libertarian views and had, on a number of occasions called out the military to quell the town's riotous population.

The town had a Grammar School, which was under the control of the Church Burgesses but this was impoverished and of little regard. In 1835, the wealthy manufacturers and professional families who were adherents to the Anglican faith, critical of the educational provision decided to establish a proprietary institution 'Sheffield Collegiate School'. A management committee was established and it was directed that the twelve members of the committee must be members of the Church of England. Shares were available for purchase and the subscription list opened. In the establishing of the Sheffield Collegiate School, the Anglican Church had now secured an influential foothold in higher education. Soon after the school opened, Henry Stephenson became a pupil. It set the scene for several generations of Stephensons and Blakes who not only remained committed to the Church of England but who were also destined to bring considerable influence to bear on the development of the Anglican Church in Sheffield and the city's future educational system. Whilst such connections augured well for the Church, there was considerable resentment and suspicion on the part of the radical Nonconformists, who viewed the development as yet another example of the Church of England exercising undue influence. Within two years, the Methodists had established their own grammar school; Wesley College which was soon to rival and out-class the Collegiate School.

However, the academic attainments of the pupils of the Collegiate School and Wesley College counted for little, only a few of them entered the universities—even though by 1837 the law restricting the admission of non-Anglican Church adherents to universities had been lifted. In Sheffield a narrower view was held. The newly arrived middle and professional class families in general determined that their sons should follow a career in their family businesses. It was therefore not unexpected that John Stephenson had a similar plan for his son, and in 1843, Master Henry, at the age of sixteen, joined the company.

In many respects the typefounders' strike marked the beginning of the end of the original typefounding techniques. Technical innovations were being introduced into the printing process. The development of the iron-hand press facilitated the application of a much more even pressure across the impression platen which made it possible to print effectively on larger sized sheets of paper, whilst the installation of a steam-driven press in 1814 at *The Times,* constructed by Koenig and Bauer, opened the way for applying cylindrical impression to the type forme and ultimately to the development of presses based on the rotary impression principle.

Although the first real, hand-operated, mechanical casting machine was the typecasting machine developed by Dr. William Church which appeared in 1822, few founders were willing to adopt it and the mechanisation of the typecasting operation did not become a commercially viable operation until the early 1850s. The first attempts were not really mechanical inventions, involving the use of a power drive, but merely methods of forcing the metal into the mould by means of a hand-operated pump instead of being poured into the mould by hand. Although the first hand-operated metal pumping device was introduced in Europe by Anthony Francis Berte, in 1807, it was Bower, Bacon and Bower of Sheffield, who developed a pump which could be applied to cast a type of reasonable quality. In 1830, they produced a precision built device which subsequently became known as the Sheffield Furnace-pump. In the following year, 1831, a similar pump which had a spring propelled piston, was developed by two Americans, Mann and Sturdevant. This was later improved upon by the incorporation of a foot-operated control mechanism. Other models were patented in 1834, by David Bruce and in 1838, by Sir Henry Bessemer. Finally, the first successful casting machine, which incorporated many of the developed casting pump principles, was invented in the United States by David Bruce in 1838. This machine became known as the Pivotal Caster. It had a mould which was pivoted and moved to and from the nozzle for each cast. In conjunction with this movement there were also combined movements for opening and closing the mould and tilting the matrix away from the typeface allowing the type to fall away when the mould was opened. These mechanical actions were originated from a series of cams which were turned by means of a hand-operated wheel. As there was no water cooling, the operator paused at a certain position in the turning cycle to allow the mould to cool. Even though productivity increased, the types still needed to have much hand finishing applied. First the tang at the base of the type had to be removed; the letter had to be rubbed on a stone or file to take off the burrs and finally, the type characters had to be set up and dressed, to remove the fragmented end of the tang at the foot, and when appropriate, planed on the front of the body to produce a nick or additional nicks.

The principal typefounders approached the idea of machine casting cautiously. Whilst the hand-powered machines based on Bruce's pivotal principle could produce an output three times greater than casting by hand, the quality of the typeface and the type body often left much to be desired. The type-size and the nature of the face of the letter to be cast frequently determined the quality of the output. The production of a physically sound typographical surface was still the paramount requirement, particularly as printing presses were becoming far more precisely engineered. Nevertheless, master typefounders were anxious to lower production costs and the introduction of casting machines offered a potential solution. Whilst each individual company sought machines which were efficient and which produced high quality type, they wanted such, preferably, at the expense of their rivals. However, as a group, the Typefounders' Association actively prepared to become joint or controlling patentees of any prospective innovations in an effort to secure exclusive manufacturing rights in order to deny those founders outside *The Ring* from developing efficient casting facilities.

From the beginning, John Stephenson had contended that it was the physical quality of type which was the key to producing a satisfactory letterpress printing and his attention to accurate production methods in both the construction of moulds and matrices had clearly paid dividends in relation to the profits of the company and its standing in the printing and typefounding industries. However, by the early 1850s, efficient typecasting machines were becoming available and even he began to recognise that, in an increasingly competitive market, productivity too needed to be considered.

Meanwhile, in 1848, Henry Stephenson, having come of age had £1,000 of shares transferred to him from his father's holding and from the 1850s onwards, he began to direct the day-to-day operations. As a child he had wandered round the foundry and knew the employees and their families closely and the seven years he had spent working in the foundry since leaving school had provided him with considerable technical expertise. In similar cautious vein to his father, Henry Stephenson continued to maintain the high standards, but recognised that if the company was to continue successfully, production methods needed to be changed. However, although he was anxious to ensure that the employees were kept in work and not forced out by the introduction of machinery, he was conscious of a distinct economic advantage; the wage rates paid to typecasters in Sheffield were lower than those in London. Consequently, while ever the merits of introducing typecasting machinery still remained in the balance and the lines between quality, costs, and methods of production, remained questionable, he was reluctant to implement change.

Finally, after much deliberation he initiated a programme of partial mechanisation. In 1852, a planing machine and a matrix-striking machine were installed. A justifying machine was also acquired to finish matrices struck from punches cut for small type-sizes such as brevier and nonpareil, and a kerning machine which facilitated the planing of kerned type bodies was installed. Finally, in 1853, John and Henry Stephenson installed two hand-powered typecasting machines.

By 1860 there were six machines in operation and by 1872 the number had grown to 40. Surprisingly, the introduction of motive power was slow. Henry Stephenson now the Managing Partner, was cautious in his approach. A number of London founders had installed steam power in the 1860s and in the steel and engineering companies surrounding the Sheffield foundry, steam power abounded. Finally, in the early 1870s, steam power was installed. An engine house was built and the appearance of the yard, with its various workshops around it changed dramatically as power shafts and driving belts began to link the steam generated power to the foundry's casting rooms.

However, the seeming tardiness in the technical development of the casting operation did not reflect the true situation. The precision of the company's working practices in mechanical engineering which John Stephenson established continued. Craftsmen engineers were employed and apprentices trained not only in mould making but in the adaptation and development of the casting machines which the company purchased. There was also an acute awareness of mechanical innovation and Stephenson, Blake often invested in new plant, primarily to test its effectiveness. Johnson and Atkinson's caster patented in 1862 was claimed to produce near perfect types in one operation. It was claimed that casting tangs were removed, and that the types required neither rubbing nor dressing. After closely examining the products of the new casting machine, the Sheffield foundry did not consider that the types were of the appropriate quality. However, when Mason, a casting machine maker, produced a mould which made a clean tang break mechanically, the members of the Typefounders' Association paid the inventor a financial premium to enable him to patent the design in Britain and the United States and restrict its use. Stephenson and Blake were quick to see the advantage of the Mason break and subsequently incorporated the principle in the design of their moulds. Although Stephenson, Blake were late in venturing into the use of typecasting machines, this cautiousness proved to be of no obstacle to the company's success at the Great Exhibition held at the Crystal Palace, in 1851. The company was awarded a Diploma and a Gold Medal for the quality of its types and in the succeeding years, were awarded similar accolades at both British and Continental trade fairs. Notwithstanding these successes, it was with a good deal of greater satisfaction that the company hosted the meeting of the British Typefounders' Association in Sheffield in August 1855. To

John and Henry Stephenson, the occasion truly marked the importance of the Sheffield foundry amongst its peers.

However, by the late 1850s, John Stephenson must have had some cause for concern as to the future succession in the business. He was approaching the age of seventy and his health was failing. Whilst Henry had taken on the responsibilities of Managing Partner, he was approaching his mid-thirties and unmarried. Finally, in 1862, at the age of thirty-five, Henry married Emma Parker, the daughter of a solicitor, and took up residence near his parents in a fine Victorian villa in Endcliffe Vale in Upper Hallam.

In 1864, John Stephenson, died at his home in Endcliffe Glen at the age of 74. He was greatly respected—having spent forty years establishing a business which was finally to become Britain's leading typefoundry. At the time of his death there were still only four partners in the business; John Stephenson, Henry Stephenson, William Thompson and Thomas Blake. The two Stephensons held a 16/30ths share holding, whilst Thompson and Thomas Blake held 7/30ths each. The capital value of the company had risen from £9,000 in 1830 to £13,000 in 1841 and £23,000 in 1848. By 1860 the capital value was reckoned at £30,000. Following his father's death, Henry became the major shareholder. Thompson and Blake remained as non-executive shareholders whilst pursuing their own interests in the associated family business.

Four years later, in 1868, Thomas Blake died and his shareholding passed to his son William Greaves Blake. Since 1831 the Blake family's interest in the typefounding business had been agreeably limited to share-holding. In other directions their wider business interests were complex. As a result of a series of marriages the Blakes had become closely linked to a number of other family manufacturing businesses in the town. In 1792, William Greaves had set himself up as a steel maker, and finally, after bringing his sons into the business, built a model factory known as Sheaf Works at the side of the newly opened South Yorkshire Canal—a development which greatly enhanced trade. The imported iron which was brought into the port of Hull was now transported by barge directly into the heart of Sheffield's growing steel industry, whilst vast quantities of coal were transported out.

The firm William Greaves and Sons were pioneers in the making of steel and in manufacturing a wide range of cutting tools. The local trade directory of 1833 described the firm's activity as 'American Merchants, Steel Convertors, Manufacturers of Table Knives, Razors, File and Edge Tools.'[1] Thomas Blake had married Elizabeth, the daughter of William Greaves and in 1823 he left the family file making business in Scotland Street to join his father-in-law and brothers-in-law, Richard and Edward Greaves, at Sheaf Works.

Fig 16 Sheaf Works, 1840 William Greaves and Sons, later Thomas Turton and Sons Limited

In 1850 the principals retired and the firm passed to Thomas Turton and his sons. On the death of Uncle Edward Greaves, William Greaves Blake, his nephew, still in his late teens, became quite wealthy as a result of his uncle's legacy. Meanwhile the marriage of Thomas Blake to Elizabeth Greaves produced six children, two sons and four daughters. However, on his death, in 1868, only one son and two daughters were surviving, hence the greater part of Thomas Blake's estate passed to his son, William Greaves Blake, which included his father's 7/30th share in the Stephenson, Blake Company.

William Greaves Blake was born in 1833, and like Henry Stephenson was educated at the Sheffield Collegiate School. In 1848, after holidaying with his father in the Rhineland, arrangements were made for him to attend a school in Koblenz in order for him to receive a wider education. He appears to have been a student for about two years, principally acquiring fluency in the German language, but letters he sent to his father revealed that conditions were particularly harsh. During 1850 he returned to Sheffield and began working at the typefoundry. As a diversion he volunteered for service in the 3rd Regiment of the West Riding Militia and in May 1853 was commissioned in the rank of Ensign. Then, as the Crimean War broke out, he was called for service as general mobilisation was ordered. He found the military life much to his liking and subsequently became a regular soldier, serving in a number of overseas stations and was posted to India soon after the Great Mutiny.

By 1864, after eleven years' service, he was tiring of the Army—particularly with the boredom of military life in an Indian frontier station. In the extensive correspondence which passed between himself, his family and his friend, Henry Stephenson, he confided that he was becoming increasingly lonely—observing that many of his friends were married and that life in India offered little opportunity for meeting a partner. He resigned his commission and returned to Sheffield. Shortly after his return he married, at the age of 33, Caroline Rebecca Watson, who was related to the Jessops, one of the town's leading steel producing families. Unfortunately, Caroline Jessop died within a year of marriage.

Within two years, Major William Greaves Blake, gentleman and widower, married the nineteen year old Rebecca Jessop, his late wife's cousin and their union was blessed by the birth of eleven children—six daughters and five sons.

Although, William Greaves Blake had inherited the 7/30ths share in the typefoundry he, like his predecessors, took no part in the direct management of the typefoundry business. He openly professed he felt no inclination to follow a full-time career in business and spent much of the remainder of his life at leisure, hunting, shooting, fishing and in the cultivation of orchids at his Sheffield residence, but he did nevertheless, maintain some considerable interests in business and commerce. He was appointed a director of William Jessop and Sons, one of the leading Sheffield steel manufacturers, of the Sheffield Gas Company and of the Sheffield and Rotherham Savings Bank.

Unlike their father, two of his children were destined to become closely involved in the typefoundry business. The second son, Robert Greaves Blake, born in 1875, joined the company in 1894, whilst Frances Blake, the eldest daughter, born in 1870, married Henry Kenyon Stephenson. It was thus that the Stephensons and the Blakes became linked by both marriage and by business. Throughout their lives, W. G. Blake and Henry Stephenson were close personal friends and although Blake took no part in the management of the company, the two were able to deliberate on many issues relating to their mutual business interests. As a result of one such deliberation in 1878, Stephenson, Blake considered that it would be in the longer term interest of the company to acquire William Thompson's shareholding. Unfortunately, Thompson died during the course of the transaction but the agreed arrangement proceeded and his beneficiaries received their settlement over a period of two years. Thereafter, with only two principal shareholders, it was agreed that Henry Stephenson would hold 2/3rds and William Greaves Blake 1/3rd of the shares—and would remain a partner in a non-executive capacity.

Chapter 9

Mutual Friends and Competitors

WHILST Henry Stephenson maintained a careful control of output, whether it was over or under production, it was a caution based on the trade fluctuations of the printing and publishing industry. The profits were generally good but the company always had a large number of creditors and considerable sums of money owing to it. The company, now increasingly under Henry's direction, continued to progress, but the London representative, Henry Bannister Smith, was giving some cause for concern. Smith, who lived at No. 149 Aldersgate, had joined the company in the late 1840s, and whilst his dealings with the customers were good and the foundry's turnover from the London market increased annually, his selling techniques and general demeanour embittered the relationship which Stephenson Blake maintained with the Typefounders' Association. Initially, Henry Bannister Smith was highly regarded and his contribution to the volume of sales was amply rewarded. He was provided with £500 of company shares and was paid a salary of £150 which equalled that of John Stephenson. Then in the late 1850s he began to contract private debts with customers which, in turn, became the responsibility of the company. He resigned in 1860, but his debts were unfortunately of such magnitude that they had to be met by John and Henry Stephenson and by the other partners and by two business friends of the family, who also acted as guarantors.

Whilst in the mid-nineteenth century a general turndown in business had affected the printing trade there was one area of activity which, from 1855, had been most lucrative. The repeal of the Newspaper Stamp Tax had brought the development of scores of local papers which had created increasing demand for newspaper body types which were relatively easily cast and profitable. Sales were high and demand was too, and whilst the foundry had expanded its production capacity, output still lagged behind and the company found the greatest difficulty in meeting customers' demands. However, the breakdown of the price-fixing arrangement of the Typefounders' Association meant that although the volume of type produced was higher, the lower prices had, overall, reduced profits.

Active membership within the Typefounders Association had brought rewards and recognition which were not necessarily of a direct financial kind. Stephenson, Blake could well be said to have become recognised as a major typefounding company by the time the Association met in Sheffield in 1855. To some extent the ill-feeling which the London representative, Henry Bannister Smith, had caused in the period 1855 to 1861, was ameliorated by careful deliberation in the meetings of the Association, but his departure from the firm left the London representation bereft. For a number of years, trade with the London printers and newspaper makers depended much on the firm's reputation rather than representation. Now although Henry Stephenson made frequent visits to London to visit key customers, there was a limit to the amount of time which could be devoted to servicing the London accounts. By the mid-1860s it was becoming increasingly clear that a London office and warehouse was necessary.

A lease was taken out on the ground floor space of a building, No 90 Newgate Street and it was opened late in 1865. The value of the innovation was difficult to assess due to a singular promising situation which came to pass coincidentally. The H. W. Caslon Company which during the previous thirty years had undergone a technical transformation, had developed some considerable new business both in London and more particularly overseas—trading in many respects, on the historic name of Caslon. Unfortunately, the H. W. Caslon company was not the most stable of organisations. Considerable difficulties had arisen in the day to day management of the business. Production was at times severely limited due to lack of co-operation and wage demands on the part of the typecasters. This state of affairs led to a serious lack of trading stability. As a result of a long drawn out dispute within the company, Thomas White Smith, one of its senior representatives, left Caslons and took up an appointment as the Stephenson, Blake London Office Manager.

Thomas White Smith and the newly opened London office and warehouse proved to be an immediate success. The trade with the London printers increased at an incredible rate and Smith's connections with overseas agents set the scene for the expansion of overseas trade. Clearly the newly

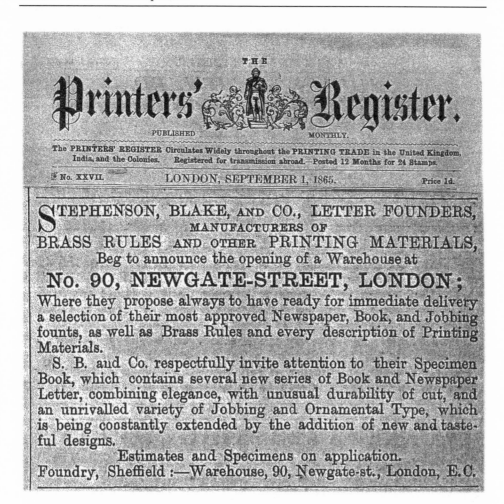

Fig 17 Advertisement, Printers' Register informing customers of the opening of the
London warehouse No. 90 Newgate Street, 1st September 1865

found trade and contracts came at the expense of H. W. Caslon and
Company. After five years, it had more than exceeded Henry Stephenson's
expectations. By the early 1870s, it was patently clear that the Newgate
Street premises had become inadequate. Whilst ideas of leasing more
accommodation at Newgate Street were considered, Henry Stephenson's
vision was of a London Office, Showroom and Warehouse of significant
and commanding proportions. Newgate Street was near the City, but prestigious premises in the square mile comprising Fleet Street and Farringdon
Road would place Stephenson, Blake in the very heart of the British printing industry. The choice of premises was settled by agreeing a lease of 21
years for No 33 Aldersgate Street on 25th March 1871.

Fig 18 London office and warehouse,
No. 33 Aldersgate Street

Thomas White Smith managed the London office for eight years with
great credit. He not only established Stephenson, Blake as a major player
in the City's printing and publishing industry he also made a valuable
contribution towards opening up overseas trade for, whilst he was at the
Caslon Foundry, he had also helped establish a representative and a warehouse in Paris, and he had also opened up negotiations with a view of
expanding Caslon sales in Europe. His efforts to establish Stephenson,
Blake in the Colonies were successful and agents and warehouses were
established in Australia—Melbourne, Sydney, Wellington and Brisbane,
and later in Canada and South Africa. However, the cultivation and development of the European market barely proceeded after 1873—a regression
which arose out of a delicate and somewhat curious situation.

H. W. Caslon and Company, in the 1820s, had been in a parlous situation. This had arisen as a result of family deaths and changes of ownership. However, throughout the latter half of the nineteenth century, following a period of stable management and a generally favourable trading climate, it had renewed itself from a near-bankrupt situation and had regained much of its former prestige. Its position in Chiswell Street in the heart of the City of London placed it in a favourable situation where it was not only able to service the needs of the London printers and publishers but promote its trade with the Colonies—for not least reason that the very name Caslon represented an essential Englishness in its associations. However, the latter day resurgence of the company was primarily due to one man: a young compositor from the West Country, Thomas White Smith. On the 24th January 1854, having completed his apprenticeship that very day, he had been invited to take dinner with his employer, a Mr. Sercombe. Also taking dinner at Mr. Sercombe's home that evening was, by coincidence, the Stephenson, Blake London representative, Henry Bannister Smith. H. B. Smith took kindly to the young man, recommended him to Henry Stephenson, who engaged him to serve as a clerk in Stephenson, Blake's counting house in Sheffield with a view to his becoming one of the firm's representatives. The young T. W. Smith at this stage in his life seemed unsuited to work as a representative and after three years left Stephenson, Blake and entered the counting house of H. W. Caslon and Company. Later, T. W. Smith recounted . . . *the only other occupants of the counting house besides the principals (H W Caslon and George Fagg) were the good old typefounder and kindly Scotsman Alexander Wilson . . .* [2]

In August 1860, after three years, he joined the 'outdoor' staff and took up residence in Leeds. For five years he worked the whole of the North of England, Scotland and Ireland and brought a great deal of business into the company. Unfortunately all was not well at H. W. Caslons, as T. W. Smith related: *Mr. Henry Caslon, the last of the name, was a man of generous impulse, but of little wisdom in business matters. He was more fitted to fill the role of a gentleman of the world, unfettered by any necessity to consider ways and means, than to own and manage successfully a typefoundry, however old and well established. The natural consequence was that the income derived from the business did not stand the demands which he made upon it, and an ill-advised attempt being made to reduce the wages of some of the workmen, a strike of those of one department of manufacture took place, followed by a lockout of all the rest. This lamentable occurrence, which led to almost total suspension of the business for eight months of the year 1865, nearly ruined it. Alexander Wilson and his brother Patrick, as well as myself, were no longer occupied in Chiswell*

Street, and whilst my old Scotch friends were able to retire on a small competence left them by a distant relative, I had to seek employment elsewhere.[3]

Whatever gentlemanly explanations were recorded of the situation, it is not difficult to surmise the sheer frustration of T. W. Smith. He was now aged 32 and in the previous five years, spent on the road as a traveller, had not only proved himself a successful representative, he had developed considerable personal self-confidence. Finally, there could have been nothing more frustrating than having clients' orders on the books and no means of fulfilling them by reason of a strike induced by the owner.

The employment of T. W. Smith by Stephenson, Blake represented a paradox. In his eight years as their representative, trade allegiances and sales were switched at the expense of the Caslon Company. The foundry strike, the loss of customers and credibility took its toll. The elderly Henry Caslon was in declining health and there was no one obvious successor. In a bid to save the company, Caslon approached Stephenson, Blake with a view to a possible merger. This proposal, at face value, looked attractive to Henry Stephenson. The foundry was modern and well-equipped with a good deal more production capacity than he had in Sheffield. There were 55 casting machines, 40 of which were steam driven, two were for the casting of script and three for large letter. There were in excess of 600 moulds, amongst which were 100 which had been made to meet the needs of the French market. H. W. Caslon and Company was indeed an attractive proposition despite its recent decline. It still had many good accounts and an overseas trade which was worth acquiring, moreover, it had a name: Caslon—this alone meant much in terms of national, colonial and international goodwill.

The proposed merger negotiations were conducted in most gentlemanly terms. However, Henry Stephenson wrote: *I should like very well to remove our foundry to London and incorporate it with yours as a matter of inclination, but the present state of typefounding is so unpromising, and the actual value of any plant so much reduced by comparison with times of higher prices, that I doubt if you would be disposed to take such a sum as the present conditions of trade would warrant my giving.*[4]

Caslon responded with a price of £15,000 plus stock at valuation. Further correspondence put the value of the stock at £26,000 and after some bargaining it was agreed that the stock would be valued at half price. The offer was attractive and the cost of acquiring such a well-equipped and in every way desirable acquisition, was relatively cheap. However, the marked success after only two years of Stephenson, Blake's venture in establishing a warehouse in Newgate Street to some extent tempered Henry

Stephenson's view of the deal. Nevertheless he did not reject it out of hand. The idea of merging and transferring his business to London would never have been seriously considered. Whilst the Stephenson, Blake Company was in the process of making its mark on the printing and typefounding industry, at home, in their native Sheffield, the Stephensons and their business associates were reckoned as principal players in a town which was developing as an important industrial centre with burgeoning civic developments in which the Stephensons were destined to play a key part.

Henry Stephenson kept his options open for several months. Finally he wrote to Henry Caslon declining his offer. It cannot but be mused whether or not he delayed the decision in the hope that he might have acquired the Caslon foundry at a lower price? It was a decision which over the next seventy years Henry Stephenson and his successors would have some cause to regret. The ambitious Henry White Smith now seized his chance and negotiated to return to H. W. Caslon and Company as manager with an agreement that on the demise of Henry Caslon he would acquire ownership of the foundry.

However, there were more pressing problems for Henry Stephenson. A trade war was now waging amongst the major typefounders. Stephenson, Blake's turnover slackened in the mid to late 1870s and the pursuit of further continental agencies was set back as great efforts were required to keep the London market sustained. The price-war and the disarray amongst the typefounders began to take its toll. As a consequence, the five leading companies came together again and the Typefounders' Association was re-formed in order to set an agreed level of prices. The resurgence of the Association was timely. A prolonged general economic down-turn between 1874 and 1889 caused a good deal of depression, although the printing, publishing and typefounding industries did not suffer quite as severely as other parts of the economy.

The Association now comprised: H. W. Caslon Company, V. and J. Figgins, Miller and Richards, Sir Charles Reed and Son, and Stephenson, Blake. The general interest of the members was to maintain a level of prices for type which would produce comfortable profits; promote the adoption of a standard measure for printers and typefounders, and take whatever action it could against the independent typefounders who were operating outside the Association, producing low cost type, using pirated designs replicated by the electrotyping process. They went further, and attempted to promote legislation relating to the assigning of copyright to the design of typefaces. In more robust terms, if the Association could buy out or drive an independent founder out of business it would. In short the Association aimed to monopolise the production of printers type.

Whilst the Typefounders' Association flourished, the price of type remained high. In the years when the members' tenuous relationships broke down, they discovered, to their cost, the damage which price cutting had caused. Having learned a hard lesson, the Association had reconvened, but the problems which now loomed were problems which, on the longer term, were insoluble. As a body they were at one in attempting to monopolise the development of typecasting machinery and the protection of typeface designs. Their efforts seemed to be in vain now that electroplating and electro deposition techniques had made it possible to plagiarise and copy designs directly from the cast letter. Electrotyping was a process on which the Typefounders' Association poured their scorn and they made much of their case—that types so produced could never have the quality of letter which had been cast from a struck matrix. Clearly, the derision and declamations by the Association and its members indicated their fears—particularly when the Association could not prevail on Parliament to secure copyright or patenting of designs beyond a period of five years.

The printing trade was ever quick to rail against the Association. Type had always been costly but during the interregnum years when the Association had collapsed there had been significant reductions in the price of type. Now the Association was reconstituted and there were ominous signs that the price of type would rise dramatically. The trade press complained and reflected the general bitterness. The publisher of the *Printers' Register*, Arthur Powell took up the cause and criticised the Association referring to it as *The Ring*. His tone and approach was deemed by the Association, to be so rude and vociferous that a libel action against him was threatened. This threat was dropped when the Association realised that many of its members' customers supported the criticism of *The Ring*.

However, the Association was made of firmer stuff and now took a different stance. The members not only owned their respective businesses, they were, in their own right, men of considerable stature in politics and in the City and were not prepared to take criticism either from printers or from the trade press. They agreed that they would not publicly respond to any criticism of the Association's pricing policy; would not refute or deny any criticism of the fact that they were maintaining a monopoly and, finally— an action which provoked many years' resentment—refused to undertake any form of press advertising. The imperious attitude of the Association caused even the normally unbiased and impartial writers of educational and instruction manuals on the art of printing to condemn *The Ring* and its practices.

However, with increasing mechanical innovation, higher output and with growing demands from a fast-growing printing industry, the latter half of the nineteenth century can be regarded as the heyday for the traditional letterfounders' businesses. What, in the earlier part of the century, had been a relatively modest operation which could be set up locally with a minimum of capital, was now an increasingly complex business requiring significant investment. Mechanisation and motive power to drive the machines was necessary, as was a need for considerable engineering expertise to meet the ever increasing demands for high quality type. Consequently, many of the smaller foundries, which had sprung up between 1820 and 1860, were unable to meet the challenge and closed. In contrast, a number of the larger printing companies and newspaper houses installed their own typecasting facilities, although these offered little by way of competition.

By the 1890s, the five great typefounding houses, represented by the Typefounders Association, created a virtual monopoly out of their capacity to produce high quality printing types. Overall their profits during the period 1875-1895 were reasonably high as the members maintained a strong hold on the prices they controlled. The master printers and the owners of newspapers railed against the high prices but the complaints fell on deaf ears. The principals of the major typefounding companies not only maintained their price ring, they were also careful to maintain their stature. Aldermen Figgins and Besley, Sir Charles and Talbot Baines Reed and Sir Henry Stephenson represented a coterie which was not to be moved. They met as the Typefounders' Association, twice a year in congenial surroundings and with a general bonhomie of gentlemanly goodwill—seemingly presenting a united front to the trade in the matter of type prices. Individually, they were jealous and suspicious of one another and of each other's business activity and social standing. To the printing industry, the superiority of the Typefounders' Association and its members, represented an intractable group. The Association would neither negotiate, nor advertise, nor justify the arbitrary—*what the market demand will stand*—pricing policy. As a result, their businesses prospered and profits remained high.

However, by the early 1890s, their end was already being foretold. Mechanical composition was being introduced. The seemingly overtly gentlemanly business of the Association gradually began to decline. James Figgins was Chairman of the Association until 1894, when during that year, a bitter disagreement involving Figgins' foundry with another member's company led to Figgins' resignation and to his company withdrawing from the Association, whereupon, the Chairmanship passed into the hands of Sir Henry Stephenson.

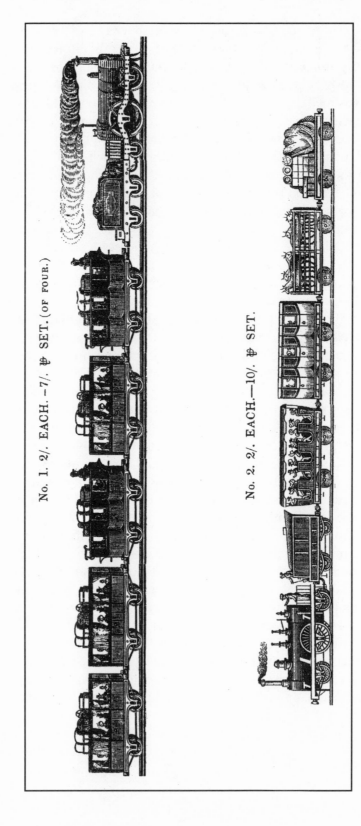

No. 1. 2/. EACH. –7/. ₱ SET. (OF FOUR.)

No. 2. 2/. EACH.—10/. ₱ SET.

Fig 19 The Coming of the Railways, pieced engines and carriages
Blake and Stephenson, 1844

Chapter 10

Techniques and Technicalities

T HE mid-nineteenth century output from typefoundries was, on one hand, geared to meet a fickle, fashion-driven but design-insensitive market; on the other, it was concerned to meet a demand for body-type from the newspaper printers and the book houses. The general market—printing and publishing businesses, demanded typographical novelties and display types and that demand seemed insatiable. The meeting of that demand was costly and required a rapid turnover of designs. For typefounders, the creation or commissioning of ornamented or decorated letter was not easy. Many typefounders resorted to design techniques which were not only aesthetically flawed but which were crude and in the worst possible taste.

In general, analysis of the fashionable life-span of a basic design of letter (such as a Sans serif, Modern, Grotesque or Tuscan) appears to have been some thirty years, from inception to the point when, either as a result of declining sales or a falling from fashion, the typeface was quietly withdrawn, or withdrawn deliberately, in order to force customers into buying newly cast letter. Frequently, a particular typeface design which, from the time of its first appearance in a specimen book, proved to be a success, would be developed beyond a point of practical and commercial reasonableness as a result of it passing through every conceivable variation of shape and strength, some of which variations were often embellished by decoration and excrescences which were both ridiculous and tasteless. Whilst the production of such varieties cost money, the market bore the cost and the founder made a profit. However, this kind of business only thrived whilst a founder could keep issuing an unending stream of new designs. Consequently, newly issued specimen books and leaflets always heralded the virtues and uniqueness of newly created designs and typographical novelties. Increasingly, the policy of Stephenson, Blake of continuing to make the finest quality type, ran contrary to the needs of many printers who often purchased cheaper type because of its ephemeral nature.

In contrast, the production of body types for the setting of text scarcely changed during the latter part of the nineteenth century. The basic design of type used was regarded, euphemistically, as Modern, but the basic design was available from every typefoundry in a wide range of weights of body, stroke, size, set-width and x-height. In the setting of text matter for book work, the average compositor and master printer believed that wide word spacing and leaded interlinear spacing was the true means of realising legibility. Meanwhile, the display, advertising and jobbing compositor's yardstick for creating an interesting design was the use of a different and a contrasting typeface on every line—the page often being crowned with an attempt to fill the entire space of the broadsheet. In contrast, the printers of newspapers were primarily concerned with the density of wording within the columns.

From the middle of the nineteenth century onwards a slow but fundamental change began to take place. The starting point was the output from the Chiswick Press. The typographical style of a number of its books appeared radically different. This change was exemplified by the use of Caslon Old Face—a type face which for almost sixty years had been considered unfashionable. Its reappearance has always been exemplified in the production of the work: *Lady Willoughby's Diary,* which was published in 1844. However, this was but one work of the period which the Chiswick Press printed in this style. In the years which followed, the H. W. Caslon company were casting the original Caslon Old Face to order, and during that time a discrete group of printer-publishers met with some success in recapturing the Aldine tradition. Then, in 1857, Caslons, sensing there might be a market for Caslon Old Face, reintroduced it. Vincent Figgins followed, and reissued a Roman which had appeared in a 1795 specimen book. These desultory innovations made little impact; the majority of books and newspapers still embraced the ubiquitous Modern typeface.

The truly typographical innovation came in 1860, when the Edinburgh firm of Miller and Richard issued Old Style, a series, in eight sizes—from pearl to great primer. It was a redesigned Old Face which had been cut for them by Alexander C. Phemister. In presenting it, the foundry explained in some detail that it had been cut to avoid the objectionable peculiarities which were inherent in Old Face. The Miller and Richard Old Style was an acclaimed success and other founders, faced with enquiries from their customers, began to cut their own particular versions. Meanwhile, Phemister left the Miller and Richard foundry and joined the Dickinson foundry in Boston, Massachusetts where he cut another version which the company launched as Franklin Old Style. Next, H. W. Caslon joined the tilt by making much, in their advertising, of the fact that their Caslon Old Face was the only truly genuine version. Stephenson, Blake not to be outdone, set their punchcutters to work on a version which was issued in 1886 and displayed in a specimen leaflet entitled, *A New Series of Old Style Types*. Other founders followed. The Patent Type Company, directed by Shanks, issued a version of Old Style whilst Sir Charles Reed's, Fann Street Foundry issued a series in 1866, which they euphemistically described as Medieval Founts. Clearly the movement away from the monotonous Modern typeface was beginning in earnest.

Whilst the generally variable state of the economy constantly affected the growing printing and newspaper publishing industry of the United Kingdom, the overall profitability of Stephenson, Blake, and their competitors tended to remain reasonably good. The need for type was making demands on the foundries and designs, whether good or bad, still needed to have punches cut and matrices struck. The difficulty in meeting the demands of the market was often to be found in the shortage of competent punchcutters. Those who were available, were in the main technician-letter cutters—and they were exactly that. There was a real dearth of artist-letter cutters who could create original designs. Talbot Baines Reed's remark on the distancing of the artist from the technician had certainly come to pass.[1] Universally they, almost unbeknowingly, shared the difficulty of being able to recreate a true Old Face which would offer an appropriate printed image. One of the problems was the changes which were taking place in the printing process. In the hundred years since Caslon's time, letterpress printing practice had changed. Printing was now undertaken on machines with a cylindrical impression. Formes of type were no longer inked by tampons but by carefully set gelatine rollers which rolled ink on to the face of the type. The impression cylinder packed with a relatively hard dressing—as opposed to the traditional soft handpress tympan dressing—by comparison, only required minimum of pressure. The substance of paper too had changed. It was no longer manufactured from rag fibres but from wood pulp fibres. The product from the late nineteenth century paper mill was smoother—unlike rag paper, which not only had to be dampened but impressed deeply into the body of the paper. Meanwhile after the 1850s, the development of rotary presses had increased the speed of output of newspapers dramatically and this had been achieved by the development of a method of casting semi-cylindrical stereotyped plates. However, the production of flongs for the casting of rotary stereotype plates was making demands on the typographical image for, as crude as the newsprint image was, readability of the newspaper was still of primary importance. The established Modern typefaces, with the delicacy of contrast of thick and thin strokes and finely bracketed serifs, did not reproduce well on newsprint printed from a stereotyped plate. The production of stereotypes for the book printing trade had for a long time been undertaken by the use of handmade, wet flongs which were impressed by brush-beating and then dried out before casting. This process contrasted greatly with the dry or semi-dry flongs which were used to press flongs for semi-circular, stereotyped plates which had to moulded and cast within a short production time-frame. Arising from these limitations, type designs suitable for stereotyping tended to be used. The essential characteristics of the designs were those of the Ionic letter design, which were medium weight faces, possessing equal and even body strokes with unbracketed serifs. They were unimaginative but practical typefaces which, when stereotyped, printed reasonably successfully.

Meanwhile, Stephenson, Blake continued to seek improvements in the casting and finishing of their type. There were still many technical problems which had to be overcome. By the 1860s typecasting machines could remove the tang 'break' automatically but there was still a need to dress the feet of the letters and this was done by setting up the characters into lines and then planing the foot of the types to remove the burrs left by the breaking away of the tang. When the members of the Typefounders' Association shared the acquired patent rights for incorporating the 'Mason break' into the mechanism of moulds this was seen as a boon and Stephenson, Blake immediately began a programme of modifying their equipment in order to incorporate the idea. However, there was still an irksome, labour intensive operation to be overcome; that of rubbing down of the newly cast types at the point where the matrix and mould had come together during the process of casting. As early as 1868, the company had seen the potential usefulness of a mechanical rubbing machine which had been developed by an American, Patrick Welch, but decided that, although the foundry believed *the less a letter was handled the better,* because of the low level of wages paid, it was cheaper to have the job done manually than by machine. However, by 1877, it was becoming clear that by redesigning the shape of the shoulder within the matrix the problem might be solved. The problem had initially been solved at the Edinburgh foundry of Miller and Richard by William Grandison, who had developed a punch profile which prevented distortion of the sidewall of the matrix during the striking oper-

ation. Grandison, a punchcutter of some repute, having been made a generous financial offer which he could hardly refuse, left Miller and Richard
and joined Stephenson, Blake.

Those members of the staff who were engaged in punch and matrix
production had an almost separate and privileged existence. The production
of matrices was still predominantly undertaken by the striking or pressing
of punches—a technique which had been proven over the centuries. The
quality of type produced was high, so why change? Whilst the casting
department pointed out, almost in vain, that the machine speeds and
high operational temperatures were causing undue wear on matrices and
much maintenance was required; their words fell on stony ground. Other
foundries were using electrolytic plating methods to enhance the wearabil-
ity of their matrices, whilst Stephenson, Blake still relied upon burnishing
the face of the matrices. If the machinery and maintenance of matrices was
a cause for concern, the cutting of punches was also. The skill of hand and
eye still remained paramount in the process of cutting punches but it was a
stage in the making of types which remained sacrosanct. The production of
new typefaces and novelties was limited to the output which could be
wrung from the punchcutter.

Meanwhile, the search continued for ideas and inventions which would
automate the whole of the casting process. In 1884, James McLaren, a
Glasgow justifier, developed a machine which automatically dressed the
type and Henry Stephenson saw that the machine had distinct promise.
Unfortunately, during the later stages of its development, McLaren died.
However, his executor was approached and the patent rights for the
machine were acquired and a McLaren dressing machine was made and set
up in the foundry. By the final quarter of the nineteenth century,
Stephenson, Blake had established a precision engineering workshop of
some significance. The latest typecasting machines and letter finishing
devices were acquired and studied. Seemingly worthwhile improvements
were incorporated into their own highly modified and idiosyncratic
machines. The workshop not only designed and built typecasting machines
but also, designed and built moulds which incorporated innovations from
other foundries.

Elsewhere, production methods were changing dramatically. As early as
1827, an American, Darius Wells, had begun making large sized type in
wood and by 1834, William Levenworth had developed a machine which
incorporated a pantograph which routed out the shape of wood letters. This
development made possible the production of wooden poster types and its
success led to the demise of large letter cast by the sanspareil matrix and
mould. By the early 1880s, Lyn Boyd Benton of Milwaukee had taken out

a British patent on a pantograph-based punch-cutting machine similar to Levenworth's except that it was designed to fashion, by cutting, master letters which could subsequently be used to 'grow' matrices electrolytically. By 1885, Benton had modified his machine to facilitate the engraving of matrices and his engraving machines were subsequently installed in the Mergenthaler Linotype Company to successfully mass produce line composition matrices. Originally, Benton had offered his punch cutting machine to Stephenson, Blake but it is said that Henry Stephenson dismissed the offer on the grounds that he did not believe the principles on which the patent was established was unique, the more probable reason being that he thought that cutting punches, and possibly matrices, by machine was a step too far and that the quality of the type produced would be compromised. Six years were to elapse before Stephenson installed a Benton-Waldo machine and even then it was at the instigation of an outsider, Emile Bertaut, a freelance punchcutter. On being commissioned to cut a new typeface, Bertaut announced that he would initially set his assistant cutting the punches on a Benton-Waldo machine and that he himself would undertake the finishing by hand. It is not too difficult to reckon the labour economics of the operation. Punchcutters were always paid premium rate wages and the idea that the outline work could be speeded up considerably by machine cutting was probably the deciding factor. There is little doubt that behind Bertaut's advice lay the influence of Elisha Pechey, the London Office Manager who had been pressing the matter for several years, along with a demand that the company should permanently employ an engraver who could produce typographical novelties in tune with market demands.

Chapter 11

Types: Gentlemen and Players

IN many respects, the London Manager and his staff became the true antenna of the company. Henry Stephenson had, from the first, repeatedly reminded them that the purpose of the London Office, the warehouse and showroom was not merely to stock and sell type; but to truly represent the company, send market intelligence to Sheffield and keep him advised of any promising letter designers and punchcutters who could be of value to the company.

At first, the departure of Thomas White Smith from the London Office to H. W. Caslon and Company, appeared to spell disaster, particularly as the showroom in Aldersgate had only been open two years. Henry Stephenson was also somewhat bemused regarding a successor for there was a distinct slackening in trade—quite possibly because T. W. Smith, contrary to a gentleman's agreement not to poach customers, moved his personal clients back to the H. W. Caslon Company. After considerable thought Henry Stephenson transferred his Chief Clerk, Elisha Pechey, from Sheffield, to manage the London Office. Pechey had for ten years been most successful and his accomplishments were not limited to the administrative function. Having served his time as an apprentice compositor and having subsequently worked in London as a highly respected Proof Reader, he brought to the company his considerable typographical expertise, designing, almost incidentally, an innovative decorative brass-rule combination border which, at the time, not only sold well but which was also regarded as typographically useful. For Pechey managing the London Office was a challenge and he knew a difficult task lay ahead. He reviewed the situation and came to the conclusion that the inner London market was well served by the representatives of the main typefounders. However, Greater London and the towns and villages of the Home Counties, with a growing urban population and with the emergence of local newspapers, hitherto of little importance, appeared to be the source of much needed additional sales. Pechey persuaded Henry Stephenson to allow him to appoint an assistant who was charged to service the Greater London area. The tactic worked, particularly as the remaining sales areas in the provinces had been reallocated and the policy of calling on customers was extended from twice a year to one of quarterly visits.

Nevertheless, Stephenson had to seriously consider the very variable trading situation. The foundry had been extended. New casting shops had been erected and equipped with the most up to date machinery. The additional sales staff who had been employed to bring in orders had done their work well. The order books were now over full which had led to a situation where, despite enlarged production capacity, customers' needs could not be met and the rate of good, but outstanding, debt was rising. In 1867, it had stood at £10,000, twenty years later, in 1887, it had risen to over £20,000. Now, almost without warning the demand for stock suddenly became unprecedented. Pechey found it difficult to meet demands from customers and was constantly pressing Sheffield to increase production. It was particularly embarrassing when the company could not supply even its newspaper customers under two to three months. From London, Pechey, in near despair, wrote to Henry Stephenson: *We are, I suppose, in a worse state with regard to stock both here* [London Office] *and at Sheffield than we ever were relatively before but there is no doubt in my mind that the efforts of your engineers and fitters must be unrelaxed to keep pace with the growth of your business . . . I am afraid this is the only foundry that has ever found it necessary to adopt stunting and repressive measures of this kind, but I fancy you have never had sufficient faith in the growth of your business . . .* [1] In Pechey's observations can be found the basis of the difficulties which the London Office faced in dealing with its Head Office and Foundry 170 miles away. Whilst at the foundry, emphasis lay in the production of great quantities of highly profitable body type to meet the needs of the burgeoning newspaper industry, the creation and production of new typefaces and commercial novelties took second place. Both Pechey and his successor, Hanson, had to compete in the London market, not only against the travellers employed by members of the Typefounders Association but also with a number of independent typefounders whose prices were much lower and who were often selling the latest typographical novelties and fancy typefaces. Henry Stephenson was less than enthusiastic. There was a good deal of inertia on his part and an even greater reluctance to take advice from the key members of his staff, particularly those based in the London office. The correspondence which passed between Henry Stephenson and Elisha Pechey indicate that relationships, whilst gentlemanly, were often less than amiable. Pechey was not one to hold his tongue and his all too frequent demands commercially and typo-graphically fell on deaf ears. An example of the tortuous nature of the rela-tionship is to be found in a letter from Pechey to Henry Stephenson, dated 29 December 1894: . . . *Your deference to my view as to the new Old Style is flattering, but puzzling. You have a more or less definite ideal in your mind, which I am afraid is different from mine. You agree as to the fatness of hairline and mainstroke and gauge being as now, and I agree to the De Vinne form of letter being adopted. My ambition had been to get a distinctly new character of Old Style, but I see no reason why I should desire to further my own views on such a speculative subject against your opinion and those you have consulted . . . My experience has taught me that the fatness, etc. of the new O.S. is what is wanted . . . I cannot claim to have got any ideas whatever from the Printers' opinions. I merely know they can appreciate an entirely new departure.*[2]

A few months later, Henry Stephenson wrote: [On the matter concerning the No. 3 Old Style] *We had persuaded ourselves into liking it, but with the reservation that it would have been improved by being distinctly wider fuller and with thicker hairlines. . . We hardly dare occupying the punch cutters with a series which we are only half satisfied with but which will keep them off other work for at least two years. Can you not suggest where the present fount fails to realise your ideal, or where the ideal has been at fault?*[3]

For almost thirty years Elisha Pechey was the mainspring of innovation and development, technically and commercially. His dedication to the company filled his whole life. Whilst he struggled against the increasingly obdurate and autocratic Henry Stephenson, at other times he could not but be totally bemused by his employer, who could be so patronisingly gener-ous and caring.

In 1900, Pechey at the age of 69, journeyed to America and Canada seek-ing to develop further the company's representation. Whilst returning from America he was taken ill and though he resumed work for a short period, he never really recovered and died in March 1902. Pechey, the London face of Stephenson, Blake, was dead. His twenty-nine years directing the affairs of the company via the London Office coincided with very different activ-ities elsewhere.

Henry Stephenson began his life in the foundry. He knew every member of the workforce and their families. He knew every alley, ginnel and building in the Sheffield crofts. As a committed member of the Church of England he worshipped at St. George's Church. The residents of the area were representative of the poorest elements of a town which was now booming and prosperous as a centre of steel production and armaments. The rise of the Stephensons from that of a respectable family of mechanics to considerable affluence was greeted either with intense envy or admiration and supportive bonhomie. In reality, the family was rapidly outgrowing its roots. What does a successful second generation business man do when at the head of a highly respected profitable business?

Henry Stephenson, now in his mid-fifties, had for long managed the company autocratically and arbitrarily—albeit with a degree of paternalism. However, as his life passed it seems evident that his role in the business was less than satisfying and he began to turn his energies, altruistically or otherwise, to local politics and social affairs. In November 1883, he was nominated as a by-election candidate for a seat on the Sheffield Town Council held to serve as a Councillor for St. George's Ward, his political leaning being reflected in his membership of the Liberal-Unionist group. Although at the age of 56 he was one of the youngest members, he quickly made his mark. Only three years later, in 1886, he was chosen to be Mayor of Sheffield and, in the year following he became an Alderman and, as 1887 was Queen Victoria's Golden Jubilee year, Henry Stephenson on Jubilee Day, 21st June 1887, was honoured by the Queen with a knighthood. Other honours and responsibilities followed. He became a Town Trustee, a Church Burgess and a Magistrate. In 1900 he was made an Honorary Freeman of the relatively newly created City of Sheffield. In 1903, he became the first Chairman of the Sheffield Education Committee created as a result of the passing of the 1902 Education Act.

Sir Henry Stephenson's record extended further. Mark Firth, a wealthy, second generation steel manufacturer and owner of Thomas Firth and Son, became interested in establishing a university extension college. He donated considerable sums of money and Firth College was established. Unfortunately, within a year, Mark Firth, the principal benefactor, was dead. The College struggled to survive until 1897, the year of Queen Victoria's Diamond Jubilee, when a subscription fund was established to enable it to become University College. Sir Henry Stephenson became its principal benefactor providing support which finally enabled the College in 1905, to become fully chartered as The University of Sheffield.

As the 1890s came to a close, the health of Sir Henry Stephenson gradually began to decline although he continued to undertake both his public duties and his nominal oversight of the foundry. Even in his early seventies, he would walk the two miles distance from his home in Endcliffe Glen to

Fig 20 Sir Henry Stephenson, KT 1827–1904

the foundry. From Endcliffe, through Ranmoor and Broomhill—the elegant Victorian Broomhill of John Betjeman's poem.[4] He would pass the opulent houses of the wealthy Sheffield steel-barons of the late Victorian age, thence leading to commodious terraced houses of the city's business folk, before finally descending the hill into Nether Hallam and St. George's Ward, the gateway to the squalid slums of the crofts, where the expanding Stephenson, Blake and Company's typefoundry was sited. As Sir Henry wended his way, he would be greeted by the townsfolk of every station. Many of the local families had known him since boyhood and he was now highly regarded as one of the founders of the emerging City of Sheffield. At the foundry he ruled, rather than managed, but his many years of expe-

rience and practical expertise were never in doubt and, whilst his workers
and senior staff often railed, his all-embracing benevolence tempered their
often held malevolence and grievances.

The factory had grown. The company had been able to buy the adjacent
near-derelict properties over a period. Behind the original house he had
occupied in his boyhood, in the now named Upper Allen Street, numerous
extensions had been built. The factory had spread across and into Marsden
Lane to provide typecasting shops. An engine house originally housing a
steam engine was superseded by a gas engine.[5] A model suite of offices
was provided for the principal and the senior managers—with ornate tiled
walls and tiled ceilings supported by decorative gilt studs, the rooms were
expensively furnished with solid mahogany desks, all of which gave an
aura of successful trading and industrial opulence. The order-clerks and
members of the counting house sat on high stools maintaining ledgers,
processing orders and keeping a close eye on the customers' credit levels.
On the south side bounded by Kenyon Alley lay the engineering department and brass rule manufacture, whilst at a later time, the upper storey on
the south side would be designated the punchcutters' room, planned to
provide north light for the engravers and punchcutters and in later years
would be augmented by electrolytic plant for the production of matrices.

The sudden demise of the first patron of Sheffield University College,
Mark Firth, had in many ways, put Sir Henry Stephenson in a difficult
position. Another public figure had to take the lead and the governing body,
of which he was a member, looked upon him, despite his age and increasing infirmity, as a natural successor. In the Spring of 1904, the task of
establishing the new university was almost complete when word came from
the Privy Council that a Charter, establishing the University of Sheffield,
was to be granted and that King Edward VII would make an official visit
to mark the event by opening the new university buildings. Sadly, for the
Vice President of University College, Sir Henry Stephenson, this was not
to be. He died on the 24th August 1904, aged 77. His death was marked by
voluminous obituaries recording his long public service. The printing and
typefounding industries paid tribute to his role; acclaiming him as the
doyen of British typefounding. There was yet another event which heralded
change: in 1904, Major William Greaves Blake, friend of Sir Henry
Stephenson and fellow owner of Stephenson, Blake, died at the age of 71.
The passing of Elisha Pechey in 1902, and of Sir Henry Stephenson and
Major William Greaves Blake in 1904, marked the end of an era.

Chapter 12

Owners in Waiting

S
IR Henry's surviving son, Henry Kenyon Stephenson, who was born in 1865, had been educated first at Sheffield Collegiate School and then at Rugby. In 1883, he joined the company at the age of eighteen. Following the pattern of his father, H. K. spent the next five years gaining practical experience alongside the punchcutters, justifiers, mouldmakers and casters. In 1888, he was made a partner and became increasingly involved in the day to day management, whilst, in 1894, at the age of 29, he married Frances Blake, the daughter of the sleeping partner, Major William Greaves Blake.

Major William Greaves Blake, the owner of a third of the share value of the company and close friend of Sir Henry Stephenson, having married Rebecca Jessop, had a family of eleven children. The second son, Robert Greaves Blake was born in 1875. Like the Stephensons, he was educated first at Collegiate School, Sheffield, at Hillborough School in Leicestershire and finally at Rugby. Family connections apart, it appeared sensible for R. G. Blake to enter the business which, for almost sixty years, had added considerably to the Blake family wealth.[1] In 1894, at the age of 19, Robert Greaves Blake began his career in typefounding and spent the next four years in learning the business. Ten years later, in 1904, on the death of his father, he, and his now brother-in-law, H. K. Stephenson, became the owners of the foundry.

These were parlous times and in the decade which followed, the two principals would be required to make difficult decisions. There were a number of technical and commercial issues facing the two partners the resolution of the uncertainty surrounding the adoption of the Point-body

System and Point-lining System; the threat of the newly introduced composing machines; innovations in matrix making which might lead to competitors producing quality letter at lower prices; and a fear that the two relatively successful foundries: H. W. Caslon and Company and the Miller and Richard Company might combine and pose a serious threat to Stephenson, Blake.

Elsewhere, there were encouraging signs. The effects of the 1870 Elementary Education Act were beginning to be felt. The literacy level of the working-class population was improving; national and local newspapers were thriving and their circulations were rising at an incredible rate. Book printers and publishing houses were enjoying a steady and sustained growth.

Within the printing trade, magazines such as the *Printers' Register* and the *British and Colonial Printer* were being seen to have a major influence on the printing trade: managements, craftsmen and apprentices alike. There was an enthusiastic thirst for improved technical knowledge—particularly relating to the new processes and technical developments which were taking place in the United States. There was also a new consciousness relating to typographic design. The magazines initiated the idea of establishing a Printers' Specimen Exchange—an innovation which encouraged craftsmen and apprentices to send specimens which were appraised and commented on in the editorial. This was an American idea which was taken up with considerable enthusiasm. Such new-found enthusiasm offered typefounders' travellers with a useful selling platform. Typeface varieties, their usage in typographical design and composing room organisation and efficiency, were matters which were related. Competitions were organised and prizes offered both in money and in kind. Travellers who could demonstrate a thorough working knowledge of these matters and a flair for typographical design, were in a strong trading position—particularly if their foundry supported them.

As for business opportunities, the growing focus of attention was the potential market in supplying printing office furniture, wooden type and sundries. Since the very beginning of letterpress printing, the process of assembling the typographical image—composition—had required disciplined storage methods and good housekeeping of the myriads of letter and typographical characters. Type had always been laid in cases with the letters arranged in a logical technique-studied order. Such types cases and racks in which to store them had traditionally been made by the local printers' joiner.

However, in the latter half of the nineteenth century, the burgeoning printing industry in America—particularly the newspaper printers—

became interested in well-designed and carefully engineered typecases set in orderly cabinets, the upper surfaces of which could provide appropriate facilities for type composition and handling of type in page form. The equipping of a well-furnished composing room was to become the yard-stick of efficiency.

In the United States one firm, the Hamilton Manufacturing Company, set the pace. High quality typecases and dust-proof cabinets constructed in hard wood attracted leading printers who reorganised and re-equipped their composing departments. The Stephenson, Blake travellers found their customers enquiring as to the availability of modern composing equipment, and the company, after determining the quality of the Hamilton Manufacturing Company's products, began to act as agents. However, the volume and value of composing room furniture sold, soon brought the principals to the view that it would be a valuable extension of the company's business activities to establish their own wood-equipment manufacturing department.

Several issues needed to be resolved before a wood equipment factory could be established. The quality of the products which Stephenson, Blake obtained from the Hamilton Manufacturing Company was considered by the principals to well equate with their own high standards. However, manufacturing timber products was an area in which the company had no expertise, whereas a number of the lesser typefounders and printing equipment suppliers had been manufacturing wood-furniture for some years. Among these was a provincial manufacturer located in Market Harborough in Leicestershire. The firm had been established in 1895, by John Haddon who owned the Caxton Typefoundry in Salisbury Square, London. The Caxton Typefoundry was ill-regarded by the Typefounders' Association, not only because it was not a member, but because it manufactured pirated type designs which it sold at prices well below those fixed by The Ring.

The wood furniture department of the Haddon Typefoundry was directed by William R. Giddins whose expertise in printers' furniture making had been acclaimed throughout the trade. An approach was made to Giddings who was invited to join Stephenson, Blake and take the lead in establishing the new venture in January 1907.

William R. Giddins was indeed much experienced. He was a master craftsman in wood, having served an apprenticeship with the firm of Ketts, who had many commissions for church restorations and ancestral homes. During the time of the South African War he had been employed in the management of Mulliners, who were specialist wheelwrights, providing wheels for artillery and timbered wagons. After the ending of the Boer War, he moved to manage the Haddon factory in Market Harborough.

Having secured the services of Giddins, the next stage was solving the problem of location for the new department. The main site of the company was now virtually a contained island bounded by Upper Allen Street and Edward Street, with a longer term potential of extending towards Scotland Street. It was considered that even if there was space on the main site to accommodate the wood manufactory, its physical presence would not fit comfortably with typefounding and its related engineering needs.

A search for a suitable factory site in the vicinity of Upper Allen Street proved fruitless. Finally, a group of old cottages and workshops on the corner of Jericho Street opposite the foundry were purchased and on completion of the contracts, work began in earnest. The site was cleared and within six weeks the new building was completed. The initial building was relatively modest. However, the site was substantial and offered much scope for the handling of deliveries of timber and supplies and equally for transportation of the rather bulky finished products. In the equipping of the factory, the company's philosophical approach to quality was applied: only the very best and most up to date of woodworking machinery was acquired. A gas engine was installed to provide motive power. As it was envisaged from the first that such furniture would be fashioned in hard wood—oak and beech—the company went to considerable expense in installing a

Fig 21 The Woodworking Department, 1911 Jericho Street-Upper Allen Street

wood-conditioning plant, designed to control, to stabilise and accelerate the seasoning of the hard wood timber stock. By June 1908, the wood material department was in production and when the costs were calculated the setting up had totalled £4,870.

From the first, the two principals realised that such a relatively ambitious venture could only be successful if it was reasonably large-scale, had volume throughput and high quality. Robert Greaves Blake, who was responsible for the project, need not have feared. News of the venture had spread quickly and the travellers had sold the new service well. Several prestigious printing companies: *The Times, The Daily News* and the Workers Printing Society had reorganised their composing rooms and had placed their orders with the company. Within months, the London Office, which had done so much to promote sales through the Aldersgate showroom was complaining bitterly at the delays in delivery and the inability of Sheffield to meet customers' needs. Although within three years the production facilities were destined to be doubled to meet the ever increasing demands of the full order books, the ideals of the company had been somewhat compromised. The cost of buying such high quality hardwood furniture was beyond the financial reach of many smaller companies and in response to customer needs, the department introduced a range of composing cabinets made in softwood, but of equal quality to meet the demands of the market.

Running in parallel with the establishing of the wood material department was the decision to manufacture wooden poster types. One of the earliest strengths of the original Blake and Garnett Company and their Sheffield rivals Bower, Bacon and Bower had been the supplying of large-sized sanspariel letter in metal. However, in 1827, an American, Darius Wells, developed a machine for cutting decoration in wooden surfaces. This invention had been applied to the cutting of wooden-type. The development was taken a stage further when in 1834, William Levensworth of New York invented a pantographic router which would cut out a type face in wood from a design set in a brass template. The casting of large-sized type gradually came to an end as precision-cut wooden letter became available and as printers installed larger sized cylinder printing presses and sheet-sizes of cheaper machine-made paper became available, the market for posters and broadsheets increased and with it came a demand for wood-letter.

Initially, Stephenson, Blake did not take the growing market in wooden poster types seriously. The company was quite content to supply the finest quality metal types in Britain and there the matter stood. However, when the travellers came forward with requests for supplying poster letter, the company sought out a potential supplier. Several firms' products were considered but amongst them, Day and Collins of London produced a letter of quality which Stephenson, Blake considered appropriate and, from 1871, they were commissioned to cut and supply letter on contract. It was an arrangement which was to last for thirty years

Then in 1902, a decision was made to embark on the in-house production of wooden letter when it seemed that their long-established supplier might cease trading. However, in 1905, an American, Barthe No 4 Casting Machine was acquired from the Western Type Foundry. This machine could cast hollow-bodied type in sizes 72 to 120 point. This meant that whilst a forme of large-sized letter might only be fractionally heavier in weight than wood-letter, the forme would be made up of types which would have a better typographical surface. The innovation proved so successful that the following year a Barthe No 3 Casting Machine was installed to enable the casting of letter from 30 to 60 points.

However, the notion that hollow cast type would only fractionally add weight to the forme of type was little more than sales talk. Large-sized, hollow metal type did not appreciably reduce the weight of the imposed type forme, therefore there was little to be gained by way of increased speed of printing on the letterpress cylinder presses. Clearly, with billboard advertising growing, particularly for entertainment: sport, theatre and cinema, there was a growing and lucrative market in producing wooden poster letter and the principals were determined to exploit it. Through close association between the Stephenson, Blake's order clerks and travellers and the staff of Day and Collins, it was learned that F. W. Ventris, the foreman at Day and Collins, had left the company, had entered into partnership and was trading under the name of Crockett and Ventris. It appears that Ventris had been given some assurance that Stephenson, Blake would place orders with him. The year was 1906. Before the fledgling company could meet the demands placed on it by Stephenson, Blake, the cutting of pantographic patterns of the Sheffield foundry's letter designs had to be completed. This task fell to Ventris himself and although Crockett and Ventris received payment for the work, the demanding nature of the clients and the sheer volume occupied Ventris for almost two years. In the end the principals of Stephenson, Blake came to the conclusion that it would be preferable to establish their own wood-letter production facility. An approach was made to Crockett and Ventris. Crockett was bought out of the partnership and Ventris, along with his machine tools, transferred to Sheffield. Initially, Ventris and his assistants were located in a corner of the typecasting department, but, on the establishing of the wood material department in its new premises, the wood-letter production too moved in alongside it. With a

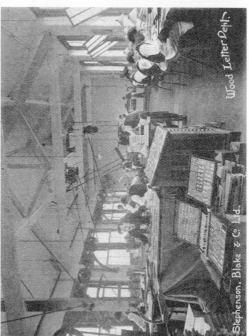

Fig 22 Production activities in the Wood Manufacturing Department, 1911

degree of panache, Stephenson, Blake were eager to announce to the trade that it was now able to offer both metal and wooden type of high quality, all of which was produced in its premises in Sheffield. Unfortunately, trading at the end of the first year produced an almost 20% loss and the partners were somewhat chastened. However, the initial gloom was soon dispelled. By late 1909, orders for wood-letter began to stream in and plans were quickly laid to expand facilities. Thereafter, the firm of Day and Collins went into decline and several members of their staff joined Stephenson, Blake, together with several of the Day and Collins machines which were purchased and installed in Sheffield. There was a good deal of satisfaction when the 1910 Specimen Book was issued with the founts of wood-letter displayed in its latter sections and H. W. Caslon and Company agreed to become an agent and displayed the Stephenson, Blake range of wood-letter in their Specimen Book. By 1914, the company could boast the availability of over 60 wood-letter typefaces.

Chapter 13

Making the Point

AS the third quarter of the nineteenth century progressed, the members of the Typefounders Association found that the bespoke nature of type founding had finally come to an end. Typecasting machines operating at high speed were now not merely casting, but breaking, trimming, dressing and delivering letter ready for setting-up, fount make-up and packing. These developments had transformed the whole operation. Precision engineering methods were now the standards of the day—even for typefounders. Unfortunately, each foundry still had its own typographical standard of measure. The sizes of type were still expressed by a range of fanciful names: brevier, nonpareil, pearl and minion *et al*. These prevailing arbitrary sizes were archaic and, in practical usage, chaotic. However, there was an accepted measure; that of pica which was recognised as approximating one sixth of an inch.

In the eighteenth century, the French typefounder, Françoise Didot had devised a system of measure for printing types which was finally regularised within the system of metric measure. The system was logical and became generally accepted throughout the Continental countries. Whilst far-sighted typefounders and printers in Britain and the Colonies looked favourably towards some agreed regularisation of printers' measure, there was little enthusiasm for its introduction. In 1841, the Sheffield typefoundry of Bower and Bower, put forward a logical approach to linking printers' measure to imperial measure but little interest ensued. Discussion continued over decades and the idea was regularly considered in the Typefounders' Association. All the British typefounders (whether they were members of the Typefounders' Association or not) publicly supported the introduction of a well-rehearsed system based on picas, nonpareils and points. But, in private, it seems they would only accept the point system if their company's pica became the standard. Nor were their motives particularly altruistic. When printers bought type, spaces and related typographic material from a particular foundry, it tended to bind a printer to that particular founder for the differential in dimensions in other founders' material meant that it was not easily interchangeable. There was also an unmentionable reason why a number of the typefounders were unwilling to enthuse over the adoption of the Point System. By the 1890s, the coming of the Linotype had increasingly depleted their easily earned profits as the sales of body-type to the newspapers began to dwindle. Even amongst the members of the Typefounders Association there were companies who simply did not have either the incoming revenue or the capital to re-equip with point-sized moulds and matrices. A stalemate existed and none would give way.

The situation was also acute in the United States. However, in 1878, Marder and Luse and Company, owners of the Chicago Type Foundry and one of the country's major typefounders, took the decision to cast type on point body measure.[1] Within a few years, others were to follow. Finally, at a meeting held in Niagra, in 1886, the United States Typefounders Association agreed to adopt the American Point System. It was to comprise two units: picas and points—72 points approximating one American inch. Hence, the pica equalled approximately 12 points and six picas to the inch.[2]

Thomas White Smith of H. W. Caslon, took particular interest in the news that Marder and Luse were adopting the long-discussed system. He made much of the advantages of the Point System in the firm's house magazine, the *Caslon Circular*, hoping to influence printers generally and his own customers in particular. He raised the matter with members of the Typefounders' Association and particularly sought support from Henry Stephenson on the feasibility of adopting it. Stephenson dismissed the idea, on the pretext that the six picas to the inch principle was purely theoretical. However, whatever Smith might have proposed at this stage would not have been acceptable. By this time the external cordiality between the two companies was but a front. The two were trade rivals and were vying for dominance.

T. W. Smith's observations on the arithmetical basis of the dimension of the Point indicates a general problem of the time. He contended that typefounders' tolerance of working were impractical beyond 1/1000th of an inch. However, the working tolerance at Stephenson, Blake was 1/5000th of an inch—a standard which had been set by John Stephenson who, on the setting-up of the foundry, had constructed a measuring device which had been in use since the beginning. Gaining little initial support, the Caslon Company gradually began to change their mould dimensions to approximate the American Point System. Then in 1895, the progressive but smaller Caxton Typefoundry—one outside of membership of the Typefounders' Association—announced its intention of casting its letter to the American Point System standard.

Such precision, at a time when letterpress printing was still a relatively inexact process, seemed unimportant. There were many typefounders and printers alike who questioned whether the Point System was really necessary. Whilst at first Stephenson, Blake were seemingly turning their backs on the issue, they were in fact monitoring developments closely. Within months of the Chicago Typefoundry's and other American founders' Point-body products becoming available, Stephenson, Blake checked the dimensions carefully and found that, across a range of various American founts, strict adherence to the so-called standard left much to be desired.

Finally, in 1898, the Typefounders' Association, after much deliberation and consultation with Master Printers, agreed to adopt what was to be known as the British-American Point System. Although the Stephenson Blake pica—approximately one sixth of an imperial inch—was relatively close to the American standard, the company was determined to cast their type to the Point-body and Point-lining standard. Quietly and almost unnoticed by customers, they renewed moulds and matrices on Point System dimensions.

Stephenson, Blake had a vested interest in encouraging the printing and the typefounding industry to adopt the Point System. A standard measure would, on the medium and long-term, release printers from ties with founders whose type body sizes were irregular. The benefits of the system would drive out the old sizes and in doing so would create market opportunities. In 1900, they acquired a machine patented and developed by Taylor and Watkinson which cast leads, clumps and other spacing material in continuous strip form. The commercial potential to the company of compatible and interchangeable spacing material based on the Point-body standard which would range with all other founders' typographical material was very attractive. The earlier the printing industry would adopt the Point-body dimension the better. Ultimately, the Taylor and Watkinson machine proved to be a boon and the cost of producing lead spacing material fell so dramatically that other founders ceased production of strip material as Stephenson, Blake cornered the market.

However, the introduction of the Point-body System and Point-lining System was not readily accepted amongst the very conservative British printing fraternity and the Typefounders' Association felt that they had to promote the idea. To further the cause, a meeting was arranged at the Regent Street Polytechnic in London, to be held on the 29th March 1904 and Henry Kenyon Stephenson was invited to speak on the subject, delivering a paper entitled, *Coming to the Point*. The Chairman of the proceedings was John Spottiswoode, a member of the nationally renowned company of bible printers, Eyre and Spottiswoode. An audience of 130 gathered for the occasion.

Beginning the lecture, H. K. Stephenson made much of the traditional method of making punches and the quality of types cast from matrices which had been struck in the traditional way. As the lecture progressed he made a number of derisory comments regarding the use of the electrotyping process in the making of matrices—abhorring the quality of the typeface cast by this method. He then made a veiled attack on an anonymous typefoundry who were using these methods and went on to condemn the process which . . . *places in the hands of unscrupulous persons a ready means of counterfeiting, without purchaser permission, the productions of typefounders who have at great expenditure of time and money designed and engraved the original punches, metal faces or matrices . . .* [3]

As the lecture progressed he laboured the issue increasingly; that these were piratical practices that the types which they produced were, in any case vastly inferior to those produced by traditional methods. In his concluding remarks in answer to questions, he contended that: *the proprietor of a new foundry had endeavoured to divert business to himself by means of a policy of aggressive abuse and misrepresentations anent the old established houses, many of whose faces he had pirated. Knowing the transparent hollowness of his pretensions, they had perhaps too long allowed his allegations to pass unchallenged.*

The somewhat biased and technically incorrect report of the event which appeared in the *Caxton Magazine* recounted *that when the lecturer had resumed his seat, the Chairman, looking grimly sarcastic, said that it had been an instructive lecture but that . . . perhaps he ought to say that had he known that the lecture was to be a disguised attack on another typefounder he should not have presided and must disassociate himself from personal endorsement of an attack against another typefounder with whom up to that time he had had happy relations*[4] John Spottiswoode thereupon hurriedly left the meeting. In the somewhat tense and embarrassing situation which ensued, James Alexander, the teacher in charge of Typography Instruction at the Polytechnic, who was the host, assumed the chairmanship. A less than serious but sardonic question was then posed by Frank Colebrook who asked: *as a matter of historical interest, whether there was any truth in the story that the Associated Founders (The Ring) had bought the first French machine-type caster, through some printers, and had taken it out to the Nore and sunk it?* H. K. Stephenson responded by saying that the story was somewhat improbable but that . . . *Figgins would be the likeliest founder to know about that.*

The evening ended on a somewhat acrimonious note. Then, in the April 1904 issue of the *Caxton Magazine*, the Editor really stirred the situation by writing a diatribe of several pages aimed at *The Ring* in general and at Stephenson, Blake in particular. It was a contentiously stinging attack implying that Stephenson, Blake was behind the times in their matrix making methods. The Editor's closing remarks were salutary: *Other points, equally telling, could be noted, did we feel disposed, from Mr. Stephenson's lecture. We did not record his lecture of a few weeks ago, at Sheffield, because a full report was not sent us. If it was as misleading as that at the Polytechnic, it is clear we did not miss anything of value, though it might possibly be of interest (?) In commenting on the latest utterance, we do so entirely in the interests of the trade and of fair play. We hold no brief— notwithstanding the industriously circulated report that Mr. Haddon runs THE CAXTON MAGAZINE—for the Caxton or any other foundry, but—as a Trade organ—we do hold a brief for the patient printer, who has been too long at the mercy of the—to put it mildly—unprogressive 'ring typefounder' That he is unprogressive is only too clearly shown by Mr. Stephenson's own descriptions of the methods followed at the foundry with which he is connected.—ED., C.M.].*[5]

Whilst the attack against Stephenson, Blake was less than accurate—the Editor incorrectly, described the *cutting of brass punches* and there were a number of instances in the text where the word punch was used when he should have written matrix—nevertheless, the editor was, in part right, the foundry was behind the times. The late Sir Henry Stephenson would not consider other methods. Pechey had constantly urged the adoption of machine-cut punch techniques and the company had only responded when Bertaut, the commissioned punchcutter, prevailed.[6]

On the question of the attack against *The Ring*, Sir Henry Stephenson since 1893, had been Chairman of the Association and had ruled it with a rod of iron. He made members agree to continue the boycotting of advertising in the trade magazines and waged a war against the typefounders who were outside the Association.

Now, H. K. Stephenson could not let the Polytechnic lecture affair pass. Within days, a 4-page response was printed and issued as an insert in the *British and Colonial Printer*, refuting and belittling the comments made by the *Caxton Magazine*. Many of the comments in the response were fair and accurate but the general tone was that of someone thrown on to the defensive: . . . *the unscrupulous person employs the electrotype process, if for no other reason, because it is the only one which adapts itself to piracy. The direct engraving process necessitates the making of original patterns, whereas all need for such skill and originality as these involve is obviated by the much less costly if ignoble system of automatic reproduction of other founders' type faces!*[7]

The reproof of the article in the *Caxton Magazine* then went on to the semantics of the development of the Point System which, considering that it had been agreed in America in 1886 and in Britain in 1898, makes it seem remarkable that a lecture on the subject should have raised such interest when the matter had been settled. Clearly, Stephenson, whose cousin, Stephen Blake had become secretary of the Typefounders' Association used the occasion to hit at Walter Haddon and his Caxton Typefoundry. As a final item in his rejoinder, H. K. Stephenson wrote: *Excellence in results is the true test of excellence in methods, and so long as the Sheffield foundry produces types which excel in finish, accuracy and durability, it will be unaffected by such criticisms as those offered by the Editor of Caxton Magazine.*[8]

The war of words was still raging the following year. In January, 1905, the company issued a 4-page, 8vo leaflet which was sent to customers with every order despatched. The heading ran: *Truth v. Fiction, Tilting at the Ring.* The final paragraph of the leaflet sums up the situation: *The proprietor of the Caxton Foundry has put about in Australia the amazing story that he has refused an invitation to join the British Type Founders' Association. Probably never were grapes more sour, and his hysterical cablegram to Sydney can be compared only to the broken gamblers' last throw. For ourselves we need scarcely say that nothing could be more distasteful to us than the association with one whose ideas on the question of commercial morality are so entirely at variance with our own.*[9]

Chapter 14

The Broken Reed

T HE invention and development of the Linotype by Mergenthaler, in 1884 made inexorable in-roads in the lucrative market for the supply of body-type for newspaper printing. By the end of the century it was estimated that there were over 1,000 Linotypes in use in London and probably the same number in the provincial news offices. By 1900, Fleet Street, the heart of Britain's national newspapers, had almost entirely (with the exception of *The Times*) adopted the Linotype for news text production.

In such a relatively short time, orders for newspaper text type had simply disappeared. All the members of the Typefounders' Association suffered. Supplying large quantities of body letter was singularly profitable but now, with orders falling, there was a surplus of casting facility. Whilst the London founders had enjoyed at least twenty years of good profits, several had failed to re-invest and modernise.

The long-established London typefoundry of Sir Charles Reed and Sons Limited was facing severe trading difficulties. The Fann Street typefoundry was unique. It had a much respected historical pedigree which embraced the English typefounding tradition across two centuries. To account for this, its genesis needs to be considered. On the death of Thomas Cotterell, owner of the Nevil's Court Typefoundry in Fetter Lane, in 1785, the business was continued by his successors until 1794, when it was purchased by Robert Thorne, one of Cotterell's former apprentices. Thorne transferred the business to premises in the Barbican and then, in 1810, relocated it to Fann Street in Aldersgate—hence the title The Fann Street Foundry. After

Robert Thorne's death in 1820, the foundry was put up for sale by auction and purchased by William Thorowgood, from Staffordshire. Thorowgood was the London agent and part proprietor of a company in Stone, Staffordshire which manufactured a Patent Roller Pump. Although it seems that Thorowgood was an outsider and was not directly connected with the world of print, he had a brother, Frederick Thorowgood, who was a printer in Cheapside. Nevertheless, Thorowgood must have been a person of some significance for, two years after acquiring the Fann Street Foundry, he was accredited: *Letter Founder to his Majesty, King George IV.* In 1828, Thorowgood also acquired the long-established Fry Foundry situated in Type Street. The foundry had been established in Bristol in 1764 by Joseph Fry, a successful medical doctor. Interesting himself in the success of Baskerville in Birmingham, he set up his own foundry with Isaac Moore, a whitesmith—a worker in silver, pewter and tin—and William Pine, a Bristol printer. Moore cut a successful series of founts based on Baskerville's design which were regarded as highly fashionable and which enhanced the reputation of the newly established foundry considerably. However, Joseph Fry was quick to discover that the main trading centre for a typefounder was London. In 1768, he transferred his business to London trading as Joseph Fry and Company and in 1782, his sons Edmund and Henry joined the business. Meanwhile, in 1782, the stock of the long established James foundry was auctioned and Fry bought a considerable portion of the stock. Joseph Fry died in 1787 and the typefoundry was taken over by Edmund Fry. By 1816, his co-partners had retired and Edmund's son Windover Fry joined the business. The Fry foundry over the years had developed an extensive range of exotic and academic language type faces, Moderns and fat blacks, and from 1824 assumed the name of the Polyglot Foundry, a title which reflected the wide and unusual range of typefaces they were able to cast. On retirement in 1828, Edmund Fry put the business up for sale and it was subsequently bought by William Thorowgood.[1]

Although Thorowgood knew little about typefounding, he had a particular bent for selling and management and for ten years ran a very successful and profitable business. In 1838, he admitted his traveller, Robert Besley, into the business and in 1849, with his retirement pending, the business was renamed Robert Besley and Company. His market was essentially London-based and competition both from provincial typefounders and later from machine casting methods, was of little consequence. In addition to his direction of the company Besley increasingly involved himself in affairs of the City of London and became a much respected Alderman. Meanwhile, Benjamin Fox, a punchcutter of some renown joined the company and shared the day-to-day management as Besley's public duties increasingly made demands on his time.

In 1861, on Robert Besley's retirement, his interest was taken up by Charles Reed and the business took the title of Reed and Fox. However, Charles Reed, like his predecessor, was greatly involved in the government of the City of London and his public service was marked by the conferment of a knighthood. He was now styled Sir Charles Reed and on the death of his practising partner and punch cutter Benjamin Fox in 1877, the firm became known as Sir Charles Reed and Sons. Unfortunately, within four years, 1881, Sir Charles Reed was dead and his sons, Andrew and Talbot Baines Reed succeeded to the business.

For some ten years, 1881-1891, the two brothers managed the business. However, during this period general trading conditions were difficult—particularly for typefounders—but even more so where, as in the case of the Reed Foundry, the quality of management and business acumen was weak. The second and third generation members of the family had grown apart from the business. Whilst Talbot Baines Reed was a highly esteemed and much revered authority on typefounding and a printing historian of considerable repute, his family business was woefully unprepared for the changes which were taking place. A crisis point was reached in 1893, when, somewhat prematurely, Talbot Baines Reed died, followed in 1894, by the death of his brother Andrew.

There had been little capital investment in new plant and, in an attempt to attract and hold customers, the company had lowered both its prices and the quality of its products. The rapidly reducing body-type orders caused by the introduction of mechanical composition and the financial prospect of the renewal of moulds and matrices which the Point-body System would have required brought the directors to a decision that the trading style of the company had to change.

In desperate straits, the business was converted into a private limited company and the directors turned it into a type broking business—hopefully selling type cast in the Fann Street foundry and type from other foundries—including founts from American typefounders who were keen to break into the British market. A decision was made to put the business up for sale and, as loyal members of the Typefounders' Association, they were anxious to abide by the agreement that if any one of the members wished to sell or cease trading, the remaining Association members would be invited, collectively or singularly, to acquire the ailing company. After much discussion and prevarication, neither the Association nor any one of its members would come to the rescue of the Reed Foundry, whereupon the directors resigned from the Association and signified their intention of putting the business on the open market.

Outside the affairs of the Association, Eliot Reed, Sir Charles Reed's grandson, now made a direct approach to Sir Henry Stephenson. His asking price was well below the market value and the value of the stock discounted at 45%. Whilst the possible acquisition of the business of Sir Charles Reed and Sons was, strictly speaking, of limited commercial value to Stephenson, Blake, Sir Henry thought there might be some merit in acquiring it, providing the price was right. Although the foundry had a number of founts which were commercially successful, it had little by way of up-to-date casting machinery. The sale prospectus indicated that the principal typecasting potential was invested in 28 casting machines, powered by a six horse power Ruston and Hornsby gas engine. However, the finishing of the type was still done by hand and there were in excess of 40 staff in employment. It seemed that the only real value might be its long-established goodwill for it was claimed that the foundry had some 3000-3500 customers, of whom 1,000 were supplied with body-type.

However, the Fann Street foundry, successor to the historic Polyglot Foundry with its long tradition, seemingly represented a prestigious jewel in the crown which might add lustre to the Stephenson, Blake business. Over a period of almost two hundred and fifty years the punches and matrices of the early English typefounders had passed, by succession and purchase, into the ownership of Sir Charles Reed and Company.

Sir Henry Stephenson responded to Eliot Reed: . . . *I am naturally at my age averse to big experiments, and although I would try and put aside this feeling if I saw clearly it would be distinctly to my son's advantage to purchase the Foundry on satisfactory terms, we really have not the means of satisfying ourselves on this point. How to carry on the Foundry, if we bought it, is a very difficult question. To keep up permanently two establishments would certainly be absurd, but any practical typefounder would recognize the difficulty of working for any length of time as one united Foundry two separate sets of Moulds, Matrices and Machinery constructed on different standard of bodies. This consideration, coupled with the fact that the Fann Street Plant, if you forgive my saying so, has become to a considerable extent out of date and would require replacing in many respects both with new Machinery and new Moulds and Matrices in order to effect the necessary saving in production, make the whole question so complex that my son admits with me the purchase would be a leap in the dark to such an extent as would be too hazardous for us to make.*[2]

Eliot Reed, disappointed with the response from Sir Henry who was seen as a friend of the family, now left with little room for manoeuvre, sold the business in 1905 to one of its former managers who immediately issued a new specimen book in the hope that trading might be improved. In many respects, the gentlemanly Typefounders' Association collectively was less than charitable towards the Reed foundry. Whilst raising capital for the purpose of acquiring it may have been difficult, the truth seems to have been that they knew, or hoped, the Reed foundry, which was nearing bankruptcy, would collapse and were waiting to bid for parts of it at knockdown prices.

During this period of negotiation, the situation in Sheffield had changed. Sir Henry was dead and H. K. Stephenson had become the managing partner. He now took the initiative and offered £5,000 for the business. The type stocks were assessed and it was agreed that a price half way between market prices and scrap value would also be paid for the 82 tons of stock.

Even for Stephenson, Blake at this late stage, the decision to acquire the Reed foundry was not altogether altruistic. The Reed foundry under new ownership had already begun factoring H. W. Caslon's type and sundries and had this arrangement continued, Stephenson, Blake may have seen their rivals getting a commercial advantage. In any case, the prestige of acquiring the Reed foundry, of making use of the existing customer goodwill and of acquiring several particularly popular typefaces justified the purchase. As for the historical matrices and punches—they were simply historical artefacts of little commercial value, coming into the possession of the company as curiosities.

The amalgamation was announced in the trade press and was effective on the 1st January 1906. It was decided that the seemingly amalgamated companies would trade under the name: Stephenson, Blake and Company and Sir Charles Reed and Sons. Several Reed employees were transferred to the London office, whilst the type, metal and the extensive collection of punches and matrices were transported to Sheffield. At an earlier time when the Reeds were endeavouring to sell the company to Stephenson, Blake, Sir Henry had clearly indicated that he had no intention of maintaining two foundries. Now that the acquisition had come to pass this was put into practice. However, if the claim that the Reed foundry had in excess of 3,000 customers was true, it was clearly necessary to make provision for supplying them with type cast on bodies relating to the Fann Street standards. The casting department at Sheffield was rearranged to accommodate a virtually self-contained Reed's foundry by installing five casting machines. The head caster, and a second caster operator, a justifier and a mould maker were transferred to Sheffield and charged with servicing existing Reed customers' needs, whilst the justifier and mould maker were employed realigning and justifying the most saleable of the Reed founts to Point-body and Point-line standards.

Unfortunately even at the very low acquisition price of £5,000 the financial returns in terms of profit were disappointing. Stephenson, Blake seemed to have acquired little from the purchase except a prestigious ancestry.

The stock of punches and matrices acquired from the Reed foundry comprised three categories: body and jobbing typefaces which sold very well and which were bought regularly by a number of book printers and newspaper houses; innumerable jobbing and decorated typefaces which were of poor design and which at the time of purchase seemingly of limited commercial value; a few historic founts of punches which had been passed down were of antique value rather than commercial. These comprised:

(a) Greek matrices, including the Great Primer Old Greek attributed to John James, formerly being part of the Thomas Grover collection of 1685.
(b) The Union Pearl fount, of the period 1770, the oldest surviving English decorated letter which originally belonged to Grover.
(c) A fount of Scriptorial matrices and a fount of Black Letter from Fry's foundry, originally an item cited by Rowe Mores as part of the Johnson and Grover auction sale of 1782.
(d) The Anglo Saxon fount known as the Elstob Saxon cited by Rowe Mores in his *Dissertation on English Typographical Founders, 1788.*
(e) The punches for Irish type cut by Joseph Moxon in 1680 and the Fry-Moxon Irish punches.

With the union of Sir Charles Reed Company and Stephenson Blake complete and with the passing of the old guard, H. K. Stephenson and

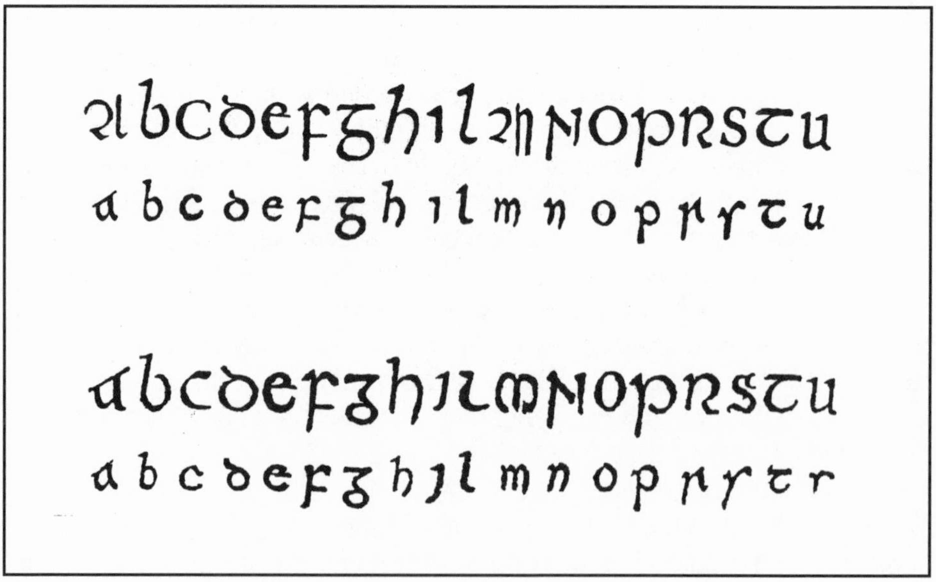

Fig 23 Irish types acquired from Sir Charles Reed and Sons Limited

R. G. Blake turned their attention to the transatlantic challenge. The mould-makers and the justifiers were set to work assiduously converting moulds and matrices to Point-body standards whilst the possibility of exchanging and trading successful designs, particularly with American typefounders, looked promising. Although as the senior partner, H. K. Stephenson assumed particular responsibility for external activities and commercial development he was increasingly involved in public affairs outside the foundry and, as much as he influenced and made the final decisions related to the running of the business, his technical understanding of many of the skills was limited when compared with those of his predecessors. Whilst he knew the workpeople well enough, he lacked a natural empathy with them—an attribute which particularly marked his predecessors' steward-ships. For much of his life, H. K's interests rested in the wider world. Meanwhile, the day-to-day direction of the foundry passed to his fellow partner R. G. Blake.

THE FOUR SIZES OF FRY'S ORNAMENTED

60-point 5 A ; about 18½ lb.

ABCDEF
GHIJKL
MNOPQR
STUVW
XYZ

48-point 5 A ; about 11¾ lb.

ABCDEFGH

36-point 7 A ; about 8½ lb.

ABCDEFGHIJK

30-point 10 A ; about 7½ lb.

ABCDEFGHIJKLMNOP

STEPHENSON BLAKE · THE CASLON LETTER FOUNDRY · SHEFFIELD

Fig 24 Fry's ornamented specimen, 1907

Chapter 15

Social Nuances

THE success of Stephenson, Blake and Company Limited not only brought the company but also its principals into the ranks of the great manufacturing industry of Sheffield, it was now also the leading British typefoundry, nationally renowned for the quality of its printing types and associated products. Its principals were regarded with that particular awesome esteem which, at that time, seemed to surround the leading figures of the printing and publishing world. The public faces of Henry Kenyon Stephenson and Robert Greaves Blake were typical of owners of a successful third generation family business. They were public benefactors and keepers of the public conscience. As informed and involved lay officers they each made a personal contribution to the management of local affairs and national institutions, They supported the establishment and in politics; the Liberal party.

Since his mid-twenties, H. K. Stephenson had been involved in public affairs and following the death of his father increasingly so. In 1905, he too was elected to the Sheffield City Council and within three years became Lord Mayor. He returned to the mayoralty again in 1910 and subsequently, was elected Alderman. In 1905, he also became a member of the Council of the University of Sheffield and served as the University Treasurer until 1910, after which he was elected Pro-Chancellor. He subsequently held appointments on many charitable bodies and was a serving director on a number of major companies based in Sheffield and South Yorkshire.

At the other end of the social scale were the workers. The Victorian mores and values relating to the relationship between masters and servants long remained evident in the company. The now wealthy Stephenson and

Blake families existed on a very different plain from their workpeople. It was not a unique phenomenon but in Sheffield the social make up of businesses and enterprises was somewhat different from other industrial cities. The great iron, steel and heavy engineering companies and the collieries which had grown and developed with such rapidity since the mid-1850s, employed thousands—great regiments of men ranging from the highly skilled to the lowly labourers. The owners and shareholders of such large organisations had become quite remote from the workers daily engaged in the dangerous business of heavy industry. Factory and mines discipline was strictly enforced and faceless upper managements ruled arbitrarily.

In contrast, there were the many others who earned a living by their own skills in cutlery, silver manufacture and the tool-making trades. They worked within a variety of contractual arrangements; in teams, or on contract, as out-workers, as casual or as day labourers. Although their employment and livelihood was often tenuous and uncertain, within the economic bounds of subsisting, they had considerable independence. Within these industrial dimensions, the Stephenson, Blake company was, in typefounding terms, a large company, yet, by local comparison quite small.

Meanwhile, the social make up of the company was almost unique. By 1914, the two principals and their several family employees were wealthy and public school educated. Consequently, economically and socially they stood apart from their workpeople and the company was, through its hierarchical structure, inimical of the age. There were winners and losers, high salary earners and those who were grossly under rewarded. Each group of workers clearly defined in social terms. If expertise was required, the company would unashamedly head hunt, invite individuals to join the firm, and offer levels of remuneration and perquisites which would be difficult to ignore. Locally recruited work people—particularly those who joined the company as boys or very junior staff—all too often found that, unless they had very special skills or had carved for themselves an indispensable niche, the management, though often benevolent, had little regard for them even though they may have been employed in the company throughout their working lives.

Whilst the owning families were at the top of a hierarchical structure, the workpeople too had a place based on a scale of economic worth and company value. The mangers who were recruited to undertake particular roles were tempted with very generous salaries and, within reason, had a degree of freedom. Frequently there were fundamental differences of opinion and whilst the principals' views prevailed, and wrong business decisions resulted, these would be quietly remedied at manager level without reference.

If key managers were suitably rewarded, the next level in the structure, the travellers, were indulged. They were expected to maintain a high standard of dress and deportment and were required, and remunerated, to reside at hotels of a standard deemed to be in keeping with the status of the company. Their salaries, commission and expenses reflected these expectations. They were seen as the ambassadors of Britain's premier typefoundry. However, if the confidence and professionalism of the travellers bred a particular superiority, this situation in no way matched the arrogance and independence of the staff in the London office. The foundry and the wood material department could produce the finest products, but the recovery of production costs and profits depended on sales. Whilst nationally, Stephenson, Blake had its fair share of the market, the business tended to driven by sales generated in London through the office, showroom and warehouse at No. 33 Aldersgate Street.

In 1898, Elisha Pechey having reigned supreme as Manager of the London office for almost thirty years, pressed H. K. Stephenson on the question of appointing a successor who could be introduced to take over the management of the London office. With some reluctance, Stephenson agreed to release E. B. Hanson, who had been recruited in 1875, to succeed Pechey at Sheffield, and he was now directed to understudy the elderly Pechey. On the death of Pechey, three years later, in 1902, Hanson took charge. Whilst Hanson was essentially an administrator, his twenty-five years' experience working in the Sheffield offices had provided him with valuable experience which he would need in London. Whether H. K. Stephenson and R. G. Blake thought that by having a loyal employee who, having spent much of his working time in Sheffield, could be directed more easily than the elderly, loyal but dominating character Pechey, is a matter of conjecture. As Hanson took control of the London office, the independent character of the office continued. Under his direction the travellers and the London office staff had to fight their battles on several fronts: keeping London and overseas sales high in the face of competition from the company's direct and most feared competitor, H. W. Caslon and Company, and from the smaller typefoundries and sundries' suppliers which had proliferated in London and the Home Counties. In addition, irredeemable sales were being lost every year as long-standing, loyal customers were installing composing equipment from the Linotype Company, the Typograph Company or the Lanston Monotype Corporation. Whilst the office staff and travellers in London regarded themselves as the sales hub of the entire company, their perception was not altogether misgiven. Both Sir Henry and H. K. Stephenson, although in daily contact by mail and telephone, were remote and not known to the customer printers. Over the

RICH
MARABOUT
STOLE

16/6
(As Sketch.)

Full Size,
BROWN OR
BLACK.

Extra Length, 21/-

In the New
MOLE
SHADE,
49/6

WARM AND LIGHT.
IMPERVIOUS TO DAMP.

Sent on Approval.

DEBENHAM & FREEBODY,
Wigmore Street, London, W.

Set in Antique Roman, Hogarth, and Cymric Border.

Engraving and Embossing FOR THE TRADE.

WEDDING INVITATIONS
CALLING CARDS
MASONIC CARDS
ANNOUNCEMENTS
LETTER-HEADS
ENVELOPES
BOOKLET COVERS, &c.

WE always have something to interest you. Don't put it off, but *write to-day* and we will give you our views of how to increase your *Trade*. Our samples are what you need.

MORGAN & SONS, 73 Font Street Avenue, E.C.

ESTABLISHED 1865

Set in Antique Roman, Hogarth, Grotesque No. 7, and Cymric Border.

STEPHENSON, BLAKE & CO.   SHEFFIELD & LONDON.

Fig 25 Stephenson, Blake, display specimen for Hogarth series, 1906

years, there were increasing pleas from the managers of the London office that the Chairman and Managing Director should be seen in greater evidence in London and be available to visit important clients. However, there was little personal touch. The directors too often operated on a level far removed from contact with customers. The travellers were the commercial face of Stephenson, Blake and whilst R. G. Blake managed the production operation, H. K. Stephenson who was responsible for the commercial activities of the company and for the London office, began to deal with his responsibilities in a very cursory way, as he increasingly involved himself in public affairs.

At the foundry the discipline and routine reflected the management style of the time. The weekly paid workers had to be at their workplaces by 8 o'clock each morning, Monday to Saturday. A worker, under scrutiny from the clerk in the time house, would pass his numbered disk to the checking clerk. Employees who were not in the factory were locked out for the day — unless they were one of that unique group of punchcutters or justifiers, in which case their irregularities were tolerated. The punchcutters were the highest paid and were an elite. Their drunkenness was tolerated by the directors, as was their *lakin*—Monday morning absence—a known aberration of absenting oneself on Mondays whilst recovering from weekend drinking bouts. Workers of a lesser status guilty of this absenteeism would be summarily dismissed. Meanwhile, girls and women were employed in the end process of assembling letter in the typecasting rooms and in the warehouse, where orders for type were made up according to prescribed fount and weight tables. The work was unskilled, but required a certain individual deftness of hand. Nevertheless, their work was disparaged, even by Hanson, the London manager, who referred to them as *those awful beings, the setters up.* Since the earliest days of the foundry, girls had been employed in this work and were paid very low wages. As a consequence, the whole of the production chain manifested a social hierarchy and in most cases each member knew his or her place. The office workers worked longer hours and had a daily lunch break of 90 minutes. The technical managers and supervisors formed another group but, even amongst this group there was a social order of skill and importance. The punchcutters and justifiers were a *corps de elite.* Their hours of work were less than those employed in the foundry and they enjoyed a good deal of freedom. In contrast, the labourers, girls and women were at the lowest level in terms of conditions, wages and esteem.

Unlike their peers employed in steel, engineering or mining, where the directors were too remote to know individual workers, or where their fellow neighbours were casually but independently employed, working at

The Offices
and part of Works

Fig 26 Across Marsden Lane A Pen drawing of the Works Yard and Offices, about 1900

the foundry was different. Almost each and every working day they were monitored, either by Stephenson or by Blake. The physical presence of the owner-directors always seemed to be there—the Blakes and the Stephensons walked the factory, checked the accounts in the offices, observed production in the foundry or in the wood material department. The directors took a pride in knowing every one of their work people's names. When workers were less than courteous to the directors and managers they were warned and instructed to improve their behaviour and their manners. Those members of the firm who were known to be active members of the Church of England were favoured, as were those who gave their time to the youth organisations and the Territorial Army.

When a worker fell ill, the firm gave support. If a wife or children of the worker fell ill, help was offered to the family in terms of money, allowed absence and support. Subjection to benevolent autocratic paternalism was the price of employment at the typefoundry which made the finest quality printing types in Britain.

By the turn of the nineteenth century, the area round the foundry comprised slum housing of the worst possible kind. It was an area which over a period of a hundred years had seen dispossessed agricultural labourers seeking employment, followed in turn by itinerant Scots, Irish and Italian families. For several generations they had found accommodation in the crofts and it was from these slums that the labourers and the women were recruited, whilst the better paid, skilled men and the office workers had moved out of the smoke-filled valley and into the suburbs of Upper Hallam. For better or worse, accepting or critical, their common bond lay in a sense of loyalty and pride at being employees of Stephenson, Blake of Sheffield.

By the end of the first decade of the twentieth century the company was both admired and envied by its competitors. The vertical and horizontal development and the organisation of it was remarkable. The principals, father and son, had aspired not only to becoming the leading British typefoundry but also the leading supplier of printing equipment. The engineering department, under the direction of J. W. Hay, the Chief Engineer, who had joined Stephenson, Blake from Miller and Richard, designed, constructed and redesigned casting machines. Precision standards were set for moulds and matrices and no expense spared in the furthering of accuracy and quality. Outside local expertise was also readily available. Both Sir Henry Stephenson and H. K. Stephenson as patrons and senior lay members of the University of Sheffield, could tap into the unique source of metallurgical and engineering expertise which was available in the University. With the best of resources and expertise, the firm's engineering activities developed almost to that of a level of an engineering research laboratory.

The horizontal development of the business had proceeded so extensively that Stephenson, Blake was no longer a mere typefoundry. It was now producing the highest quality composing room furniture, ancillary equipment and wood-poster types. It was also moving into becoming an agent for a number of proofing and printing presses. Short of the supplying of large-scale printing machinery, the company's travellers could offer an unparalleled range of typographical equipment and sundries.

Meanwhile, within *The Ring*, there were now only two other companies remaining: H. W. Caslon and Company and Miller and Richard of Edinburgh. The gentlemanly half-yearly luncheon meetings of the Typefounders' Association were less than genuine. Over the years the personal relationship with Thomas White Smith had deteriorated. For almost thirty years Stephenson, Blake had cause to rue the day the H. W. Caslon Company, near bankrupt, had approached them with a possible merger or buy out. Not only had this opportunity been missed but it had also meant the loss of the very astute London Manager, T. W. Smith. On being tempted back to the H. W. Caslon Company, Smith, in his autobiography, was to write . . . *I was not placed beyond temptation in the way of remuneration; and, seeing possibilities in the future of the old business in Chiswell Street whose owner had no son to succeed him, which did not exist elsewhere, I was quite ready to accept the advantageous offer.*[1]

T. W. Smith had breathed new life into the H. W. Caslon Company, much to the discomfiture of Stephenson, Blake. The name Caslon was still held in high esteem—particularly in the British Colonies. Yet both foundries could lay claim to using the name Caslon—H. W. Caslon through a continuous company line of occupancy at Chiswell Street foundry; Stephenson, Blake through the historical acquisition of the William Caslon IV foundry in Salisbury Square.

However, in the somewhat middle-class judgmental social circles, T. W. Smith was regarded with suspicion. In 1896, having introduced his three sons, Albert, Sydney and Harold, into the business, he proposed that the family name be changed from Smith to Caslon. To outsiders this was regarded as being somewhat pretentious. T. W. Smith, explaining his reasons recounted that in view of . . . *feeling . . . regret that the honoured and historical name of Caslon should die out . . . and having experienced inconvenience and some annoyance from the possession of so common a Sir* [sic] *name as Smith . . . I urged my sons to take the necessary legal steps to add the prefix Caslon to their own . . .*[2]

Whilst the change of the Smith family name to Caslon may not altogether have appeared altruistic, on finally acquiring sole ownership, Smith had some grounds for his action. In July 1874, the declining Henry Caslon had written to him: *I was very pleased to see your sales for June so very good. Verily the old House is itself again under your able guidance. I can assure you it is a great comfort to me to know that I am succeeded by a gentleman, and one who so ably fills the position so long held by the Caslons. May you have many prosperous and happy years, and, when past work, resign the 'ribbons' to a chip of your worthy self.*[3]

Ten days later, Henry W. Caslon—the last of the line—was dead.

The earlier acquisition of the Sir Charles Reed foundry put the other two founders on their mettle. If Stephenson, Blake feared a merger between the H. W. Caslon Company and Miller and Richard, how did the two view the situation? In 1904, on the retirement of Thomas White Smith, Sydney

Fig 27 Thomas White Smith, Chairman, H. W. Caslon and Sons
Limited, 1835–1907

Caslon proposed an amalgamation of the three foundries. However, from
the first, Stephenson, Blake rejected it, reasoning that the foundry in
Sheffield was preoccupied with a massive realignment and restructuring
of moulds to enable conversion to Point-body and Point-lining and amalgamation might interfere with this development. The truth was that
Stephenson, Blake were well ahead in their adoption of the Point System
and were at a tremendous advantage over the other two in terms of
modernisation.

The amalgamation issue was again raised by Sydney Caslon in 1913,
the basis of his approaches being a plea for the rationalisation and
economies of production. After considerable negotiation the amalgamation

was rejected by both Miller and Richard and Stephenson, Blake, largely as a result of the pessimism displayed by Sydney Caslon as to the future market prospects for typefounding. The three parties continued to consider amalgamation in one form or another. Meanwhile, in Sheffield, it was decided to put the firm on a more appropriate legal and financial foundation. The use of the business appendage; Sir Charles Reed and Son was finally left to lapse as, in April 1914, the company became registered as a private limited company: Stephenson, Blake and Company Limited. H. K. Stephenson and R. G. Blake became the sole directors with G. Redfern registered as Company Secretary.

The company was now in a very impressive position and as part of the company's image-making programme a visit to the foundry was arranged for the benefit of the delegates attending the Imperial Press Conference. The visit was so well received that the firm's policy began to change radically. In May 1914, the company commissioned a large stand at the International Printing Exhibition held in London. Type, sundries and composing room furnishings were displayed to very eager crowds of viewers and the company received congratulations and accolades from the trade and from fellow-exhibitors. The crowning glory of the season was the Annual Conference of the British Federation of Master Printers held in Sheffield during June 1914. Stephenson, Blake entertained the Conference and the delegates who visited the foundry and the wood material factory were more than suitably impressed. However, the euphoria of the Directors, the workpeople and those who had visited was soon to be dashed.

Chapter 16

Punchcutters and Engravers

T HE technique and the work of the punchcutter had changed very
little since the beginnings of the invention of letterpress printing.
The work entailed dedication and skill in working detail and shape
into a somewhat inhospitable material.[1] Expertise in the techniques of
punch cutting was gained by systematic and sensitive training, guidance
and a period of extended practice. However, many punchcutters lacked a
sense of aesthetic sensitivity and a natural feel for letter design. As technicians, the majority, were superbly skilled and could copy or recreate an
image of an alphabet, but lacked the creative bent of trained artist-design-
ers. As copyists, as technicians and as embellishers and decorators of
alphabet, they were accomplished. In a nineteenth century typefoundry
they were indispensable and reigned supreme.

In the original Blake and Garnett foundry, Garnett, who had trained as a
silversmith, possessed the necessary artistic skills in addition to his ability
to cut punches. However, during the early days of the foundry, the stock of
letter acquired from the William Caslon typefoundry and the output of
Garnett sufficed. Although John Stephenson was sufficiently skilled at
letter-cutting, apart from cutting a small quantity of letter, his skill was
used primarily to make good the many punches which became damaged
during the matrix striking operation. As the foundry developed, punches
were purchased from independent letter-cutters, or punches were cut by
copying other founder's designs. Type production fell into two distinct
areas, text or body type for newspaper printing and for book printing or
jobbing and display letter for the commercial and general printing market.

For the better part of fifty years the design of body type was based on the design of Roman which Firmin Didot, the French typefounder, had popularised which took on the generic appellation of Modern. Over an extended period letter-cutters re-cut and recreated designs of Modern in a wide range of possible variations: in weight, x-height dimension, in width, and in both condensed and expanded forms. Such variations did not require a punch engraver to possess aesthetic qualities but a high standard of engraving, copying and re-cutting skills. The range of typefaces, as offered in Stephenson, Blake's specimen books, was representative of most of the other typefounders. The Sheffield foundry's designs were no better or no worse than most of its British contemporaries—the uniqueness of Stephenson, Blake lay in the physical quality of its types.

In contrast, the capturing of new designs for jobbing and novelty type faces was effected very much on an opportunity basis. Other founders' designs were adopted or copied and variations and embellishments added to produce a semblance of originality. Lettering images culled from fashionable or Continental ephemera were imitated and recreated in type form. When a rival founder issued a design which attracted enquiries from customers, an attempt was made to issue a similar design. Although at Stephenson, Blake, the arbiter as to whether to pursue production of a particular design of typeface lay in the minds first with John Stephenson and later with Henry Stephenson, it was, for many years Elisha Pechey, with his distinct ability in typography who endeavoured to moderate, or otherwise, the owner's opinions—particularly as Pechey and his successor, Hanson, were in a position, as managers of the London office, to know what the firm's most important customers wanted.

The ultimate key to producing a successful typeface lay with the punch-cutters. Over a period of some one hundred and thirty years, Stephenson Blake hired them in a variety of contractual situations. A minority were trained through an apprenticeship. Others were employed as improvers. Some were approached and tempted from other foundries whilst others, wishing to maintain their own independence, would contract to work piece-work and be employed to cut a particular fount or series. Very few records exist relating to the earliest Stephenson Blake punchcutters. When the foundry was established most of the punch cutting was carried out by William Garnett. Later, John Stephenson, having acquired some skill over a period of several years set to work with another punchcutter, James Ross and sharing the work, cut Antique No 1, some time between 1831 to 1834, the Great Primer size being cut entirely by Ross in 1835.

The mid-nineteenth century skilled punch engraver was not merely a key member of a typefoundry, he was also a rarity. Stephenson, Blake employed would-be punchcutter apprentices but many had neither the ability nor skill, or the personal quality of sheer determination to achieve. Consequently, such apprentices were according to their ability transferred to the lesser occupations of justifier, mould maker or caster. Although one such apprentice punchcutter, John Hemingway, began his employment in 1842, it would appear that during the twenty-year period, 1840 to 1860, not more than two punch-engravers were employed on a full-time basis at any one time. Meanwhile, freelance engravers were commissioned to undertake work and the company bought in founts of punches from other type-founders both at home and abroad. However, the prospect cannot altogether be dismissed that between 1830 and 1850, William Garnett and his son may also have worked on some of the founts.

Employment as a punch-engraver in the foundry of Stephenson Blake was far from easy during the period 1820 to 1900. The output of punches, matrices and type was always under the critical scrutiny of either John Stephenson or Henry Stephenson, both, without exception, knew the detail and the finesse required in a well-cut punch and a well-punched matrix. The two principals' demands in their striving for perfection must at times have been singularly wearing and soul destroying. The records of absenteeism and alcoholism amongst this elite group is testimony to the situation. In 1869, in a memo addressed to the casting room overseer by Henry Stephenson, having returned from a short holiday expressed his anger: *I am very much annoyed this morning to find the men—with hardly an exception—had taken advantage of my absence and gone off drinking almost from the day I left. Several of them are off even yet. The casters to whom the moulds were entrusted having been—as usual the worst.*[2]

As the foundry developed in the latter part of the nineteenth century, the need for the services of punchcutters increased and those punchcutters who were in full-time employment were not only exceedingly well rewarded financially, their hours of work were appreciably less than the remainder of the foundry. Whilst the company did what it could to both train and educate apprentices,[3] it still had to resort to making punch cutting contracts paid for at piece work rates and contracts with freelance cutters either for whole or partial founts.

Unashamedly, the company poached other typefounders' staff. William Oliver first joined the company in 1857, having been tempted from his employment at Figgins. He was paid twice the amount of wages he had received at Figgins and was constantly being induced to remain in Sheffield. Even as late as 1872, he was party to a new contract: . . . *that during the space of five years from the date hereof as above specified the said William Oliver engages to reside in Sheffield and to work as a Punch cutter diligently and exclusively for the said Henry Stephenson and his Partners . . . at the following rate of remuneration, namely 8 shillings per punch for Roman, Italic and Antique of all sizes below Two-lines Pica, subject to the approval of the Punches by Henry Stephenson or his successor in the management of the said business and at a proportionate rate of payment for other work not comprised in these classes. That the said Henry Stephenson engages to find the said William Oliver full employment on the terms and conditions above mentioned for the period of five years as before stated but in the event of Henry Stephenson or his Representatives in case of illness or decease wishing to terminate this engagement before the completion of his term it shall be competent for him or them to do so at any time by giving six months notice of such intention and by payment to the said William Oliver of the sum of £20 as compensation.[4]*

Oliver worked for Stephenson Blake until 1878. His twenty-one years' service were not without incident. He had drink problems and was regularly called to account by Henry Stephenson. Often such admonishment led to much argument and amazement on the part of other employees—for Oliver was not only bad-tempered but incredibly insubordinate—much to the consternation of Henry Stephenson. By 1876, he had become so heavily in debt that he was made bankrupt to the sum of £650. Henry Stephenson attempted to come to his rescue with a loan, but the bank refused and Oliver was referred to the Bankruptcy Court. Even at the time of his ceasing employment in 1878, he was in the company's debt. With all his faults, Oliver's work had produced results. The standard of his punch making was exceedingly high and under his guidance the whole of the punch cutting and justifying staff gained much skill and expertise.

Meanwhile, James McLaren, who had been trained by Miller and Richard of Edinburgh, joined the foundry as a mould-maker. It was soon found that he had great all-round experience and under the tutelage of William Oliver, became a first-class punchcutter. He was engaged in the cutting of several key founts and engraved the combination series of ornamental brass-rules which Pechey had designed. Sadly, his path followed that of his punch cutting mentor, Oliver, McLaren too became an alcoholic and his employment came to an end.

With the unstable situation with Oliver and McLaren, Henry Stephenson was increasingly desperate to replace them with more reliable staff. M. Jean Rochaix, a Parisian letter-cutter, had previously been commissioned by the company to cut several successful founts and in 1873, he was invited to join the company in Sheffield on a permanent contract. However, the arrangement was less than satisfactory. He disliked the close supervision of his work. Henry Stephenson considered him ill-mannered and was appalled by his constant grumbling and his wish to return to Paris, whilst the tenor of his relationship with his colleague, Oliver was less than harmonious. After completing some of the sizes of the Saxon Black his employment came to an end.

However, Rochaix did not return to Paris but settled in London and for two years worked for H.W. Caslon until he set himself up as an independent letter-cutter. The voluminous correspondence conducted between Rochaix and Stephenson, Blake in very stilted English, interspersed with commentaries in French, reveal him to have been an individual who did not take kindly to authority; either in the employ of Stephenson, Blake or H.W. Caslon. Whilst his work was not highly thought of, because of the shortage of punchcutters, he continued to be employed on a freelance basis and during the period cut punches for Saxon Black, Old Style Grotesque, Elongated Latin, Latin Condensed, Antique No 2, Classic and Old Style Italic. At the time, Henry Stephenson was struggling to free the company from the difficult relationship problems which existed in the punch-cutting department. McLaren had suggested that William Grandison, one of Miller and Richard's letter cutters, might be tempted to come to Sheffield. Grandison was approached, but as he was under a rather tight contract with Miller and Richard the idea was not pursued further. The situation then changed. Two years later, with the sudden departure of Rochaix, a fresh approach was made to Grandison, who was by then working as a freelance for Miller and Richard and for a number of American typefounders. In 1877, he was persuaded to move to Sheffield and for about a year worked for Stephenson, Blake and for other founders. His work was of such a standard that Henry Stephenson took him into permanent employment. He was much favoured by Stephenson, paid a salary of £420 per year and allowed to work at home. These conditions gave Grandison a remarkable standing. His technical knowledge of typefounding was immense, and like his fellow Scot compatriot, was a credit to the Edinburgh company Miller and Richard. Sadly, Grandison's health declined as tuberculosis overtook him. In 1883, he moved, for health reasons, to the Isle of Wight, where he continued to cut punches for the foundry until his death in 1884.

The search for reliable punchcutters was almost an eternal quest. The replacement for Rochaix led Pechey to seek out Frederick Tarrant who, although independent, was fully committed to work for both Figgins and the Fann Street, Fox Reed foundries. However, as Tarrant was so heavily committed, he declined the offer. The rapid demise of Grandison was viewed with a good deal of trepidation and Stephenson pressed Pechey to approach Tarrant once again. Tarrant agreed and he and his son—who also

Fig 28 The foundry at work in the late nineteenth century: Punch engraving; Punch hardening, Casting type, Brass rule making

showed promise in punch-cutting—came to Sheffield in 1883. He was paid £420 per year and another £55 to continue the training of William Meggitt—Grandison's apprentice—and the junior punchcutter, Francis Tice.

However, there were doubts. Pechey knew of Tarrant's shortcomings as far as technique was concerned and he seems to have been warning Henry Stephenson from the start that should Tarrant join the staff, not to force his usual all-demanding high standards on him. Grandison was consulted and his view was that although Tarrant was a good punchcutter, he did not have a good eye for form and that he was getting old and nervous. Grandison expressed these opinions after inspecting his work and interviewing Tarrant at the foundry. The views of Pechey and Grandison were borne out. Tarrant's work was never particularly outstanding and after a number of years it became increasingly poor as a result of his drink problem.

The departure of Rochaix must have thrown Henry Stephenson into desperate straits. He considered that whilst one long term solution would be to advertise a post for a trainee punchcutter, he realised full well the problem. The expense of several years' training often came to naught. Francis Hayes Tice, a young man in his twenties, employed as an engraver by Thomas De la Rue and Company, responded to the advertisement. Stephenson had him cut a trial set of punches and being disappointed with the result rejected him. Some nine years later, in 1885, Tice, who was now an accomplished punchcutter, on learning of a vacancy for a punchcutter applied for the post and was appointed to not only cut punches but also to cut brass masters for making electrotyped ornaments. Five years later, he resigned due to critical views of his work expressed by the management.

At the loss of Tice, Henry Stephenson was again thrown into despair. It is not too difficult to visualise the situation. The autocratic, but benevolent, Sir Henry, now in his sixties, was, like many of his kind, unwilling to pass on any real responsibility for the management of the company—even to his son. He was still attempting to manage the day to day work of the foundry, but was now often irritated when business affairs intruded on the time and energy which he wished to devote to his involvement in public affairs. Tice's departure was yet another problem and inconvenience. The search for another punchcutter began via a very circuitous route. The Stephenson, Blake traveller for Scotland came to hear of an improver punchcutter who was seeking an appointment. The young man's father was a Scottish punchcutter who, having trained at the firm of Miller and Richard, had subsequently found employment in a German typefoundry and having married a German, had a son, William Kirkwood, who was trained by his father in the skills of letter cutting and then encouraged him to seek a post in a British typefoundry. Kirkwood joined the staff in Sheffield and proved not only to be a master of the punch cutting skill, but also that he had an eye for well-designed letter. He also had another useful attribute: his German upbringing had provided him with a good command of the German language which enabled him to converse with German punchcutters and typefounders with whom Stephenson, Blake were increasingly involved.

Kirkwood joined the foundry at a very crucial time. The British typefounders were caught in a rush to offer designs of Old Style type. Unlike the H. W. Caslon company which for some years had been able to 'blow the dust off' the original Caslon Old Face punches and matrices, the Sheffield foundry still had to originate its own Old Style. Pechey set to work creating an Old Style design and Kirkwood cut the punches. However, there was a good deal of heated discussion on the final form of the Old Style characters, Pechey as a typographer knew what was wanted and told Sir Henry in no uncertain manner. Kirkwood must have been very patient as the middle man in situ—particularly as he had Sir Henry and H.K. Stephenson virtually breathing down his neck daily whilst, Pechey, in London, would be commenting on smoke samples and on prints from early strikes from a distance. Kirkwood appears to have accommodated well to the exacting standards set by his three masters though he found working with H. K. Stephenson difficult and in 1902, he decided to return to Germany.

Shortly, after he had returned to Germany, Sir Henry wrote to him . . . *The Old Style promises to be a success and great credit is due to you for having caught Mr. Pechey's ideas so happily.* Later, whilst still undertaking work for Stephenson Blake, H. K. Stephenson wrote to him: *I do not forget your skill in never failing to catch my meaning when I was making my criticisms by word of mouth and I feel sure that if you will patiently look with my eyes as you used to in Sheffield you will interpret my meaning.*[5]

Notwithstanding what must have been a most lucrative but inhibiting appointment, Kirkwood had a most successful and prolific output. In his ten years at Sheffield and later, he could claim to have cut Old Style No 3, Condensed Athenian, Condensed De Vinne, Freehand, Veronese, Olympian and the Booklet Italic founts. Kirkwood continued to undertake some work for the foundry, although, after the death of Sir Henry Stephenson in 1904 the connection tended to lapse.[6]

With the departure of Kirkwood, the firm were again on the lookout for a punchcutter. As a young man, Emile Bertaut had joined the staff of Sir Charles Reed's Fann Street foundry and had trained as a punchcutter under the direction of his father who was also employed at the Fann Street foundry. After a number of years Bertaut set himself up as an independent punchcutter and engraver. From time to time Stephenson Blake had engaged him to cut specific founts. Pechey had a high opinion of Bertaut and, working through him, connived to get Sir Henry to acquire a Benton punch-engraving machine. It was agreed to approach Bertaut with an offer to join the staff at Sheffield but he initially expressed a reluctance and an agreement was reached that he would cut punches exclusively for Stephenson Blake. Sir Henry and H. K. Stephenson were less than happy with this arrangement and with a little coercion and with the offer of a good number of perquisites, Emile Bertaut accepted a five-year contract and in 1894 took up his work in Sheffield. He found his sojourn in the foundry difficult. He resented the close inspection of his work by Sir Henry and H. K. Stephenson and found their criticism difficult to bear. Sir Henry was getting increasingly old and Bertaut resented what he considered to be uninformed criticism of his work by the young and somewhat dogmatic H. K. Stephenson. He returned to London at the end of his contract. The ending of Bertaut's contract was regarded as no great loss—particularly as the future succession seemed assured.

The home-grown punchcutter, William W. Meggitt, who had been trained at some cost under Grandison, Tarrant and Kirkwood, had developed into a singularly competent punchcutter and during the next three years much of the work began to pass to him. However, by 1902, Meggitt had other family business interests in prospect and resigned. Fortunately, William Kirkwood came to hear of the vacancy and recommended one of his own apprentices, Karl Görner whom he had trained in his Frankfurt workshop. Görner was the last of the line of traditionally trained punchcutters and served in the company from 1907 until 1959.

In the period 1900 to 1914, an in-house trained punchcutter, J. E. Uttley, became the chief punchcutter and ultimately the manager of the punch and matrix production, the lesser skilled punchcutters and justifiers being busy preparing for the introduction of point-body and point-lining types. Meanwhile, on the death of Sir Henry Stephenson, the adamantine rule set by him that the company would never sell a type design to another foundry, was allowed to lapse. Even on his death bed he had directed that a request from the Inland Type Foundry in Chicago to purchase the rights of the Athenia Expanded series designed by Pechey and punch-cut by Kirkwood be refused.

H. K. Stephenson and R. G. Blake as junior members of the management had for some time despaired at lost opportunities and now that the ownership of the business had passed to them, some of the outdated ideas had to change, particularly in the area of punch-cutting and matrix making. It could now be seen, in the light of the burgeoning of newly designed type-faces, many of which were emanating from the United States, that it was the artist-designer who created letter forms not the punchcutter. Technically, the majority were superb craftsmen, but their ability to create typeface designs by trial and error methods in an increasingly design-conscious environment, was passing.

Chapter 17

Types of Influence

A S the twentieth century opened, there was a new design consciousness abroad amongst the printing and publishing fraternity. The
Private Press Movement in Britain and America was bringing a
much needed influence to bear on publishing houses and printers. The
output of works from such enterprises as the Doves and the Ashendene
presses and the influences of individuals such as T. J. Cobden-Sanderson,
Emery Walker and the pioneering art education work of Lethaby at the
Central School of Arts and Crafts in London did much to further the cause.
Meanwhile, in the United States, the movement influenced by such presses
as the Merrymount, Camelot, Riverside, served to sharpen opinions and set
standards of design both in America and in Europe. The shift from the use
of the monotonous Modern typefaces which had started slowly with the
creation of Old Style by Miller and Richard had, by the 1890s become
widely accepted. For better or worse, founders now in terms of the quality
of letter designs, began to issue Old Style in many variant forms; some
almost pirated from other foundries, others designed and cut with variations in set, weight and x-height. There was a conscious awareness amongst
typefounders on both sides of the Atlantic that shared designs either
bought, sold or traded, was to their mutual advantage. The wealthy Private
Press printers, particularly in America, had designed and commissioned
founts which were in many respects often superior to those produced
commercially. In 1927, Beatrice Warde, writing under her *nom de plume* of
Paul Beaujon, put the matter quite succinctly: *It seems that so far this
century has failed to establish one new type face to distinguish its books.*

*There is a new style, but Caslon and the other stand-bys have been cast for
three generations before ours. There are new advertising faces that represent faithfully our age and ideals: so faithfully that they are altogether unfit
for book printing.*[1]

The extensive collection of punches and matrices from the Sir Charles
Reed foundry had been brought to Sheffield and put into storage in one of
the cellars of the house in Upper Allen Street. Out of a genuine personal
interest and later, as result of encouragement from leading typographers, R.
G. Blake began in earnest to assess in detail the stock which had been
acquired. When leading typographers and typefounders enquired about
seemingly long lost eighteenth and early nineteenth century typefaces
which had disappeared from public view, Blake was able to respond. His
diligent researches revealed that the company had acquired a much richer
source of typographical material than was at first thought. Suddenly, the
seemingly ancient, outdated and worthless Reed stock was revealing
typographical jewels of great potential. Admittedly, the punches and matrices were all too often not in a condition which made them immediately
usable, but Stephenson, Blake held the originals which could be refur-
bished to match the current production methods. A number of the Reed
founts were highly popular and as a result, Ronaldson and Italian, which
were known to be very saleable typefaces were quickly rejustified and cast
in Point-body sized moulds. The Reed foundry's Old Style and Clarendon
series were reissued and they attracted a good deal of attention and sold
well. Under the new partners, a brisk policy of issues was planned in an
effort to keep ahead of competition. Now that the Typefounders'
Association had agreed to end their trade advertising ban, Stephenson,
Blake began designing and printing insets for the trade magazines and
displayed type specimens. A typeface which had been cut originally at
Fry's Foundry in the 1770s was presented as Georgian Old Face in a specimen booklet issued in 1907. A great deal of effort was then made to
finalise a series of Old Styles, created in-house and these also appeared in
1907. The series showed promise, but unfortunately the design was over-
shadowed by the appearance and universal acclamation of the Cheltenham
series from America.

In the bids for acquiring popular American typefaces, competition was
intense. The three members belonging to the Typefounders' Association
now vied with each other to obtain design rights. An example of this arose
in the case of the Cheltenham series which caused Stephenson, Blake
considerable disappointment. The typeface had been designed by Bertram
Goodhue in 1896, for Daniel Berkeley Updike, for use at the Cheltenham
Press, New York. The design attracted a good deal of attention in America

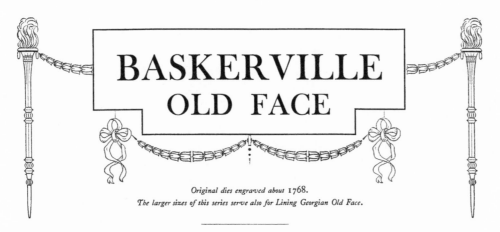

BASKERVILLE
OLD FACE

Original dies engraved about 1768.
The larger sizes of this series serve also for Lining Georgian Old Face.

72 POINT.

DECEMBER
Renovation

60 POINT.

HARBINGERS
Rustic Maiden

48 POINT.

CUSTOM HOUSE
Historic Research

STEPHENSON, BLAKE & Co.   SIR CHARLES REED & SONS.

Fig 29 Stephenson, Blake specimen leaflet, Baskerville Old Face, 1907

and was being taken up commercially by the American Type Founders company, where it was subsequently developed by M. F. Benton who produced a full series with eighteen variations. Its commercial appearance became an instant success and it was a design which Stephenson, Blake particularly coveted. However, Sydney Caslon, much to the chagrin of H. K. Stephenson, had made his bid by cablegram and successfully obtained the design rights for production of it in Britain. The Cheltenham series became an instant success in Britain and brought both profit and credit to the Caslon Company. The Sheffield foundry urgently needed a similar face in order to compete with Caslon. The Windsor series, which had been designed by Pechey and launched after his death, was a characterless and somewhat stylised Venetian roman which, although it was launched in 1905, looked singularly weak when compared with Cheltenham. To counter the situation, Hanson, the London manager, H. K. Stephenson and R. G. Blake studied the Cheltenham design and developed a version which was, after considerable correction and modification, produced under the direction of J. E. Uttley, the chief punchcutter. Whilst the principals congratulated themselves on devising a 'Cheltenham style' of letter, which they issued in 1909 as the Winchester series, in a later age, the company may well have had a case of plagiarisation of design brought against it. However, for the time being they had at least kept abreast of their main competitors—H. W. Caslon.

The now constant stream of new typefaces coming on to the market was not universally acceptable. The members of the Arts and Crafts Movement and more particularly the Private Press Movement had, for over twenty-years, taken somewhat puritanical stances both in their writings and in the books which they designed and printed. Whilst William Morris and his followers basked in mediaevalism and the art world expressed its delight with the works of the Kelmscott Press, it was the productions of the Private Presses which would have the greater influence on both designers and printers. As the twentieth century opened it was with a good deal of contempt that the designers, artists and literati viewed many of the type designs which the typefounders were offering.

On the 28th September 1911, *The Times Literary Supplement* printed an article entitled *The Influence of the Kelmscott Press*.[2] The nature of it was a review of a group of five books produced respectively by Cobden-Sanderson; St. John Hornby; the Oxford University Press (a book printed from a Greek fount designed by Robert Proctor); Philip Lee Warner, printer to the Medici Society, and a work produced by Chatto and Windus. They were essentially products of the influencing Private Press Movement even though two were run-of-the-press editions. The author carefully reviewed each of the five works and usefully analysed, compared and contrasted them with Morris's typography and book production. Having set the scene with a very scholarly appraisal, the author then proceeded to comment on typefounding: *We must add a word about typefounding. There is no more dismal sight than the pages of a modern typefounder's specimen book which seems to gather together some of the worst examples of the taste of the nineteenth and twentieth centuries in a kind of museum of horrors. The first typefounders formed their types from the beautiful which they found in contemporary or early manuscripts . . . when the alphabet became cast in lead, its growth presently ceased, and with its growth its life. Though new founts and new fashions in types have been invented from time to time, they have been inspired from no living source. The mummy keeps the form of the living body, but, twist and turn and robe its limbs as we may, it has neither comeliness nor life.* The author having finally reflected on the work and influence of Morris pleads: *May we not hope that our typefounders may also come under the influence of the movement, and that the modern calligrapher may design alphabets formed naturally and beautifully, not slavishly copied from any model, however fine, free from affectation and from eccentricity, which may fulfil all the practical requirements of modern book type?*[3] The *Museum of Horrors* article caused both consternation and anger within the Typefounders' Association. This was hardly surprising. Even though the elderly Sir Henry Stephenson who had dominated the Association for so many years was dead, H. K. Stephenson and R. G. Blake virtually held sway within *The Ring*—now embracing but three member companies. Stephenson, Blake were particularly annoyed for they regarded the article as a slur on the Sheffield foundry. Whilst the attack did not directly cite Stephenson, Blake, it was clearly directed at them and linked to their then recently issued 1911 specimen book, the contents of which had been well-publicised in the trade press. As a riposte to the adverse comments, a separate specimen booklet was prepared entitled: *Old Style Book Letter.* In presenting it, the commentary heralded: *Every British printer has, for the first time a series of eighteenth century book letter, which, while enabling him to please the taste of his most fastidious customers, will not oblige him to forgo the labour-saving advantage to be derived from types cast on point-bodies.*[4]

H. K. Stephenson was not to be outdone by the TLS. He wrote to the Editor of *The Times* and suggested that an article be written on the economic and cultural success of the city of Sheffield. On the 22nd November 1911, a feature appeared with the heading: SHEFFIELD—*the Industrial Capital of Yorkshire.* There was no specific reference to Stephenson, Blake or to typefounding, but there was a reference to Sir

Henry Stephenson and the contribution which he had made to the establishment of the University of Sheffield. The article also had other uses.
Early in 1912, the company issued a booklet entitled: *The Story of Sheffield
and Typefounding.* The preface carried a reprint of *The Times* article of the
previous year.

The article which appeared in *The Times Literary Supplement* was in
some ways an honest reflection of the period. A good deal of hypocrisy had
arisen amongst both typefounders and printers relating to the influences
which had become manifest. When it suited the case, there was much admiration for the works of the Kelmscott and the Private Presses; at other times
they voiced their opinions that the works of the Private Presses were nothing more than products of dilettantes who had little idea of the real world
of commerce. In truth there was a place for both fine-book production and
commercial printing, but the attack by *The Times Literary Supplement*
touched upon an internal weakness, that of a lack of typographical sensitivity on the part of typefounders and, in the case of the Stephenson, Blake
foundry, on the principals who owned it. However, Stephenson, Blake, in
common with other founders, facing ever-reducing orders for text types
realised their market was changing. The company needed to orientate itself
to meeting the needs of printers and advertisers and their eagerness for the
latest fashion in display and jobbing types. The rights for producing
Hallamshire Old Style, Flemish Condensed and Expanded were acquired
from the Inland Type Foundry of Chicago; Washington Text from the
Keystone Type Foundry and Westminster Old Style, De Vinne, Spartan and
Clearface from the American Type Founders. Although the throughput of
the new founts was quite remarkable—demanding a quicker turn round of
prepared matrices and cast type—the newly made arrangements for sharing and acquiring popular typefaces for which there was a ready market
eased the problem of the search for creative punchcutters and designers. It
was now a situation of following the typographical fashion of the time and
of acquiring production rights in advance of other founders. Whilst acquiring new typeface designs by purchase or exchange was one method,
another was copying or plagiarising. During Sir Henry Stephenson's time
as managing partner, he was ever ready and willing to buy any designs
which he thought had commercial merit, but flatly refused to sell or trade
any of his own foundry's stock. He maintained this strategy within the
Typefounders' Association where he led the strongest of efforts to get legislation tightened to protect typeface designs. In practice, double standards
existed. Whilst publicly Stephenson, Blake fought tenaciously for legal
protection, they were not averse to pressing the margins of plagiarisation to
the limit, particularly in respect of the Windsor series. The matter came to

a final though unsatisfactory conclusion in 1916. The typefounding and engineering company of Legros and Grant had been asked to supply matrices to a printing company, Roberts and Newton. The designs which had been requested closely resembled the Windsor and Chatsworth series, two typeface designs to which Stephenson, Blake were entitled to protection under the terms of the copyright Act of 1911. Legros and Grant contended that the design protection covered the whole of the seventy-six characters and symbols *per se* and argued the case that registration and copyright related to the whole and not to every individual character. Stephenson, Blake contended that the use of any or all was an infringement of the copyright. Mr. Justice Eve, in summing up presented ambiguous findings and granted leave of appeal to both parties to challenge what appeared to be a very negative decision. H. K. Stephenson made every effort to take the matter into the Court of Appeal but Counsel seems to have advised against it. Consequently the matter was quietly dropped.[5]

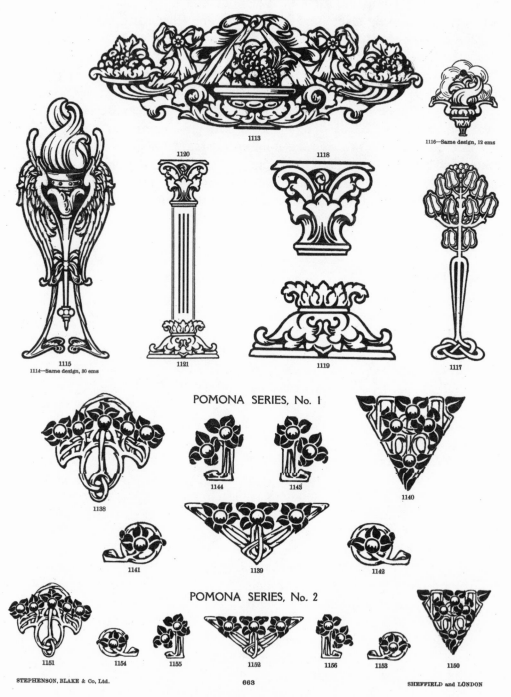

ART ORNAMENTS AND POMONA SERIES

For Prices see Current Price List of Electros

1113

1116—Same design, 12 ems

1120

1118

1115
1114—Same design, 30 ems

1121

1119

1117

POMONA SERIES, No. 1

1138

1144

1145

1140

1141

1139

1142

POMONA SERIES, No. 2

1151

1154

1155

1152

1156

1153

1150

STEPHENSON, BLAKE & Co, Ltd.

663

SHEFFIELD and LONDON

Fig 30 Art Ornaments of the 1920s, from the Stephenson, Blake 1924 Specimen Book

Chapter 18

The Call to Arms

D URING the early summer of 1914, the company had bathed in
considerable glory and the future augured well. However, by the
end of July the scene began to change dramatically as Britain went
to War. The immediate impact caused by the mobilisation of Reserve
Forces and Territorial Army units meant that the Managing Director, Henry
Kenyon Stephenson, Colonel of the 3rd (West Riding) Regiment, Royal
Field Artillery, was, within days, called into war service.

During the previous ten years the two directors had shared management
responsibilities. When Stephenson, Blake became a private limited
company, H. K. Stephenson, assumed the role of Chairman and Managing
Director responsible for overall business policy, including the London
office and overseas trading. Unlike his father, much of his time was, and
would continue to be, devoted to interests far removed from the work of the
foundry. In contrast, Robert Greaves Blake, from the earliest time of his
joining the company had become deeply immersed in the oversight of the
factory organisation and production. He had carefully planned, and seen to
fruition, the wood material department and managed the day-to-day operation of the foundry. Now that H. K. Stephenson was with his regiment in
France, the management of the company was in Blake's care, and he was
having to deal with new problems. Within days of the declaration of War,
orders for type and wood-equipment began to fall dramatically.

Despite the exigencies of war, Blake still managed to spend a few days
of leisure away from the foundry. In a letter to Lieutenant Colonel H. K.
Stephenson serving with the British Expeditionary Force in France, he
writes, on the 28th September 1914: *My Dear Harry . . . Would you drop*

me a line at the Devonshire Arms at Bolton Abbey [as] *I am shooting on the Duke of Devonshire's moors on Wednesday and Thursday. Francis* [has joined us and] *was splendid. I think he too enjoyed his day. There were many birds. 176 brace; 180 brace; 100 brace were bagged. R.G.B.*[1]

Francis was H. K. Stephenson's eldest son, Henry Francis Blake Stephenson. He was born in 1895 and educated at Eton. After leaving school he was sent to Berlin where it was intended that he should gain experience whilst working in a major printing and publishing house. However, this arrangement quickly came to an end. On the outbreak of war, in August 1914, he was repatriated and returned to Sheffield. Meanwhile, his weekend shooting trips with his uncle, R. G. Blake also came to an end; early in 1915, he volunteered to join his father who was serving with his regiment in Flanders.

At the foundry problems began to escalate. Not only those members of the company who had served as reservists or who were members of the local Territorial Army units had been mobilised, but, as there was also a great patriot clamouring, many of the young men in the company—and the not-so-young—volunteered for service in the British Army. By December 1914, thirty members of the foundry had volunteered and as the war progressed others were called up as a result of the Conscription Acts. The course of the war and the casualty rate was stressful both for those serving on the Western Front and for those at home, particularly at the time of the on-going Battle of the Somme. Blake, writing to Sydney Caslon on the 16th of August 1916, recounted: . . . *Stephenson and my brother* [Stephen Blake] *are in the thick of it near Albert. The former is now a Group Commander and has several Brigades under him.*[2] Later that same month, Blake wrote to Alan Richard of Miller and Richard: . . . [Colonel Stephenson] *is in the thick of it near Thiepval as is my brother. I hope your boys are safe and well. It is a very anxious time.*[3]

It was an anxious time too in the business. By the end of 1916, the London office which had a pre-war establishment of nine, was reduced to three: a traveller, a clerk and an assistant. Adding to the increasingly difficult labour situation in the foundry was the departure of skilled men; engineers, fitters and toolroom mechanics who left to take up lucrative jobs in the Sheffield steelworks which were producing munitions. The pressing need for men put the foundry in difficult circumstances and the stringent Conscription Orders continued to deplete the workforce. The trading position was tenuous. For the first three years of the war, orders for type and furniture dropped dramatically. Whilst the loss of staff either into the Army or into munitions factories lowered the wage bills, the remaining staff worked part-time. The weekly hours worked were cut from 54 to 34 and only 47 casting machines out of a total of 111 were in production. Those male employees who were either unfit or too old for military service or who felt unable to face a change of workplace began to suffer. The wages earned as a result of working short time—a 34-hour week—left them with a very poor living wage and representation was made to the management to increase the number of hours worked. The plea did not go unanswered and R. G. Blake agreed to raise the weekly hours to 40, so their pay rose from 26 shillings to 30 shillings per week for married men, whilst single men's wages rose from 15 shillings to 18 shillings per week. In many respects the general level of wages had escalated, particularly in Sheffield where munitions production was booming. By 1917, Stephenson, Blake in common with its rivals, could no longer contain the rising costs in a situation where sales had fallen away so dramatically.

However, wages were not the only cause of increased costs. The production of ammunition required enormous quantities of both lead and brass—the two metals which were the lifeblood of a letterfoundry. Lead and spacing material production was halted due to the shortage of metal, the acquisition of which, was subject to strict Government licensing. By early 1918, the national situation with regard to the supplies of lead had become so critical that the Government required all printers and typefounders to declare the extent of their stocks of metal in order to determine a rationale for allocating supplies.

Although Colonel Stephenson was on active service, he wrote voluminous letters, almost weekly, enquiring, relating and advising Blake on business affairs. On one particular aspect the directors of the company felt particularly aggrieved: the company's trading losses which the war was causing. Many of the directors' friends and contemporaries in the Sheffield steel and engineering industries were making enormously high profits from war materials production, whilst the products of the foundry could make little contribution either to the war effort or to the profitability of the company. The best the company could do was produce some lead products for filling shell cases whilst the wood material department was contracted to make powder boxes for the Royal Ordnance factories, and boxes and crates for local firms engaged in the production of artillery shell cases. The opportunity for the company to profit from the wartime situation was limited, but with the coming of peace, the securing of several Government contracts for equipment to set up printing units in France for the British Expeditionary Force who were occupying the Rhineland and, a prestigious order in 1919 for type and equipment destined for the printing works being set up to service the 1919 Peace Conference in Versailles, went some way towards ameliorating the management's sense of grievance.

There must have been a good deal of relief on the part of R. G. Blake on learning of H. K. Stephenson's release from his military duties. For five years Blake had striven hard to keep the business in production, and, whilst profits had declined, he could take satisfaction from the fact that he had at least kept the firm together. His optimism was soon to be dashed. Colonel Stephenson was nominated as a Liberal Party candidate to contest the Sheffield Park Division in the 1918 Parliamentary Election—the khaki election—winning the seat by a huge majority. In 1919, he was also elected to serve as Master of the Cutlers' Company in Hallamshire—a peculiarly Sheffield institution. Meanwhile, in 1923, his service as Member of Parliament came to an end as the Liberal party was disastrously defeated. In 1936, King George V conferred a Baronetcy to mark H. K. Stephenson's long record of public service.

With the ending of hostilities, orders began to flow into the company from printers at home and abroad whose type stock had severely deteriorated over the previous four years. The control of the supply of metal quickly came to an end, and as men were demobilised the labour situation improved, although a number of previous employees found conditions in the local steel and engineering firms more to their liking and never returned. By the end of 1920, the number employed exceeded that of pre-war. There were 233 workers in the foundry; 55 in the wood materials department and 29 salaried staff. However, post-war relationships with the workpeople were less than harmonious. The directors believed that the remuneration of its workpeople was fair, but at shop-floor level this was not the case. The management constantly cited the wage rates paid in other foundries—including the fact that provincial wages were traditionally lower than in London. In the period 1917-19, local wages were exceedingly high. There were many variable rates, the war and inflation had resulted in bonuses, cost of living adjustments and special payments. Questions were raised relating to consolidation of these payments into the normal wage rates. Meanwhile, the many women employed in the foundry and the warehouse were paid at rates relating to the employment of juvenile workers and whilst the men engaged in typecasting had a trade society to press their case for improved wages and conditions, the women had none. In 1917, the Government Arbitrator awarded a 66% increase in the wages of the warehouse girls which uplifted their wages to a range from between 10 shillings to 18 shillings per week.

Although H. K. Stephenson as joint Managing Director was heavily engaged in outside activities, he still played a major role in the overall organisation of the foundry and must have found the negotiations with the workpeople who were supported by the Amalgamated Typefounders' Trade Society and by the National Amalgamated Union of Labour singularly irksome. Already known for his obduracy and quickness of decision, his illustrious war record—gaining the Distinguished Service Order—had

Fig 31 Colonel Sir Henry Kenyon Stephenson, Bt. DSO 1865–1947

neither softened nor ameliorated his understanding of the problems of the workers. The company's policy of patriarchal benevolence was severely tested in a climate of conducting wage negotiations with organised labour. Stephenson wanted to introduce a profit-sharing scheme, whilst the trade association wanted a Whitely Joint Industrial Council setting up, charged to negotiate wage rates at national level and wanted the piecework arrangements ended. The directors countered by offering to reduce the number of hours worked from 51 to 47. A demand was made for an increase in the basic wage of 10 shillings per week and the Society pressed the case in view of the fact that Caslons had been forced into accepting it.

The company's order books were full and customers were demanding service and delivery. It was April 1919 and the men, taking advantage of the situation, decided to strike. The company continued to uphold the concessions made earlier in the year and no more. Meanwhile, with no other means of supporting their families, the strikers returned to work in early July after a period of almost two months, on the promise that further concessions might be negotiated. In September 1919, the typecasters were working a 48-hour week for which they were receiving approximately 67 shillings per week, although those who were employed on a piecework basis were earning much higher wages. The engineers were paid at the same rates as those agreed by the local unions, whilst a number of other workmen were paid approximately 110 shillings weekly. Boys—young men between 14 to 18—were paid approximately 30 shillings and the women 30 to 50 shillings, according to age. By the early 1920s, inflation was running high and the rates for typecasters and dressers rose to almost 80 shillings per week. The summer of 1921 brought the beginnings of recession. The cost of living index began to fall dramatically. This was linked with the general decline in the economy and a period of industrial depression began to set in. In the company, there was a slackening of orders, both for type and equipment, and the directors sought ways of cutting production costs.

For the two principals, the immediate economic problems were only part of the overall situation. In the decade leading up to the War, they had come to the conclusion that the company must diversify. The golden age of type-founding was over. The first stage of this process had already begun, when in 1914 the company became a private and limited corporation. The war delayed the implementation of any other further developments but now, with the ending of hostilities the situation was reviewed. The company was carrying an excessive amount of capital and the principals decided to invest elsewhere. The joint Managing Directors, brothers-in-law, decided in the early 1920s, to purchase Thomas Turton and Sons Limited, the long estab-lished Sheffield steel maker, converter and manufacturer which now became a wholly owned subsidiary. The two principals also withdrew some of their share capital from the business and invested elsewhere.

The acquisition of Thomas Turton and Sons was of particular importance to Colonel H. K. Stephenson. He had four sons and four daughters to provide for. The typefoundry would provide for one or more, Turtons like-wise. A further investment was made in the cutlery firm of Butler and Sons Limited, again a venture providing diversification and occupational oppor-tunities for members of the family.

Meanwhile, for a number of years, since the death of Sir Henry Stephenson, the family had moved from Endcliffe Vale into nearby Banner Cross Hall, Ecclesall, close to the family residence of the Blakes. Now, with the freeing of capital from his share of the business, Colonel Stephenson, Member of Parliament, purchased Hassop Hall and the Hassop Estate, near Bakewell in Derbyshire.

Chapter 19

Ambiguous and Ambitious Strategies

E VEN in the midst of World War I, the three member companies of the Typefounders' Association continued to discuss and negotiate amalgamation. Miller and Richard although interested, would not seriously consider the idea on the grounds that key members of their company were serving in the Armed Forces. In 1916, Sydney Caslon, choosing to ignore the negative response from Edinburgh, approached R. G. Blake with a proposal that Stephenson, Blake should consider purchasing the H. W. Caslon foundry on a basis similar to that of the acquisition of the Sir Charles Reed foundry. Under the wartime conditions, both companies were suffering from a downturn of trade. Supplies of metal were short and shipping difficulties were affecting the overseas trading of both companies. The main thrust was coming from H. W. Caslon's directors. Originally, H. W. Caslon and Company had been located at No. 22 Chiswell Street, but shortly before the outbreak of the war in 1914, the company had geographically divided its activities. The typefounding operation had been relocated into the outer London suburb of Hackney Wick and their offices and warehouse transferred into newly built and prestigious accommodation at No. 82 Chiswell Street. The prospective amalgamation negotiations, which took place in the period 1916-19, were mainly conducted by Sydney Caslon and R. G. Blake, with H. K. Stephenson remaining usefully in the role of the Sheffield company's final arbiter. Amalgamation negotiations began to be conducted in earnest. Both firms' accountants valued the two companies and their reports revealed two very different approaches in terms of capital investment. It soon became evident that Stephenson, Blake had continually invested in capital equipment and as a result was better equipped. However, Caslon's production capacity was greater and more efficient, although in the view of the Stephenson, Blake directors, their type lacked the quality of the Sheffield foundry. The respective company accountants entered into very detailed analyses of costs, profits and values. There were times when agreement on a merger looked possible and then, one or other of the parties would raise an objection. Stephenson, Blake's directors thought the Caslon sales approach was particularly effective, coveted some of the excellent and profitable typefaces which it issued, and envied its overseas accounts, but now, having gained a considerable insight into Caslon's marketing and production potential as a result of the discussions, were able to see few strengths and a number of weaknesses in the business—one of them being the divorce of the typefounding operation from the sales and administration as a result of the company being located on two sites.

Investment by H. W. Caslon and Company had taken a different direction by providing, as it did, at No. 82 Chiswell Street, a high-profile and singularly costly head office and showroom. In the comparison of ongoing costs, H. K. Stephenson and R. G. Blake were appalled at the expense of maintaining the fine Caslon London offices and showroom. Although they envied Caslon's prestigious premises, they considered they were far too expensive to maintain, particularly on learning that they were costing £1400 per annum compared with the cost of No. 33 Aldersgate Street, the annual costs for which were under £300. However, during the negotiations, R. G. Blake did consider that, if the two firms came together, the prestigious nature of the Caslon head office would be most appropriate for a combined operation which could truly dominate the British printing and newspaper industries. This was a long-cherished wish of both Stephenson and Blake who had felt, for some time, that their company was handicapped as a result of not having its head office in London. Though there were other times when they frequently congratulated themselves that although they were far removed from their London office, they were immediately on site and in control at the Sheffield foundry. At one point, discussion was focused on the feasibility of moving both Stephenson, Blake's and Caslon's casting operations into a rural situation, in order to reduce labour costs. The idea was raised as a significant number of printers formerly located in the City of London had successfully moved out into the Home Counties. In May 1919, R. G. Blake, writing to Caslon reflected . . . [Even] *Sheffield seems to be too expensive a town just now to have business in.*[1] Negotiations dragged on for a few more weeks until finally, in July 1919, R. G. Blake wrote, quite unequivocally . . . *in any amalgamation we would not be second fiddle or take a subordinate position.*[2] Once again the two companies went their separate ways—even though the principals were still friendly and, on a number of occasions, met socially as members of the Typefounders' Association.

Meanwhile, the fortunes of H. W. Caslon began to show some improvement. The company's foundry at Hackney Wick had, during the war, been engaged in the production of munitions and this had given the company something of a financial fillip. As the 1920s approached, H. W. Caslon, with what appeared to be a new lease of life, sought to take advantage of the fact that the original William Caslon Letter Foundry had been in existence for two hundred years and decided to mark the event by commissioning the writing of a history of the company and publishing it in the finest possible style. John Findley McRae was invited to author the work and George W. Jones, the eminent typographer and the proprietor of The Sign of the Dolphin Press in Gough Square, Fleet Street, was commissioned to design and print it.

The launch of *Two Centuries of Type Founding, Annals of the Letterfoundry established by William Caslon in Chiswell Street, London, in 1720,* caused a stir of admiration.[3] Not only was it a credit to the H. W. Caslon company, it was also commendable testimony to the work of George W. Jones. Never before had the Original Caslon Old Face been displayed so beautifully. The eulogies from the trade, the printing literati and the trade magazines, flooded in—much to the annoyance of the Stephenson, Blake directors. Here was a company with which the directors had long been in gentlemanly negotiations regarding a possible merger, stealing a march on them. The directors were on their mettle. Caslons had taken on a new lease of life, they had a prestigious head office in London and many more overseas customers than Stephenson, Blake.

The public face of the relationships between the members of the Typefounders' Association was that of much bonhomie. Privately they were waging a war. Stephenson, Blake had long set its sights on establishing trade supremacy and was bent on either seeing H.W. Caslon and Company Limited cease trading or of acquiring the company at a very low price. As far as Stephenson, Blake was concerned, something had to be done to counter Caslon's *tour de force*. Clearly, a starting point would be to consult a designer. George W. Jones was ruled out from the beginning. He was known in Sheffield, having spent a number of his early years as a traveller for a less than significant local printing company, he had become typographical adviser to the Linotype and Machinery Company and had only too recently produced the bicentenary piece for H. W. Caslon and Company.

The directors' attention was turned to an up and coming typographer: Robert Bertram Fishenden, who was a rising star in the printing industry. At the age of twenty he had been appointed Works Manager of the leading process engraving company; Gee and Watson of Birmingham and two years later he had become Head of the School of Printing in the prestigious Manchester College of Science and Technology. Now, at the age of forty-one he was approached to become the Assistant Manager London with special responsibility for the preparation of specimen sheets. The appointment of Fishenden was not without its problems. It meant displacing the authority, of Hanson the then current Manager, and it came as something of a personal slight but, as an assumed loyal servant of the company, he was expected to accept Fishenden gracefully. Shortly afterwards, in 1923, Hanson retired after serving the company almost fifty years. Meanwhile, the terms of Fishenden's contract needed to be agreed. In June 1921, when negotiations were afoot to secure his services, much discussion centred around the amount of salary he was to be offered: *Dear Fishenden . . . in view of the fall in the cost of living, I think and hope you will consider the salary offered as sufficient. It is as much as we can afford at the present time. As for your house—the sooner you can go to London the better. Surely, you can sell or let your house?*[4] Fishenden and his family moved from Manchester to London and found, after two years, that the cost of living was rather expensive and asked for a significant increase in salary. Blake responded: *Dear Fishenden, The photograph of your son is charming. Surely the little lad is worth striving for. He ought to go to a first-class Public School. It all costs money. Your wife's ideas on money are shocking! I hope you don't agree with them—if so God help us at Aldersgate Street! R.G.B.*[5]

The directors insisted that Fishenden's first task was to produce a counter to Caslon's celebratory piece. A sixteen-page booklet, entitled: *Letter Founding*, in an almost identical style to that of the Caslon's history was prepared. To indicate to customers and rivals that the Sheffield Foundry could raise founts of an age equal to Caslons, the work was type-set in Fry's Baskerville Old Face and, as if to stamp the mark of seniority, a family tree diagram was drawn up; linking the Sheffield foundry to the earliest English printers and typefounders—even down to Wynkyn de Worde. This was but an interim measure; Stephenson, Blake and Company Limited were not to be outdone. Having completed the production of *Typefounding History,* work began on what could be reckoned as the Stephenson, Blake *magnum opus*. Under the closest of monitoring from H. K. Stephenson and R. G. Blake, Fishenden was directed to compile copy, design and supervise the typesetting of the specimen pages for a

Fig 32 Stephenson, Blake: Printing Types, 1924

projected book of typefaces. For many years, typefounders' specimens had been prepared according to certain unwritten rules. A founder seldom displayed the whole of the characters in a fount, particularly in the case of typeface sizes above 18 point, lest rivals should copy or plagiarise the design. Displayed words in capitals were to commence on a strong letter such as D F E H K L M N P R to ensure a line began with a full vertical downstroke. It was also preferable that the ending of displayed words contained a mainstroke on the right of the character: H M N, whilst letters and words which possessed open counters and which in combination created visual problems, A T V W Y, were to be avoided. Names of people were not to be used unless they were obviously historical. Texts taken from certain literary works were not to be used unless they were clear of Copyright Acts. The copy for any displayed typography which might be construed as advertising had to be fictitious and no dates were to be included lest the specimen book should rapidly be seen to be out of date. Such were the nature of the initial constraints put upon Fishenden. When the copy and designs had been agreed upon, the pages were typeset by compositors working in the London showrooms. Proofs were sent to the foundry in Sheffield where, under the critical eyes of Stephenson and Blake, they were duly approved—or otherwise. There were many arguments and much discussion. Fishenden was an expert and was not to be browbeaten by the directors as punchcutters and staff had been in former times.

With typographical composition of the 700 handset pages complete, they were dispatched from Aldersgate showroom to the foundry and works in Upper Allen Street, Sheffield and thence to the West Street premises of J. W. Northend Limited in Sheffield. It was here that the printing and finishing of the Specimen Book was undertaken. Two, handfed, quad-demy Miehle, two-revolution presses were commissioned and were tied up for months during the printing operation. Pages were imposed and formes transported on to the machine bed with the utmost care. Painstaking make-ready was undertaken and the formes proofed. The sheets were then taken to the foundry by a compositor or an apprentice, who would then wait—sometimes a whole day or more—whilst H. K. Stephenson and R. G. Blake would pore over each letter, comma, or typographical sign with a high-powered magnifying glass. If any character failed to print, showed damage or was defective, half-a-dozen replacement characters would be passed to the Northend workman. When sheets had been finally approved, the machines rolled slowly and carefully, each sheet being interleaved and dried before perfecting took place. During the print run Mr. J. W. Northend himself would extract a sheet from the delivery and repeat the same rigorous inspection of the printed image. Many years later, William Northend, the son of the founder was to write: *my father would be seen many an hour standing at a raised desk with two bright electric lamps clamped to it and a jeweller's glass screwed in his eye, poring letter by letter over a double medium sheet, making sure that no damaged letter would pass his scrutiny . . . The result was perfection and excellence. Although cost was no object, with machines standing idly by whilst pages were checked minutely there were times when his commercial patience was sorely tried . . .* [6]

Printing Types is probably the finest type specimen book ever produced. Subsequent reissues of it, or specimen books produced by other type-founders, never equalled the quality of this particular example and it is representative of the highest standards of commercial letterpress printing of its time. Ten thousand copies were printed and subsequently the sheets were bound and finished. Several hundred copies were full-bound in leather and each of these was hand-gilded on the head, tail and fore-edge.

The new specimen book was received with universal acclaim. Frederick Warde, Director of Typography at the Princeton University Press wrote: *I was dazzled by it, I think it is the most magnificent book of its kind that I have ever received and I know of no other letterfoundry book of types that makes such a splendid showing.* [7] Similar appreciations from other sources could be added in large numbers. R. G. Blake summed it up in a letter to a friend: *The new edition of the firm's specimen book is generally looked upon by printers and publishers as being the best thing of its kind that has ever been produced in this or any other country in our particular trade. It has even earned a review in the 'Times Literary Supplement', an unusual distinction for a trade catalogue.* [8] Reviews also appeared in the trade press during April and May 1924. *The British Printer* commented that: *Most of . . . the typefaces are of special beauty and design and in full accord with artistic taste of the present day, whilst, it is needless to say, cast with all the accuracy, precision and quality of metal which have established the productions of this celebrated firm . . . the actual printing has been carried out with special care and skill by firms who are noted for the perfection of their work . . .* [9]

However, *The British and Colonial Printer* was not so ready to eulogise over the work. It observed that: *. . . the materials used . . . the thought, ingenuity and sense of beauty lavished on its pages . . . gives evidence that no pains nor expense have been spared . . .* (but) *of course there are a few typefaces and other things which we think might well be consigned to the limbo of forgetfulness, as they represent tastes which the printing industry are happily out growing . . . it is only a matter of time, however, before the demand will cease, the public taste having been universally educated to*

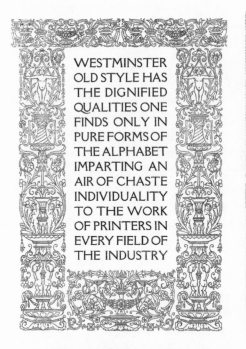

WESTMINSTER OLD STYLE HAS THE DIGNIFIED QUALITIES ONE FINDS ONLY IN PURE FORMS OF THE ALPHABET IMPARTING AN AIR OF CHASTE INDIVIDUALITY TO THE WORK OF PRINTERS IN EVERY FIELD OF THE INDUSTRY

Winchester

A comprehensive family of type faces that may be utilized in every phase of printing and advertising. There is always a type of the Winchester Family that is ideally suitable for a certain job, whether the work is for a connoisseur or for a commercial man

WINDSOR

The comprehensive range of this family will prove a reliable asset to all printers who desire a related group of type faces for continual use on all commercial work

MCMXXIV

THE
CHATSWORTH FAMILY

AN INVALUABLE TRIO
FOR COMMERCIAL
TYPOGRAPHY

STEPHENSON, BLAKE & CO. LTD.
SHEFFIELD AND LONDON

Fig 33 Stephenson, Blake's twentieth-century Old Styles, from Printing Types, 1924

dislike such things as fantastic typefaces that have neither legibility nor beauty to recommend them . . . Meanwhile, it is gratifying to notice the way this firm is keeping pace with . . . the popularising of the highest typographical standards. (Stephenson, Blake's) *efforts . . . have been strengthened by the recent acquisition of Mr. R. B. Fishenden . . . whose influence we think we (*can*) trace in the new specimen book . . .*[10]

Whilst *Printing Types* represented a personal typographical triumph for Fishenden, the choice of content, the writing of suitable copy and the design and layout were tasks which were not undertaken without considerable heart-searching, arguments and differences of opinion between Fishenden and the two Directors. Fishenden was determined to bring a fresh approach to the design of Stephenson, Blake's typographical specimens whilst the Directors, alarmed at Fishenden's seemingly aesthetically pleasing but uneconomic bent, were determined to ensure that the whole range of the company's stock should be included whether that stock was fashionable or not.

However, there were other good reasons for producing such a specimen book. In prospect was the British Empire Exhibition scheduled to be held at Wembley during 1924. It was envisaged that there would be visitors not only from home and abroad but also influential visitors from the Colonies in substantial numbers. Whilst for many years the company had taken space and exhibited at commercial and trade fairs and had gained awards for the quality of its typefounding products both at home and abroad, the British Empire Exhibition appeared to be an event on which they could capitalise. This event was seen as an ideal opportunity to influence new customers and provide a means of projecting the company and its products in the Dominions.

Reviewing the opening of the British Empire Exhibition, the *British Printer*: . . . *confidently expected that through the medium of the Paper and Stationery Section an opportunity . . . such as is rarely offered to the public, will be given to visitors . . . of realising the importance of 'various activities of the trade'.*[11] After the Exhibition had come to a close, the *British and Colonial Printer* observed: *Master Printers from all over the World have come to London for the great event and have learned more of what this country can do in the way of printing and supplying the needs of printing houses.*[12] However, that part of the Exhibition planned for the printing industry was somewhat limited and came to be dominated by the paper-making trade which arranged a fully operational paper-making machine to form the central attraction, whilst the printing machine manufacturers, printing companies and allied trades tended to be relegated to a supporting role.

Did the leading British typefoundry believe its money had been well-spent? The Stephenson, Blake stand at the British Industries Trade Fair had attracted a reasonable number of visitors. Those who appeared to be there with serious intent were invited to the London showroom in Aldersgate Street where they were suitably entertained. Whether the company won orders or gained more customers is not known. However, British type-founding trade figures published at the end of December 1924 indicated that in the previous nine months, 146 tons of printing type valued at £50,958, had been despatched abroad compared with the corresponding period in 1923 when 139 tons, valued at £49,289, had been exported.

On reflection, the cost of producing *Printing Types* had been expensive—bordering on extravagance. Initially, the cost was somewhat justified by the successful trading results arising from the company's activity at the seventh International Printing Exhibition held in London in 1925. But, at a meeting of the Board of Directors held towards the end of that year, there was considerable dissension. Whatever kudos had been gained, whatever enhanced trading success had accrued; under the cold light of the smoke-laden skies of Sheffield, there remained the inescapable fact that *Printing Types* had cost the company too much money. It was agreed that never again could the company afford such an expensive specimen book. The palmy days of the mid-1920s boom were over and the scenario of the international economic collapse of 1929 was already being set.

The unknown printer of *Printing Types* and the many succeeding specimen books, leaflets and type specimen sheets—no imprint allowed—was the firm of J. W. Northend Limited of Sheffield. The company had been established back in the 1890s, by a young print manager, John William Northend of Sheffield—a friend of George W. Jones. Northend was one of the new breed of designer-typographer printers. From the very beginning, he had set high standards of typesetting and presswork and it was his accent on the quality of the printed page which brought his company to the attention of the most influential typefounding company in Britain. Consequently, Stephenson, Blake, whose foundry and manufacturing operation was based in Sheffield, found it particularly convenient to have a high-quality jobbing printer situated less than one mile away who was able to undertake its printing needs. Equally, J. W. Northend was proud and more than delighted to print for such a prestigious, though exacting, customer. However, for many years, patronage by Stephenson, Blake carried a *sting in the tail*. In 1919, J. W. Northend and his sons, Edgar and William, desperately needed to invest in some form of mechanical composition. After years of threatening to withdraw their custom if Northend acquired a mechanical composing system, Stephenson, Blake reluctantly agreed to the installation of a line composing machine—an Intertype—installing Monotype being deemed totally out of the question. When even-

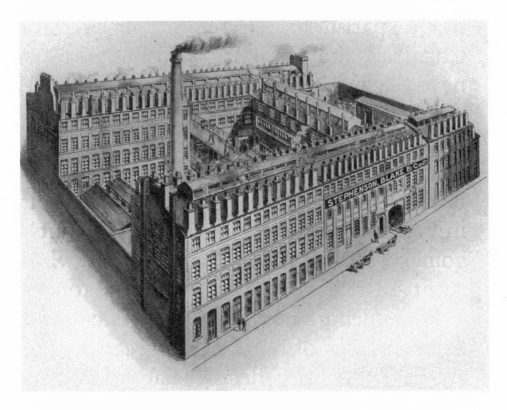

Fig 34 Stephenson Blake and Company Limited 199 Upper Allen Street, Sheffield 1924

tually in the 1970s, J. W. Northend Limited installed Monotype, not only was the heyday past of the all-embracing typefounders' specimen book and traditional typefounding all but dead, hot metal composition too was also rapidly passing into history.[13]

Meanwhile, there was a certain degree of disunity in the company's London office and the relationships with the directors in Sheffield were not too harmonious. Lockhart, the assistant London manager, loyal to the principals in Sheffield, regarded Fishenden as something of a maverick, particularly as he had, from the first, severely criticised the way the London office was organised and conducted. These criticisms were regarded as gratuitous back in Sheffield. The London managers had always been singularly independent yet diplomatic in their dealings with the directors in Sheffield. In the case of Fishenden, the directors had other views. They felt he was not aggressive enough with the travellers. The situation was not helped by Fishenden who constantly grumbled about some of the company's out-of-date and ill-designed typefaces which he thought should be consigned to the scrap heap, particularly as he had often been over-ruled on the choice of content when compiling *Printing Types*. After counting the cost of producing *Printing Types* the directors did not, in any case, intend continuing the production of such expensive publicity. In the March of 1929, Fishenden asked for another significant increase in salary—drawing attention to the directors that he had received an offer of a three-days per week appointment at the same salary that Stephenson, Blake were paying him.

The new junior director, Francis Stephenson, was sent to the London Office to discuss the matter and subsequently wrote to his father, H. K. Stephenson: *My Dear Dad, Mr. Fishenden . . . he says his expenses have increased at home; that he hasn't enough money to play golf or entertain his friends and he says we suffer by it . . . he says he can earn more money elsewhere, Francis.*[14] After the next meeting of the Board of Directors, Francis Stephenson was able to write informing Fishenden that his salary had been advanced by £100 per year. [R. B. Fishenden was now earning a salary of £900 per annum.]

Later in 1929, 'Bob' Fishenden resigned by mutual agreement. In the interests of his career he moved on to become a highly respected figure in the printing and graphic arts industry, but if truth is to prevail, the directors were not too sorry to see him go, not only on grounds of financial economy. For Fishenden, as rewarding as his sojourn at Stephenson, Blake had been, he had, nevertheless, found the style of the company's management very difficult to accept.

Chapter 20

Humane Resource Management

T HE unquestionable belief of the directors, the travellers and the sales staff of Stephenson, Blake in the superiority of their company and its products, stemmed from their assumption that the quality of the printing type which they produced was the finest in the world. In many respects it was a justifiable belief. Unfortunately, the observations which members of the company often made relating to alternative methods of type composition and developing techniques in punch and matrix making, both before the First World War and afterwards, revealed a tardy unwillingness and reluctance to change. In the outside world of printing and publishing, there were those customers who consistently supported the view of the surety of the physical quality of Stephenson, Blake type—though sometimes less so in respect of the design of the typefaces. To others in the printing industry, who had installed Monotype Composition and Supercaster equipment, the use of expensive typefounder's material was costly and inefficient.

Prior to 1914, the foundry at Sheffield was still using time-consuming traditional methods of producing punches and matrices, even though its own in-house engineering department was at the forefront of technology. Although after the death of Sir Henry Stephenson, changes were made, the company was still exceedingly cautious in taking up innovations. Partial machine-engraving of punches was introduced at the beginning of the century, but it was not until the 1920s that a punch and matrix cutting machine was acquired from the Western Type Foundry in St. Louis after its amalgamation with Wiebking and Hardinge. Whilst Stephenson, Blake railed against the use of electrotyping methods which made piracy of designs relatively easy, it was itself unwilling to introduce the technique to the company's own advantage. It was only in 1925, after the directors had paid a visit to the Monotype Corporation Limited at Redhills in Surrey, that they came to the realisaton that the electro-deposition of harder metals could prolong the life of matrices. The company negotiated with, and subsequently engaged, a local specialist, Richard Grah, to install, train staff and provide consultancy in nickel plating techniques. Grah was induced to enter into a contract which specifically prevented him from offering his expertise in the plating of matrices to other typefounders. Grah accepted the work but would not sign the limitation of the contract, maintaining the view that a gentleman's agreement should suffice!

When H. K. Stephenson entered a contemporary discussion via the trade press on the perennial typographical problem of type distribution—*dissing*, his response, came in the form of an analogous reply which likened the use of an in-company casting machine, to that of a household buying a cow, instead of using the services of a dairyman. His reply created a deal of merriment in the trade press but did little to enhance the image of the company, indicating as it did, a certain lack of appreciation of the direction in which the industry was moving. Were there chinks appearing in the armour of the knightly Stephenson, Blake Company?

Whilst there was on the part of Stephenson, Blake—principals and employees alike—a certain impish relish in the long-term prospect of the decline of the other British typefoundries, the main threat was coming from the Monotype Corporation Limited. The early critical views of the Typefounders' Association against Monotype were essentially fuelled by Stephenson, Blake. Great play was made on the weaknesses of the system. The Monotype composition metal was too soft and wore away during long print runs; the high em-quad spacing system was ill-regarded because the lines of em spaces all too frequently were given to rising from the forme during the printing process. The typographical surface lacked sharpness. All manner of trivial reasons were raised against the Monotype system. However, the early problems of Monotype composition were soon rectified and, with the inescapable evidence of the increase in the number of installations, debates on the application and virtues of adopting the point-lining system and point unit-set standards made little impact outside the shrinking world of the traditional typefounder.

That Stephenson, Blake were so often seen to be pursuing ideas which were outdated raises a view that the company's entrenched methods of type production lay not merely with the directors but also with the managers and travellers whose views of the product and of methods of type manufacture

Modern No. 20

48 Point

EMOLUMENT
Financial advertising

36 Point

NORTHERN LIGHT
Scandinavian pleasure cruises

30 Point

MOUNTING
New Government
Chinese mandate

30 Point

CONFOUND
Grand instrument
Classical overture

24 Point

LEGAL CUSTOMS
Silver mine development
produced splendid results

24 Point

FEDERAL NOTE
Inciting popular feelings
Sold aromatic perfumery

18 Point

NOTED SCIENTIST
Wonderful secrets explained
concerning former existence

18 Point

LOCAL EXHIBITS
Models of grinders advancing
suitable for knife machinery

14 Point

AMATEUR DETECTIVES
Capture daring criminals after hard
struggle in an underground labyrinth

14 Point

CHARMING MANSIONS
Now deserted by their several owners
who prefer convenient modern cottage

THE SMALLER SIZES OF MODERN No. 20 AND MODERN No. 20 ITALIC ARE SHOWN IN THE BOOK LETTER SECTION

STEPHENSON, BLAKE & Co. Ltd. 176 SHEFFIELD and LONDON

Fig 35 Modern No. 20 specimen sheet, a nineteenth century revival

were too narrow. What was never really appreciated was that the exceptionally fine quality of the Stephenson, Blake type was frequently not only unnecessarily of too high a quality for the relatively hit-and-miss process of general letterpress printing but also of little use for the printing companies who were engaged in printing from type matter which had been machine set. Printers were beginning to buy specific designs of founders' type only to meet either the demands of typographic fashion and display advertising or, to meet designer's specifications.

The development of the Ludlow and Elrod machines based on slug-composition principles gave little cause for concern. Such machines were the domain of the newspaper printing industry and that market for type sales had been lost earlier. However, the Nodis and the Thomson casters were flexible support systems which, with not too much of an expertise requirement on the part of an operative, could produce both display type with acceptable typographical printing surfaces and spacing material. However, the greatest threat came from the Monotype Supercaster on which reasonably high quality display letter could be cast in sizes from 18 point to 72 point by hiring matrices from Monotype's extensive library of well-designed typefaces.

By 1929, the general economic situation was in serious decline. The immediate post-war years had seen the wage rates of Stephenson, Blake employees escalate although expectation had moderated somewhat as the cost of living had fallen in the mid-1920s. Whilst a number of the workforce were trade union members they were not within the customary type-founding trade societies but in local branches of the National Union of General and Municipal Workers, whilst the women in the warehouse were members of the National Amalgamated Trade Society of Operative Printers and Assistants.

The travellers and managerial staff were in a different position. For long, they had been well rewarded. They were allowed generous out-of-pocket expenses, and commission on sales, whilst the London office and its management—whose projection on the London scene was vital to the directors—were particularly favoured. But the depression of 1929 brought a need for real economy. Although salaries had to be cut and staff rationalised, travellers had to be encouraged to improve sales. The situation was not new. Every time there was a slackening of sales, the directors applied pressure in a manner customary of the time.

From the time of Henry Bannister Smith, the first Stephenson, Blake traveller, the owners had insisted on the highest performance of good and decorous manners, the maintaining of a social station and impeccable behaviour. This requirement often seemed to be at odds with the little back-

Fig 36 Robert Greaves Blake DL, 1875–1947

street printers on whom the travellers called. Some members of the trade
were at times quite over-awed by the travellers' confidence and apparent
affluence. This was hardly surprising for the travellers' pay, as early as
1913, ranged between £400 to £600 per year. Managing the London-based
travellers was a different matter, particularly as they covered the all-valu-
able London sales. The travellers knew their worth and there were times
when some of them took considerable liberties. As a consequence, the
directors in Sheffield were very wary and either avoided upsetting them or
passed responsibility for disciplining them to the London Manager. In a
letter to the London Manager dated October 1913, R. G. Blake wrote . . .
*to put it bluntly, a traveller who is paid to that extent must share our bad
times as well as our good times.*[1] In the year following, Blake was to

respond to a traveller seeking an increase in salary . . . *how do you propose to be paid? Results at the present time do not justify keeping a traveller on the road . . . I may tell you privately that the whole of the South ground last week only produced something like £3 worth of orders . . . and did not even amount to the wages paid during that week.*[2]

The situation relating to the conduct and expectations from the travellers continued to exercise the directors. In July 1914, R. G. Blake having returned to Sheffield from London wrote : *Dear Mr. Hanson, I got your note at the Savoy at 6.30, Friday night . . . we now await a detailed report which we thought would be here this morning. What did Washington Wood say about Mr. Larder's character? Your mention of 'women and wine' needs an explanation . . . it is now time something was written to Larder and you had better see him. R.G.B.*[3]

The saga continued. Letters kept arriving from Sheffield: *Dear Mr. Hanson, I felt too annoyed at your letter to reply. It was so unlike anything either the firm or I have ever received before from one of its servants that I thought it best to hide my feelings. Is Mr. Larder a fit and proper person for us to employ or not? I want proof— you were given two months to make enquiries. Whilst you say 'the man's name stinks in the nostrils of the printing trade in London', it was you yourself* [who] *told me sometime ago that he was not well known in the trade. How is it that he has suddenly become so notorious? R.G.B.*[4]

The London Manager, must at times have been sorely tried. Like his predecessor he had served his stint in the offices in Upper Allen Street and was accordingly fully acquainted with the foibles of the directors: *Dear Mr. Hanson, Mr. Dyer has sent in his resignation. He intimates his intention to leave us in a four line letter! . . . has he mentioned the matter to you? If he has not, it is only additional proof of his want of savoire faire and courtesy and good breeding . . . R.G.B*[5]

Even after four years of war in which many of the staff had served in the British Army, the tone of address was still formidably authoritarian. Writing in October 1921, Blake is less than sympathetic with the difficulties of the Southeast London traveller: *Is it characteristic of Mr. Paul to squeal every time he is up against it? Last year he got a large income without effort . . . as to the giving of presents, I have said before that this cuts no ice with us. We hate this bribery and corruption and it is done absolutely against our wishes and knowledge. If we can't do business without this sort of thing we are better without it . . . R.G.B*[6]

A request was received from Aldersgate Street for an increase in salary. The response from Sheffield, dated July 1922, ran as follows: *Dear Jean, I see your earnings for 1921 were £549 and that the average for 1920-21*

*was £625. In view of this I am much surprised at your begging letter. Has
Mr. Paul put you up to this? If you had a little more backbone and thought
for yourself it would be to your advantage.* [7]

In October 1925, a vacancy had arisen for another traveller to cover the
London area and R. G. Blake writes to advise the senior traveller of his
view of the candidate: *Dear Mr. Weight, I have written to Mr. Porter saying
we have an immediate opening . . .* [but] *I think he might be of best use to
us <u>inside</u> especially in a place like London. I doubt he would be any good
outside as he is Teetotal. Mind you, I don't like a man to drink—but I do
feel that as a man he is perhaps peculiar and, displays one side of his religion if he declares himself TT. In other words, if he is one, he should not
say so . . . it is a confession of weakness—especially as if he has signed the
pledge.* [8]

The upholding of the firm's rules and conventions was not restricted to
the two principal directors. Senior managers too played their part as
guardians of good manners and social etiquette. As late as 1947, the
Company Secretary, upbraided, James McEwan, the representative for
Scotland: *Dear Sir, In reply to your letter of the 7th instant, we must just
say how surprised we were to see that you do not appear to know the
correct title and address of your own Directors. It is our own experience
that most people like to be addressed correctly. If you fail to address your
director in a proper way we wonder what you must do when writing to your
customers. All who have no title should be addressed by their initials and
Esq. after their surname. When they have a title either Military or Civil,
then these should be employed and some trouble taken to find out the
correct ones. In the case of our Chairman, to whom you appear to have
addressed this letter, it should have been Lt. Col. Sir H. K. Stephenson, Bt.,
DSO. Luckily for you he is ill and did not see the way you had mangled it
. . . Yours very truly, Frank King.*

THE BIG red fox

JUMPS at the

LAZY dog 48

THE BIG BLACK

FOX JUMPS 5

OVER THE

DOG jumps

Past the !

Red fox

THE BIG black dog

JUMPS over the

LAZY foxes!!

ABCDEFGHIJK

Fig 37 Granby Series

In 1930, Stephenson, Blake introduced Granby in order to be able to offer a roman-set sans-serif design—a fashion which had been set in train as a result of the issue of Monotype's Gill Sans. Granby was a hybrid design created in-house. A comprehensive series was developed which finally comprised four weights of Roman and Italic, and a Condensed together with Cameo, Inline and Shadow versions. Founts were cast in sizes ranging from 5-point to 72-point

Chapter 21

Cat and Mouse

IN a somewhat strange climate of good manners and gentlemanly conduct, Stephenson, Blake and H. W. Caslon continued to share expertise and, occasionally, each other's specialist services when it was mutually convenient, although, after the publishing of the Caslon bicentenary history, there was some cooling of the friendship on the part of the directors of Stephenson, Blake, which worked against any closer relationship between the two companies.

Following the death of Ralph Sydney Caslon, in 1923, H. W. Caslon and Company began to slide into a series of trading losses. Drastic economies were implemented in order to reduce standing costs. One successful aspect of Caslon's trading had been the factoring and manufacturing of printing machinery and the supplying of it under agency terms. In order to safeguard this part of the business it was decided to float this activity as a separately registered business: Caslon Machinery Company Limited. In 1926, in an attempt to raise capital, Caslons approached Stephenson, Blake, offering the sale of some debenture stock linked to possible amalgamation on terms similar to those discussed some eight years previously. Little came out of the protracted negotiations except that Caslon agreed to close down its wood letter production and Stephenson, Blake agreed to market machinery supplied by the Caslon Machinery Company Limited. By 1927, negotiations were being conducted at two different levels. Whilst H. K. Stephenson was discussing possible amalgamation arrangements, R. G. Blake was involved in talks, over dinner, with Harold Caslon and his wife regarding the possibility of the exchanging of his and his wife's stock in return for a £1500 annuity. It was reckoned that such a deal would have given

Stephenson, Blake a near controlling interest in the affairs of H.W. Caslon and Company Limited. Blake was at some pains to press Harold Caslon for a copy of the audited accounts, the sales figures, enquired about the extent of his son's shareholding and finally, how quickly could the exchange of shares be effected?[1] As a safeguard, R. G. Blake reserved his position by reminding Harold Caslon that such an arrangement would have to have the agreement of H. K. Stephenson who was already in discussion with other members of the Caslon family. The negotiations petered out yet again.

However, despite rationalisation, H. W. Caslon and Company Limited, was still losing money and the future of the company remained unresolved. In 1930, Daniel Caslon then proposed that Caslons should cease casting type, transfer punches and matrices to Sheffield and allow Stephenson, Blake to undertake all H. W. Caslon's typefounding, but, even this proposal came with strings attached. By 1933, the directors at Sheffield were becoming distinctly impatient with the Caslon family's prevarications and R. G. Blake wrote to Daniel Caslon stating that Stephenson, Blake . . . *would not consider any form of amalgamation.*[2] The only arrangement would be that of undertaking the casting of type. In a letter dated 16th October 1933, R.G. Blake observed . . . *but I would just say we all feel considerable reluctance at trading with your people whose Fathers and Grandfather have been in such close and friendly touch with us so long. Frankly we much prefer to see your company carry on under your own sail. The future of the trade is uncertain—you know the powerful competition we have to face and it is questionable therefore whether we are wise to invest much more in Typefounding.*[3]

Talks continued into 1934. In desperation, the directors of H. W. Caslon approached Stephenson, Blake for a loan in order to keep their business afloat. As a result, it was agreed that a number of staff from Stephenson, Blake would pay a visit to their foundry in Hackney Wick to survey the scene. On returning to Sheffield, they reported their concern to the directors. The plant and machinery was in a much reduced state. There was clear evidence of a lack of investment and, whilst the security for the projected loan would have been more than adequate, the two principal directors felt that if the H. W. Caslon company had subsequently gone into liquidation, it would have been to the detriment of Stephenson, Blake's own interests. On the 12th September 1934, R. G. Blake wrote a response: *Dear Caslon . . . the Colonel has seen your letter . . . and is definitely not prepared to reopen negotiations, in fact we are not in a position to do so . . .* [in the] *case of your failure, not only should we have been liable to some stigma but we might also have been saddled with your foundry which would be a great embarrassment.*[4]

Faced with a dire situation, the Caslon directors took immediate action. The foundry at Hackney Wick was closed and sold and the foundry operation transferred to the upper part of their building in No. 82 Chiswell Street. However, even such radical steps could not stem the decline in a period when the typefounding trade was struggling with a lack of orders. H. W. Caslon and Company continued trading at a loss until 1936, thereafter, finding it could no longer continue. The polite and gentlemanly game of bluff was over. Stephenson, Blake's main competitor had drifted into voluntary liquidation.

By February 1937, Stephenson, Blake and Company Limited had acquired the goodwill, the punches, matrices and stock of the best selling Caslon typefaces and could now proudly add the time-honoured by-line to their company name: *The Caslon Letter Foundry*. In Edinburgh, Miller and Richard remained. Meanwhile, Ralph S. Caslon joined the staff of the London office. The overseas goodwill which Stephenson, Blake had long aspired to was now confirmed. The Caslon connection with the Crown Agents for the Colonies was well maintained by Ralph Caslon, who effectively strengthened these ties to the distinct trading advantage of Stephenson, Blake.

There were other typefoundries still in existence but these were of little consequence, and it was only a matter of time before these too would fall. The absorption or closure of smaller competitors had been taking place long before the collapse of H. W. Caslon and Company Limited. In 1928, an approach was made by the non-associated London foundry of P. M. Shanks and Sons Limited. R. G. Blake visited the firm and although the company's typecasting machinery was of little technical value, Stephenson, Blake did have a passing interest in the technical operation of Shanks 'Long-casting machines'. Negotiations took place on the subject of a merger but the talks broke down. Shanks looked attractive. It had a fair turnover of stock, but the purchase price was regarded as being far in excess of what had been paid for the Blackfriars Typefoundry, and purchase could not be warranted even though R. G. Blake was attracted by the potential opportunity to fill surplus casting facilities at Sheffield. After almost four years of discussion, Shanks withdrew and amalgamated with R. H. Stevens Limited. However, even the relatively newly amalgamated Stevens, Shanks and Company found that with the declining sales continued trading was becoming unrealistic and approached Stephenson, Blake with an offer to sell. Although the firm had a number of commercially useful typefaces and a considerable collection of historic and ancient letter, including Gaelic and Greek founts, Stephenson, Blake did not feel disposed, even after much negotiation, to accept the offer.

Meanwhile, in Scotland, Miller and Richard, finding trading increasingly difficult, began to off-load a number of operations. In 1938, they closed their London warehouse and gradually transferred their casting operations to Sheffield. In 1952, on the death of Alan Miller Richard, the last partner, the once esteemed Miller and Richard Typefoundry closed its doors. Stephenson, Blake Company Limited of Sheffield had now become the last of the traditional English typefounders.

These were truly disastrous times which portended the future. It was calculated that before 1914 the United Kingdom typefounding industry produced 3,000 tons of type annually—Caslon, Stephenson, Blake, and Miller and Richard Limited accounting for 2,000 tons. By the 1930s, the total output had fallen to 2,000 tons. By 1939 it had fallen yet again to around 1,000 tons per year.

Chapter 22

The Changing Face of Type

T HE precepts of the Arts and Crafts Movement, of William Morris
and his disciples, and the Private Press Movement began to bear fruit
in the period 1925 to 1975. Design creativity and aesthetic ideas
which had seemed in the generation earlier to stand apart from the practice
of typography and printing were brought into play. The emergence of
educated and trained artists, designers and typographers who were able to
bring practical understanding to a highly sensitive medium had begun.
Working in the United States and in Europe, either independently, or for
the few remaining typefounders and machine composition manufacturers,
their output of both text and display letter designs over the half century
was prodigious. The pre-1914 pioneers made a contribution to the understanding and practice of typography but such were not without fault. Now
there was a better understanding of the relationship between the typographical image and the appropriate choice of paper. In practice, the original
Old Faces printed well on specific surfaces, such as antiques and imitation
handmade papers, whilst the newer Old Style designs appeared better on
smoother machine-made papers. In their endeavours to recreate the Venetian
and Aldine period typefaces, even the letter designers commissioned by
the Private Presses were often not as successful as they might have been.
Cheltenham, designed by Goodhue and developed as a series by M. F.
Benton, was different, popular and, as far as typefounders were concerned,
profitable—as was the Gloucester—the Caslon company's version of
Cheltenham, but as successful as the series was, amongst the more discerning typographers it fell short of the true Venetian-Aldine characteristics.

Meanwhile, in the realm of mechanical composition, the Lanston Monotype Company—that organisation most feared by the typefounders—presented its almost definitive version of Old Style, Monotype Imprint. The first issue of *The Imprint* magazine which appeared in 1913 had been typeset in Monotype and the Lanston Monotype Company, having been persuaded to develop this new fount of Old Face, designed by John Mason, made it available for the newly launched journal. As the introductory commentary to *The Imprint* explained: *The newly designed type in which our pages are presented to the reader was cut by the Lanston Monotype Company at our instance. We are exceedingly pleased with it, and congratulate the Monotype Company on having produced the finest face that has been put on the general market in modern times.*[1]

This was not the kind of success the Sheffield foundry cared to hear about. The Windsor series, on which Stephenson, Blake congratulated itself, was drawn by Pechey, the London Manager and punch-cut by the Sheffield staff under the supervision of the chief punch cutter, J. E. Uttley. The company had struggled with the design in a bid to keep abreast of its competitors but it never quite came up to expectations and soon paled into insignificance, particularly when R. G. Blake, having delved into the treasures acquired from the Reed typefoundry, revived and issued in 1907, Georgian Old Face, and followed this success with Fry's Baskerville in 1909. The Clarendon series, which had been withdrawn from the Reed's specimen book and had lain dormant for decades, was also successfully relaunched but, as customers were increasingly influenced by American typography and typefaces, there was a constant search for opportunities to acquire issuing rights.

However, in Europe, developments on the typographical scene came to an abrupt halt with the opening of World War I. At Stephenson, Blake, shortages of both staff and orders meant that the preparation of new founts was all but abandoned, although there was still a considerable flow of correspondence with typefounders in the United States relating to the prospect of Stephenson, Blake acquiring designs, punches or matrices. With the coming of peace in 1918, the trade in new type faces began again in earnest, even though there was to be a decade of economic uncertainty. In 1921, R. B. Fishenden urged R. G. Blake to secure the rights to cast a redrawn Venetian Old Face from the Leclede Type Foundry in the United States. It appeared under the name of Verona and proved to be one of the most successful of the Stephenson, Blake Old Style range. Throughout the economic depression of the early 1930s, the issue of new typefaces continued, even though the volume of type sales slackened, then, almost inexplicably, business began to improve and, by 1939, the company was finding

BOLOGNA

THIS new series, although based on humanistic lettering as are so many of our most appreciated type faces, is not a revival of an old face or a mere copy of a hand-written original. It claims, however, to surpass previous efforts in its recapture of the spirit of the Renaissance so much admired in Italian manuscripts of the fifteenth century. The Caslon Letter Foundry, Sheffield, in this latest production offers to the printer of to-day an opportunity of reviving the glories of the past with an ease afforded by the use of modern type and equipment unknown in the Middle Ages. It will be observed that this interesting specimen, although printed from moveable types still retains the characteristic charm of mediæval writing.

Fig 38 Stephenson, Blake, specimen from booklet introducing Bologna, 1946

difficulty in meeting the demands of customers requiring type—seemingly vindicating its policy of persisting in the search for new typefaces.

The identifying and commissioning of typeface designs was not always straightforward or lightly embarked upon. When, in the 1920s, P. Ribadeau Dumas of Paris, revived Garamond's sixteenth century design, the attention of typophiles became focused on the founts of Claude Garamond. In 1923, Deberny and Peignot, the American Type Founders and the Monotype Corporation issued a series also called Garamond which Morison contended did not follow the original but was in fact the letter cut by Jean Jannon in 1612, for the Imprimerie Nationale. A good deal of debate ensued as to the accuracy of the recreated design. Beatrice Warde's scholarly essay which traced the development of the Garamond genre and of the true origins of French Old Face did much to draw attention to the relatively ephemeral and ever changing nature of letter design albeit in the form of cast type. According to Stanley Morison, the Ribadeau Dumas version came the closest to the original. However, R. G. Blake disagreed with Morison and thought that the American Type Founder's version was the better of the two. Blake declined to buy the rights from Monotype and then, inexplicably, approached Deberny and Peignot with a view to their casting it on behalf of the Sheffield foundry. However, the Paris founder demurred on the grounds that they felt unable to cast type to the same alloy standard as Stephenson, Blake but suggested a compromise: Sheffield should cast the Roman and Paris would cast the Italic.

For Stephenson, Blake, the Garamond saga was further complicated by George W. Jones who suggested that they should acquire the rights of the highly acclaimed Granjon from the Linotype Company. Jones had been closely involved in the development of the face and Morison had commented that he thought that it was the most accurate, commercially available version of the original Garamond letter. Finally, Stephenson, Blake made a deal with the Linotype Company, exchanging the rights of Fry's Baskerville for Granjon which they intended modifying with the help of G. W. Jones for their proposed Lamesle Old Face, but it was a projected issue which never came to fruition.

Meanwhile, other typefaces were brought to life from the Reed and Caslon acquisitions. In July 1926, Stanley Morison who was busy writing an account of the work of John Bell, persuaded R. G. Blake to search the Reed collection of matrices for the Roman which had originally been cut by Richard Austen for Dr. Fry's foundry but which had been hidden since the early nineteenth century. After a long and exhaustive search the Bell characters were found and sample founts of 14 point were cast for Morison, the Cambridge University Press and for D. B. Updike. The fount met with approval and in September 1929, the foundry cast a large quantity of 12 point which it supplied to the C.U.P. for the typesetting of Morison's book, *John Bell*. Encouraged by the success of the new Bell Roman, Morison opened up negotiations with Stephenson, Blake and the Monotype Corporation suggesting that the two should jointly develop the series. After a great deal of discussion and consideration of the related italic, the series was successfully launched. Stephenson, Blake found that sales of the body sizes of the Bell series to printers for hand-composed text setting, both in the United Kingdom and in America were surprisingly good.

In contrast, a somewhat vexatious situation arose in the late 1920s. The availability and popularity of Eric Gill's sans serif, which the Monotype Corporation had developed, left Stephenson Blake singularly unprepared and a slightly Germanic version was issued as the Granby series. However, not all ventures into the creation of new typefaces were successful. Working closely with Eric Gill, Stephenson, Blake cut experimental punches and matrices for Jubilee but, as a typeface, it was never really successful and was withdrawn. Meanwhile, other experimental work was taking place. Eric Gill had several designs cut and cast in connection with a joint venture between Stephenson, Blake and the Monotype Corporation, from which the successful Perpetua series emerged.

The appearance in 1931-33 of Stanley Morison's newspaper typeface, Times New Roman, attracted considerable attention worldwide. Here was a typeface in the exclusive domain of *The Times* newspaper, its development facilitated by the Monotype Corporation Limited. Under licence the design was allowed to be shared by both the British Linotype and Machinery Company Limited and its counterpart in the United States, the Mergenthaler Linotype Company. The trade typesetting houses and the suppliers of Monotype display types enjoyed an almost exclusive position as Monotype users, much to the discomforture of Stephenson Blake who, as a consequence, were not able to offer the Times New Roman series until 1955.

A mainspring in the creation of new type designs was to be witnessed in the 1920s and 30s. The letter designs of Bruce Rogers, Eric Gill, Jan Van Krimpen, Stanley Morison and a multitude of other designers raised the design quality of both text and display type to new heights. The long-standing debates and discussions amongst typefounders of the bases on which designs were created and the issuing of new faces *ad nauseum* without due thought—save for the prospect of profit—had come to an end. Henceforth, the main initiative for the introduction of new type designs, would rest, not on the remaining typefounders, but upon the three main manufacturers of mechanical composition machinery, Intertype, Linotype and Monotype.

Of these, the Monotype Corporation reigned supreme. At the end of the first quarter of the century, Beatrice Warde had observed the fact that no single original type face had emerged to mark the twentieth century. By the middle of the century, the Monotype Corporation, of which she was a part, had facilitated not one new typeface, but scores and continued to do so until the last quarter of the century. The importance of Stephenson, Blake as facilitators of new type faces could but pale into insignificance. The Monotype Corporation in the last phases of letterpress printing had not only captured the hearts and minds of the designer-typographers, but also of the printers to whom they sold their machines.

In 1938, Robert Harling, the Editor of *Typography* and of *Alphabet and Image* became a consultant adviser to Stephenson, Blake. He oversaw the reissuing of the former wood-letter design, French Antique under the name of Playbill, and conceived the idea of opening with a graver, the body strokes of a design of early nineteenth century Bold Latin Condensed which resulted in the issuing of the very successful Chisel series. Other series followed, Union Pearl originally cut by Grover was issued on the advice of Stanley Morison and a series of shadow capitals cut by Robert Thorne about 1812, appeared as Thornes Shaded.

However, there was one area of type production in which Stephenson, Blake had long had a deserved reputation: the production of angular bodied script types. Cast by Stephenson, Blake from 1900 to 1970, the range of angular bodied scripts and rondes was unparalleled as the company bought in designs from both American and Continental designers and type-founders. The physical quality of their script types was exceptional. They were cast from a particularly strong alloy which included additional anti-mony and a two per cent addition of copper which served to strengthen the delicate kerns and strokes of the characters. The issue of the in-house designed, Palace Script, was an immediate success, filling as it did a gap in the range of scripts which had changed little since the 1840s. Following this success, a variation appeared in 1936 as Marina Script. In 1948, there appeared to be a need for an informal script and the model for this was based on Lady Frances Stephenson's handwriting which was issued as Francesca Ronde. By the early 1950s there seemed to be a market for a script with a more definitive strength. This was needed to meet the needs of clients in the advertising industry. The traditional versions, with their very fine pen line strokes, did not duplicate well enough either for rotary letter-press or photogravure production methods of the 1950s. This shortcoming was successfully met by the development of the Youthline script series.

In trading terms, the post-war scenario was beginning to change. By the 1950s, the copy writing, design and production of advertising pages for

Fig 39 Scripts and Rondes

both the national press and periodicals had passed to specialised marketing and advertising agencies who were aware of the limitations of in-house typesetting in terms of typographical quality, ranges of typeface designs available, coupled with a growing requirement to incorporate graphic and photographic material within their commissions. This area of activity was particularly orientated towards meeting the needs of the Fleet Street newspaper production and the periodical production market now dominated by national and multinational product advertising. The Stephenson, Blake London office was now to become a focal point in this activity and provision was made to provide a service to meet the growing and brisk trade in supplying these requirements to the advertisement typesetting houses.

Ken Dickinson, the Chief Typographer at McCann Erickson, one of London's leading agencies, became a consultant typographical adviser to the foundry and saw a niche in the market for a versatile Clarendon style typeface and, after considerable dialogue with Sir Francis Stephenson, Benjamin Fox's mid-nineteenth century Fann Street Typefoundry success, was resurrected yet again. Commissioning it was not too difficult, as Stephenson, Blake had, fifty years earlier, revived it shortly after acquiring the Sir Charles Reed typefoundry punches and matrices. The design was now carefully extended into a comprehensive series. Naming it proved a little difficult as Clarendon had become an accepted term within the printing and publishing industry as a generic name for a bold typeface used for emphasis. Whereupon, an associate, Geoffrey Lee, suggested that as the design had first been created in the early Victorian period and had traditionally been used in book work to accompany roman book letter, Consort might be an appropriate name. The Consort series launched in 1956, again became an immediate success—a hundred years after the appearance of its predecessor.

However, as the years progressed, it was becoming increasingly clear to the directors of Stephenson, Blake that investment in new typefaces by trading, purchase or by in-house designing could no longer be justified. When in the early 1960s Adrian Frutiger's Univers emerged from Deberny and Peignot and M. Miedinger's Helvetica was issued by the Haas foundry, both typefaces quickly became international successes. Stephenson, Blake could offer no acceptable alternatives. There was also an added difficulty. Now when new faces were released they quickly became available not only to the users of mechanical composition systems but also to the emerging photo-composing systems and advanced electric typewriter users. This was competition to which even the most efficient typefounders were unable to respond.

To promote some sales interest and as the only cost-effective way forward, the foundry successfully re-issued a number of founts of sans and grotesques. The last new founts to be cast and marketed in metal were Impact, Lectura and Adonis. Impact designed by Geoffrey Lee was issued in 1965, whilst Lectura was launched in conjunction with the Typefoundry Amsterdam. The Adonis design had originally been created for Typefoundry Amsterdam by André Cretton for use as a photo-composition typeface in 1962. Stephenson Blake acquired the design and issued it in metal type form in 1971.[2]

Chapter 23

Dynastic Succession

B Y the mid-1930s, the company had passed its centenary and it was still wholly owned by the intermarried Stephenson and Blake families. Its principal owner was Sir Henry Kenyon Stephenson, Baronet, the third generation of the family of typefounders. Henry Francis Blake Stephenson, his eldest son, who had been educated at Eton, joined the business and in 1926, at the age 26 became a director.

In contrast, the direct line of succession of ownership of the Blake financial interest had not been continuous since the early days. However, there had always been members of the Blake family associated with it. When Robert Greaves Blake joined Stephenson, Blake in 1893, this was the first working partnership since the 1830s.

Even in the 1920s there was little prospect of there being a direct Blake successor. Robert Greaves Blake's, wife, Lydia Bamford, gave birth to a daughter, Sheila, but there was no son. Stephen John Blake, R. G. Blake's youngest brother joined the business shortly prior to the Great War with a view to eventually succeeding his brother. Born in 1893, he was educated at Harrow and, after spending two years with the Parisian typefounding company, Deberny and Peignot, joined Stephenson, Blake in 1914. On the outbreak of the First World War, he volunteered for service with the Army and joined Colonel H. K. Stephenson in the West Riding Royal Field Artillery, serving in France from 1914 until 1919. After the war he rejoined the company. Sadly, he never married and in 1933, became critically ill with viral pneumonia and died.

Meanwhile, the Blake succession had already been strengthened. James Barbour Blake, born in 1914, was R. G. Blake's nephew—son of his younger brother, Philip Jessop Blake. James Blake was destined to follow his uncle from an early age. He too was educated at Harrow, and subsequently joined the typefoundry of Hermann Berthold AG, in Germany, to gain experience in typefounding. He returned to Sheffield in 1931 where he was assigned to assist his uncle, R. G. Blake in the management of the foundry, and in 1937, he too became a director.

Unfortunately, while both the two senior directors were still active and continued to control and manage the overall affairs of the business, little real responsibility was passed down to the junior directors. With the best of intentions, Sir Henry Stephenson and R. G. Blake bestrode both the affairs of the typefounding industry and the local political and social scene like Colossi.

Nevertheless, despite almost a decade of general economic depression, they served the company well. Stephenson, Blake had survived where others had failed but, there was still the long-term threat to the business from the developing machine composing systems and the associated display type and space-casting machines which were available. However, with the demise of H. W. Caslon it appeared that a balance might now be struck between these rival systems and the continued use of foundry cast type.

As the decade progressed, a greater threat loomed. Another major war seemed inevitable and when, in September 1939, war was declared, the company was placed in a difficult trading position. Immediately, the two junior directors, Francis Stephenson, then aged 44, and James Blake, aged 25, as members of the Territorial Army serving in the Queen's Own Yorkshire Dragoons, were called for military service as part of the general mobilisation. Major Francis Stephenson was second in command of the Yorkshire Dragoons, but shortly after the unit had been mobilised, he became its Commanding Officer and was promoted to the rank of Lieutenant Colonel.

Meanwhile, at the foundry, Sir Henry K. Stephenson, aged 74, and R. G. Blake, aged 64, as joint managing directors, continued to manage the business. It became something to be seen as a personal challenge—*they were doing their bit for the war-effort!* As the duration of national emergency began, apart from the two junior directors and a number of staff who were members of the reserve forces, the labour force was not initially affected but it soon became clear that there were those who were likely to be scheduled either for early call-up under the Conscription Acts or drafted into essential war work.

Within weeks, orders fell dramatically as many small printing companies closed down. However, R. G. Blake put to use his experience of the previous war and employed the available foundry staff in casting stock. By 1940, the situation had worsened considerably. In the printing industry, paper supplies became tightly controlled and staff shortages severely limited production. Gradually, the demands of the Ministry of Labour reduced the number of men in the foundry and the wood department as they were drafted elsewhere, either into His Majesty's Forces or into essential war work. Fortunately, the reduction of the work force reduced labour costs in a situation where orders had been reduced to almost nil.

One particular production area was causing considerable difficulty: the manufacture of wood-letter. Following the ending of the First World War, the long-established London firm of Day and Collins which manufactured wooden poster-types went out of business. This had brought customers to Stephenson Blake, particularly as a wood-letter specimen book had been well distributed at the Printing Trades Exhibition in 1914 and latterly to regular customers. Between the period 1910-39, the production of typographical posters had continued, despite the fact that both auto-lithography and chromo-lithography was being used successfully to produce large colour posters, the letterpress poster still had a place and wood-letter was needed.

However, as H. W. Caslon began to rationalise in the late 1920s, an agreement was reached that Stephenson, Blake would acquire Caslon's wood-letter patterns and manufacture wood-letter for them, enabling Caslon's to draw their wood-letter production to a close. It was an agreeable decision for it made it possible for Stephenson, Blake's productive capacity to be maintained at a profitable level. Then in 1926, Miller and Richard made an approach with a view to having some of their wood-letter made in Sheffield. Finding the arrangement satisfactory, they too finally agreed to cease manufacture and leave the production of their wood-letter designs to Stephenson, Blake.

With the bulk of the British wood-letter production capacity now held by two companies alone, Stephenson Blake and Robert De Little of York, the wood letter department at Sheffield could be reorganised. Throughout the early 1930s the orders for wood-type were reasonable and they kept production capacity working at an optimum level. However, by 1939 it was becoming clear that the level of wood-letter sales was declining. In September 1939, wood letter production almost came to an end due to the lack of orders, then, in 1940, the call-up of staff under the Conscription Orders completely denuded the section of manpower and talks began with De Little on the possibility of taking over Stephenson, Blake's production. Finally it was agreed that the whole of Stephenson Blake's wood-letter manufacture would be passed to the long established and much-revered York company, but even Robert De Little found manufacturing under wartime conditions difficult. At one stage the company was reduced to eight rather elderly workmen.

With the ending of the war in 1945, the De Little Company benefited from the postwar boom and continued to trade at a modest level until the end of the twentieth century. Finally, the successors to the company quietly closed the business and its relics are now in the safe keeping of the London Type Museum.

With the problems of wood-letter production solved, R. G. Blake turned his attention to maintaining company staffing levels. After the first wave of call-up for military service, these had remained stable, for the firm had been placed on the Register of Protected Establishments but, in 1941, as the manpower situation worsened, this advantage was withdrawn and many key staff were directed to war work. The number employed fell from 324 to 162. Thereafter, R. G. Blake was in a constant battle with the Ministry of Labour struggling to keep a cadre of skilled staff in order to maintain some production. In 1942, after Blake had made strong representation to the Government, the firm was again given some measure of protection when it was granted an Essential Works Order.

The retention of labour was only one aspect. The supplies of type metal and other nonferrous metals began to be tightly controlled and the Ministry of Supply directives caused acute problems. There had always been a turnover of worn type which was returned by printers and for which they were allowed credit. However, not only were such supplies of scrap type dwindling but any re-melted metal needed refining and new metal adding—particularly antimony and tin—in order to maintain the character of the alloy.[1] To add to the difficulty, the Board of Trade Non Ferrous Metal Control issued a national directive that printers were required to review their type stocks and dispose of surplus metal for the war effort.[2] This meant that yet another source of scrap metal had come to an end. The stocks of lead, tin, antimony and brass were almost depleted. At this point, R. G. Blake reluctantly made the decision to trade off the hundreds of brass sanspareil matrices which had lain unused since the 1850s, saving only representative characters for the archives—mainly letter Ms. Adding to the problem was the acute fuel shortage for the boilers and supplies of wood for the wood manufacturing department. Finally, after 1942, there was some easement of the situation. Metal and other material licences were granted which enabled the firm to continue production.

On the outbreak of war in 1939, anticipating problems which might come to pass, R. G. Blake made the decision to remove all the historic collection of matrices and punches from *The Tomb*—the basement storage in the foundry which accommodated the Reed, Caslon, Blake and Garnett and Stephenson, Blake collections—to his home at Castle Hill in Bakewell, Derbyshire, some twenty-five miles from Sheffield. He also removed four hand-casting machines which were kept in full working order in case of emergencies.

The London office too posed problems, not only from the threat of air raids. As a result of the dramatic fall in orders, R. G. Blake was much concerned with keeping costs of the London operation to a minimum. By late September 1939, Lockhart, the Manager, who had been responsible for hiring a driver and a van to deliver the London area orders discovered that the cost was rather more than he had expected. Knowing that the management in Sheffield would grumble, he was nevertheless obliged to report this. Blake responds: *Dear Lockhart . . . stop using the van; I had no idea we were paying for this. We should have thought that all the type that you have sold per day since the war started could have been sent out on a wheelbarrow. You will have to explain to printers that we are short of labour . . . the prescription is—that they will fetch it—or not get delivery!*[3]

The orders for H. W. Caslon's type, whether for the English market or for overseas, came through Ralph Caslon at the London office. Ever since they had taken over the Caslon goodwill, Stephenson, Blake had been anxious to show that their service equalled that of their former competitors and gave such orders a high priority. Unfortunately, the foundry was not too well organised to deal with the situation. The matrices and moulds from Caslon had only been in the hands of the foundry some eighteen months before the war started and now, with the problems of a wartime operation, the situation was getting out of hand. Poor Mr. Lockhart who had been struggling hard to keep the Caslon customer sales high was shocked by the sudden paucity of orders. Despairing of the situation he wrote to R. G. Blake, who replied: *. . . in regards to the Caslon section, the drop in their trade is nothing like the drop in ours and when all is said and done, there is more work attached to meeting Caslon's foreign orders than our own country ones.*[4]

From May 1940, after the fall of France to the Nazis, Britain was under threat from air raids—London in particular. Despite the air directed towards the heart of the City, the Aldersgate Street office and showroom escaped a direct hit and although much of the property surrounding it was razed to the ground, all No. 33 suffered was repeated blasts from the bombing which destroyed the windows. The staff, although much reduced, survived the raids even though a number had their homes destroyed as a result of the bombing. Life too was stressful for the remaining elderly staff, who were required, by the Civil Defence regulations, to undertake all-night fire watching duties, sometimes more than once each week.

The foundry at Sheffield appeared safe apart from a few stray German aircraft which unloaded their bombs on the city, that is until the nights of the 12/13th and 15/16th December 1940, when two air raids, planned to hit the Sheffield armaments industry, were launched. On both occasions there was widespread damage—particularly in the city centre and the commercial area but, in the main, the steel production and armament engineering factories escaped with minimum damage. However, bombs fell on property in the vicinity of the foundry causing extensive damage. Whilst the foundry and wood-manufacturing works suffered little, apart from lost windows and roof tops damaged by anti-aircraft shrapnel, the whole production came to a standstill as gas, electricity and water services were lost. After a few days the water and sewage services were restored and a few casting machines were brought into operation, their metal pots being heated by the use of oil burners and blow lamps. Meanwhile, the four hand-operated casting machines prepared at R. G. Blake's home were brought into operation for casting urgent orders. By the end of January 1942, the gas and electrical power had been restored and production recommenced. The supply of gas was vital as the company's machinery was still powered by a central gas engine and gas was used to heat the metal pots of the casting machines.

Meanwhile, in 1942, whilst serving in the North Africa campaign, Colonel Francis Stephenson, at the age of 47, suffered a head injury, was subsequently discharged as medically unfit and returned to his family. He was anxious to take up his duties in the company, but the two joint managing directors were less than accommodating. They had run the company for over forty years and they had no intention of relinquishing their authority—even though Francis, the senior Stephenson son had seen considerable service and had commanded his regiment. Consequently, Francis Stephenson's return to civilian life and business was hardly satisfying.

By 1943, the threat of invasion had passed and business conditions began to improve a little. Although since the opening of hostilities trade had been very poor, orders began to come in from new sources. There were a number of orders from the War Office for complete printing units for use in the field, His Majesty's Stationery Office was expanding and needed type and equipment and the Ministry of Information was in the process of facilitating the setting up of printing establishments. Difficulty now lay in the labour and materials shortages. Whilst licences for supplies of material, both wood and metal, were granted, the deliveries were irregular and the material—particularly the timber—below prewar standards.

By early 1945, neither the British printing industry nor Stephenson, Blake in particular, could meet demands which were being put upon it. The demand for type from customers at home and abroad left the foundry at least six months behind schedule. The greater problem was that the Coalition Government had called for a General Election, but what had not been foreseen was the lack of an up-to-date Electoral Register. The compulsory drive for scrap type metal made in 1942 had led to the scrapping, nationwide, of the thousands of pages of type bearing the Electoral Registers. Whilst the bulk of this typesetting was done by machine composition, there was still a demand for foundry cast type, spacing material and leads. Consequently, the control of type metals had to be relaxed immediately and printers and typefounders serving in His Majesty's Forces were given early release from their units in order to return to work preparing the new Electoral Registers in readiness for the General Election.

In 1945, with the war all but over, a number of the older members took their leave and retired, Lockhart the London Manager being one of them. Ralph Caslon had been appointed to the London Office since 1937 in a key, but somewhat ambiguous, role. Now that Lockhart was retired, Caslon took his place with the added title of London Director. On his new appointment, R. G. Blake wrote to him: *Dear Ralph, now that you are in entire control at Aldersgate Street our correspondence can be carried on without restraint . . .*[on the issue of members of staff seeking to return to their jobs in the London office following war service] . . . *Plant has not yet written to ask to return but young Mr. (X) has, but ??? I had better not finish. He is only young—I fancy he is a communist . . . RGB.*[5]

Not unexpectedly the senior directors of Stephenson, Blake had for some time been labouring under difficulties and, although they would not have admitted it, needed support. Clearly, the strain of managing the business over six years of war had a telling effect on the two elderly directors and now, history was to repeat itself. At the turn of the century Sir Henry Stephenson and W. G. Blake had both died in 1904 and now, in 1947, R. G. Blake died in the February followed by Sir Henry Kenyon Stephenson, Baronet, in the September. Sir Henry, like his father, had not only served the company well, his tireless dedication to a wide range of public and charitable duties in the City of Sheffield and to the University of Sheffield had been exemplary and exceptional.

Robert Greaves Blake had played his part too, as a Magistrate, as a Deputy Lieutenant for Derbyshire and as a director of a number of local utilities and steel companies. However, his greatest contribution passed unnoticed. R. G. Blake not only steered and managed the company through two great conflicts and the economic recession between the wars, he had totally immersed himself in the typographiana of the Old English Letter Founders. He examined, annotated and listed most of the stocks of punches and matrices. Of Fry's, Caslon's and Reed's stock—he was familiar with almost every fount, punch and matrix. His relationship with the likes of Stanley Morison, Eric Gill, George W. Jones and with the owners of the principal continental typefounding companies such as Deberny and Peignot, the Amsterdam Typefounders, Enschedé en Zonen of Haarlem and the Bauer Foundry of Frankfurt was testimony of his great interest, lifelong knowledge and commitment to the art of typefounding. Succession now passed to Henry Francis Blake Stephenson, Baronet—Sir Francis—and to James Barbour Blake.

Chapter 24

Postwar Changes and Reorganisation

T HE ending of hostilities in 1945 did little to improve the immediate trading situation. Whilst there was an acute shortage of materials, labour and fuel and restrictions on production, there was no shortage of customers needing to renew equipment and type. However, there was an even more pressing problem: the future development of the company. Henry Francis Blake Stephenson having succeeded to his father's baronetcy in 1947, became Joint Managing Director, sharing responsibilities with James Barbour Blake, Robert Greaves Blake's nephew. Meanwhile, Sir Francis's son, Henry Upton Stephenson, on completion of his military service, joined the company and became a director in 1951, as did his cousin, Charles L. Stephenson who also joined the company after military service, becoming a director in 1959.

As Britain celebrated its *Festival of Britain* in 1951, a public token of its postwar resurgence, the principal British typefounding company with its full order books, appeared to have a promising future—even though there was a potential threat of competition from typefounders in France and Germany once their postwar reconstruction was complete.

However, the situation was not altogether favourable. The typefoundry and the wood manufacturing department after six years of war needed both renewal and reorganisation. The typecasting at the end of the 1940s was mainly undertaken on Bruce pivotal casters which had either been adapted or built within the company's own engineering department. There were also some American-designed and Sheffield-adapted *sliding body principle* casters. Although these machines were much slower, they were favoured as

Fig 40 Sir Francis Stephenson with dogs, Hassop Hall, 1950

the finished types came from the machine as assembled lines of letter, eliminating the post-casting process of setting-up which was traditionally labour-intensive women's work. However, the Bruce machines produced a better typeface and a denser type body. The challenge was: could the type-finishing feature of the sliding body mechanism be applied to the Bruce caster? As the modernisation and development of casting machines was specific and specialised, the possibility of such a development being commercially attractive was hardly viable. It was decided that the redesigning should be attempted within the company. William Hetherington, the Chief Engineer—a design and precision engineer of distinct ability—set to work on a prototype caster using the principles of the Bruce metal pumping system combined with an ejection and a cast letter assembly mechanism. Several adaptations and improvements were made to the early models until finally, a machine emerged which produced fully finished letter in lines ready for fount make-up and despatch.

Other innovations followed. The casting machines which had hitherto been powered via a mass of overhead driving shafts and belts from the gas engine were replaced, as individual electric motors were installed for each machine. Since the middle of the nineteenth century the foundry had been run on gas; for motive power and for the heating of the metal pots. At the time, this was regarded as an innovation as gas was cleaner than coal and coke burning. There was also a favourable management connection with the supplier. Both the Stephensons and the Blakes were Directors of the Sheffield Gas Company Limited—Sir Henry K. Stephenson being the Chairman until the company was nationalised. However, by the late 1940s, this method of heating the caster metal pots was hopelessly out-of-date. The gas heaters were unreliable, as was the control of the metal temperature. Electric heater elements which were thermostatically controlled were incorporated, together with automatic ingot feeders to supply a controlled influx of metal into each casting machine metal pot. Whilst experts in mechanical composition—particularly Monotype specialists—were cynical on hearing of these innovations, what was not appreciated by those outside the company was that the composition of Stephenson, Blake's typecasting alloy was significantly different from that used in the Monotype casting operation, particularly in respect of the percentage of copper and antimony, which required a much higher working temperature and greater pump pressure during the casting cycle.

Meanwhile, in 1958, Charles Stephenson, on a visit to American Type Foundries incorporated, had been impressed by their production of a specially hard type known as Service Type, the durability of which emanated from a balance of zinc within the type alloy. Several Continental typefoundries, including the Bauer Typefoundry, Frankfurt, had endeavoured to produce hard alloy types, with little success. Now, Stephenson Blake began experimental casting with various zinc-based alloys. William Hetherington, Chief Engineer, and Victor Harrison, the Casting Department Manager, conducted a number of trials. Alloys of varying proportions were used which involved higher casting temperatures, increased pump pressures and variations in the speed of operating of the casting machines. The work was successful and specially hard wearing type was made available for sale under the description of Mazak.

Meanwhile, the work of the engraving department also needed to be rationalised. For many years, the engravers had been located not in the main building but in a studio workshop which formed part of the wood manufacturing department located on the opposite side of Upper Allen Street. This location was purely historic and was due to the location of the original pantographic pattern cutting equipment used to produce wooden poster type. Apart from the inconvenience of having the department some distance from the foundry, the making of matrices had changed significantly. In general, it could involve four operations: punch cutting and

Fig 41 Joint Managing Directors:
Henry Upton Stephenson and James Blake, 1969

finishing, pantographic matrix engraving, electrolytic plating and matrix justification. This work was now brought together and located in a new extension which was built parallel with Kenyon Alley. A reorganisation of the warehouse too had become a necessity. Since the takeover of the Caslon business, the handling of large quantities of stock had been difficult and as the postwar boom in foreign sales leapt from 7% to 25% of the output, space was needed both for stock storage and, more particularly, for despatch preparation.

Facing the foundry across Upper Allen Street, was the Wood Manufacturing Department, established in 1911. It had been a reasonable commercial success for many years. To employees and regular visitors it had become known by reference as 'the wood side' as the premises were located opposite the main Stephenson, Blake complex. Its products were in the main composing room cabinets, with their assorted range of type cases and ancillary equipment, such as register tables and imposing surfaces. In addition, the pressed steel composing equipment which was fabricated elsewhere was assembled and despatched from the Wood Department. Meanwhile, although the general success of the department was variable in terms of productivity and profit, it had gradually been making some contribution to the company's turnover—although at one stage, the directors simply saw the development as being an additional service to customers, within the greater activity of the company. At the beginning of the 1920s it was generating 6% of the firm's total profits; by 1939 this had risen to 17%. The reason for this upsurge during the 1930s stemmed from a number of developments in the planning and design of composing rooms. In the United States, the Hamilton Manufacturing Company had designed a flexible unit system by which a range of composing room facilities could be brought together to make up composing frames to form specialised bespoke work areas. Stephenson, Blake adopted these ideas and made a feature of offering in-company advisory and planning services which were supported by the preparation of a detailed composing equipment catalogue.

The situation was not to last. Within weeks of the outbreak of the Second World War, the Wood Manufacturing Department came to a standstill. There were cancellations of work ordered, few orders coming in and the making of stock was impracticable due to the bulk problems of storage. With a minimum of orders and reducing staff as the men were either called-up or drafted into war work, production continued at a very reduced level. Often the orders which were received were merely for renewing or making good printing installations which had suffered as a result of bomb damage.

Early in the 1950s, Henry Upton Stephenson, having become a junior director assumed responsibility for the commercial activities of the Wood Manufacturing Department. Under his direction, the work activity which was becoming increasingly hybrid, was reorganised and the department renamed the Wood and Steel Department. The volume of trade began to improve and there came a steady influx of orders resulting from changes in composing room practice. Several initiatives were to influence the developing situation. In the general printing industry there was a movement towards improving and increasing productivity. Letterpress was still the main printing process. The cost of machine-down time and make-ready time on the presses—particularly where two or more colours were being printed—was driving production costs higher. A Government-sponsored Productivity Council team consisting of representatives from the British

Fig 42 Charles Lyon Stephenson, Director,
High Sheriff of Derbyshire, 1984

Federation of Master Printers and from the Printing and Kindred Trades Federation, made an extensive tour of leading printing companies in the United States and produced a report which highlighted a need for a more scientific approach to the letterpress printing process. The use of precision aids and better operational techniques was recommended. While the report laid particular emphasis on printing machine make-ready techniques, it advised that there needed to be a more precise relationship between pre-press typesetting and forme preparation. Printing equipment manufacturers rose to the challenge and produced equipment aimed at improving both composing and machine printing practice. Stephenson, Blake was in a strong position to explore the development and manufacture precision aids. Its own engineering department was able to work to very fine engineering tolerances whilst the same precision also applied to the production of wood-based products. The company had for a number of years supplied Striped Mounting boards and specially planed Chestnut mounts. This line was now extended and Dowelmounts were manufactured under licence. The designers in the engineering department turned to the development of Calibrated Precision Galleys, Lining-up and Close Register Tables and Precision Proofing Presses with considerable success. Sundry items too were remodelled. Where the company either lacked expertise or production capacity, arrangements were made with other suppliers. The firm of Notting Limited in Bowling Green Street, London supplied steel quoins and other high quality steel products. The supplying of cast steel imposing surfaces was a very specialised area of manufacture and after fruitless searches for a reliable supplier, most of the postwar orders were placed with Pye and Company Limited. A number of the postwar innovations had been planned earlier. In the 1930s, a decision was taken to build proofing-presses under licence granted by the American press manufacturer Vandercook and manufacturing arrangements were made with Victory Kidder and Company Limited. These arrangements continued until 1939, when the contract was then switched to the Western Manufacturing Company Limited, Reading in conjunction with the PrePress Company, also of Reading. During the postwar period several different sizes of press were developed, including a powered precision proofing press.

With the growing emphasis on precision, it was becoming clear that the market for accurately produced wooden spacing material would soon disappear, particularly as the rival supplier, Cornerstone Limited had entered the market with a high quality range of anodised aluminium spacing material. As Stephenson, Blake could cut and finish wood spacing material to a fine degree of accuracy, a search was made to find alternative materials for spacing and type-forme furniture. Finally, Resolite, a laminated plastic made by the Imperial Chemical Industries Limited was found to be suitable as it could be cut and machined accurately on the existing wood-manufacturing equipment.

In the furnishing of Composing Rooms, Stephenson, Blake offered two kinds of equipment: high quality hardwood composing furniture (invariably made in English oak) and similar units in pressed-steel. The pressed-steel units were fashioned to the same designs as the corresponding units in wood. However, all the units had one thing in common: metalwork and specific 'ironmongery'; pressed steel galleys, racking, handles and case irons.

Since 1911, there had been a long-standing arrangement with the London engineering company of Estler Brothers Limited who had undertaken the supply of metal composing cabinets, but on the death of one of the principals, organisational problems had arisen and in 1936, Stephenson Blake transferred production to the London firm of C. F. Moore Limited. Moores continued supplying Stephenson, Blake into the immediate post-war period but, in the early 1950s they began developing, with the close cooperation of James Wright, the highly regarded Head of the Department of Printing at the Camberwell College of Arts and Crafts, London, their own particularised style of composing equipment. These new designs made an immediate impact on the printing industry and Stephenson, Blake faced considerable competition. Clearly, there was a clash of interest and the directors came to a decision that they would have to diversify and acquire an appropriate manufacturing facility of their own. The C. F. Moore equipment had without doubt, increased the demand for pressed steel equipment and related sundries. Clearly, a decision was needed either to establish a specialised engineering subsidiary or to acquire one. After much discussion, the directors decided to purchase the principal shareholding in Farnworth Engineering Limited, located in Joseph Street, Farnworth near Bolton, Lancashire.

Meanwhile, a number of German equipment manufacturers were also redesigning steel composing cabinets. James Blake saw these in the factory of Stempel, the German typefounders and equipment manufacturers based in Frankfurt and an agreement was reached to allow Stephenson, Blake to offer their version of the Stempel designs. These were made in the engineering works at Farnworth and subsequently assembled in Sheffield in the Wood and Steel Department from the pre-manufactured parts.

The sales of both wood and steel equipment now began to grow steadily, particularly from the mid-1950s onwards when significant contracts from local education authorities began to materialise as facilities for printing education were modernised and expanded. One of the most significant of these was the furnishing, in 1958, of the Composing Room in the School of Printing at the Sheffield College of Art. The attention given to this local project was amply rewarded for the company had available locally an exceptionally well-equipped printing school which could readily be shown to prospective customers. Following and arising from this project, came the designing and re-equipping of the new Composing Department of the London College of Printing at the Elephant and Castle. Stephenson, Blake supplied cabinets, furnishings, equipment and type to more than forty colleges and educational institutions within the United Kingdom as well as to countries within the British Commonwealth.

Throughout the 1950s and 60s orders for supplying composing and pre-press equipment continued. Two of the most significant were to be seen in the planning and equipping of Percy Lund Humphries Limited, Bradford—

a project which required special typecases designed to accommodate Chinese and oriental language type. The success of this resulted in a contract to refurbish the Composing Rooms of the book printers, R. and R. Clark Limited in Edinburgh.

The heyday of letterpress printing had not yet passed. In the late 1960s, the re-equipping of Composing Room facilities also extended to the national newspapers. One of the largest and most spectacular orders received was that of re-equipping St. Clements Press in Fleet Street, which printed the *Financial Times*. The planning and supplying took almost two years and the manufacturing of the imposing surfaces, some of which extended forty feet in length, taxed even the most skilful of composing-room designers. Finally, the last and largest order ever received for supplying equipment came in 1973, when Stephenson, Blake was commissioned to re-equip the Composing Room of *The Sunday Times* and *The Times* on their relocation from Fleet Street and Blackfriars to new premises in Gray's Inn Road.

Fig 43 'Fleet Street', 1959

The relocation and re-equipping of the St. Clements Press in Cannon Street and Distaff Lane to the south of St. Paul's Cathedral created problems. The building of industrial premises in the heart of the City of London was strictly controlled. The architects were not allowed to erect a multi-storey building which would overshadow the prospect of the cathedral. As a consequence, the ceiling height of the workrooms was low which presented equipment installation difficulties. The Imposing Surfaces for the pages of *The Financial Times* were made in cast steel and bolted together to form 42 feet long Surfaces with feeder plates positioned at right angles. This was one of the most challenging of Stephenson, Blake's 'Fleet Street' commissions. The picture shows the Surfaces stacked in Distaff Lane awaiting installation. The occasion created an incident. The City of London Police challenged the Stephenson, Blake's London representative, Reg White, not with blocking the pavement but with causing the footpath and the street to sink! The ruined, bomb-damaged church shown in the background is that of St. Nicholas Cole Abbey—the first City church built in 1677 by Sir Christopher Wren following The Great Fire. It was restored in 1962.

Chapter 25

The Ending of the Gutenberg Galaxy

BY 1955, the Stephenson, Blake management team comprised the joint managing directors, Sir Francis Stephenson and James Barbour Blake supported by the two junior directors, Henry U. Stephenson and Charles L. Stephenson. At this point, Frank King, the long-serving Company Secretary retired. This had been anticipated earlier when Denys Edmonds, a Management Accountant and Consultant, who had experience in the engineering industry was appointed Assistant Secretary. Edmonds now became Company Secretary and was charged to plan a programme of cost reduction and manufacturing diversification.

Meanwhile, the printing and publishing scene was beginning to change radically. In the twenty years since the end of the Second World War, the letterpress process which, in 1945, accounted for some 70% of the total output, was in decline. By 1965, it was estimated that offset lithography accounted for 50% of the market, with letterpress 40% and other processes accounting for the remaining 10%. By 1995, the offset lithography process accounted for 85% of the market, the remaining 15% represented all the other processes—letterpress printing having been almost totally eclipsed.

These fundamental changes in the processes affected both mechanical typesetting and pre-press methods. Although the change from letterpress to offset lithography now required the preparation of high-quality printed proofs of text matter—camera ready copy, for the subsequent process of plate making, the main manufacturers of composing machinery had, since the late 1950s, been adapting and redesigning their hot metal systems to provide for a photographically generated typographic image. By the mid-

1960s, commercially viable, but expensive photo-composing systems became available from the three principal manufacturers. Many printing companies viewed the changing scene with some apprehension. Whilst a number scrapped their traditional hot-metal type setting and composing departments, others still clung to the preparation of high quality letterpress proofing and camera ready copy, believing that this practice would continue for some time.

In view of the impending changes, Stephenson, Blake, sought to acquire the marketing rights of a manual photo-setting system which could be used to compose, in photographic form, lines of displayed letter, in the belief that this would possibly offset the losses sustained by the diminishing sales of type. After considering a number of models and systems the company finally acquired the rights for the German made, Letterphot system. Clearly, developments in offset lithography were increasingly being driven by the availability of improved photographic chemicals and new techniques in graphic reproduction. It was at this time that the directors also decided to establish a commercial photo-setting service in the Aldersgate Street premises, as the location afforded good and ready access to the London-based advertising community. From singularly modest beginnings the operation grew until, encouraged by its success and potential future, the directors agreed to join a consortium. This was launched and a new company was registered as Rush Filmsetting Limited. Membership comprised Stephenson Blake, Crosfield Electronics, the Heidelberg Company, the Sun Engraving Company, C. & E. Layton and Company and *The Daily Telegraph*.

The filmsetting operation was supported by the installation of a Lumitype system. One of the principal consortia members was *The Daily Telegraph* which used the service for the typesetting of their weekly colour supplement. Each week, the completed typeset output of text on film was despatched to the photogravure printers, Bemrose and Company Limited of Liverpool, where the page-make-up was completed, gravure cylinders etched and where the colour supplements were finally printed and distributed. The success of the filmsetting venture moved the directors into establishing an agency aimed at supplying filmsetting equipment and a Graphic Equipment Division was created, based on the marketing and selling of the American Alphatype system, linked with the Letterphot headline filmsetter.

Meanwhile, a change of policy was made relating to the sale of type. Although the company was beginning to embrace filmsetting, it recognised that there was a market need, particularly in the London area, for offering a sorts service. Stephenson, Blake had long resisted the sale of sorts—the arrangement whereby a customer was able to purchase specific letters, words or sentences of a given typeface. This resistance had emanated from the huge quantity of split and broken founts which the company had acquired over the years as a result of the various takeovers of other type-founders' stock. Now in the late 1960s, with printers and advertising agencies requiring words or sentences in order to produce pasted-up originals, a sorts service was established to operate from the London office. There was also a steady trade in supplying the specially hard type cast in Mazak alloy for use in the soft-plastics manufacturing industry and for hot foil processing. This led the directors to believe that there was still a small, but worthwhile market in which to sell typefounders' type.

However, the scene in the City of London was also beginning to change dramatically. The Aldersgate area was scheduled for redevelopment. Since the end of the 1940s, the London office, No. 33 Aldersgate Street—never a particularly auspicious building—had stood starkly alone as the old properties and wartime bomb-sites were cleared. Finally, in 1969, the property and the freehold site was sold and the London office relocated to Graphic House, Southwark Street, south of the Thames.

Other changes were afoot. Stephenson, Blake had come to a watershed. Sir Francis Stephenson, the senior joint managing director was 72 years of age and somewhat reluctantly took his retirement. In many respects this was understandable. He had reached the age of 52 before he had succeeded to the headship of the family business and his twenty years in that role, had been fraught with disappointment and with the difficulties of directing a company which was in general long-term decline.

James Blake and Henry Upton Stephenson now succeeded as joint managing directors. Robert Blake, James Blake's elder son had joined the company and several other members of the family became directors. In the face of increasing financial losses there was still, within the two families, a wish to keep the typefounding business alive and every effort was being made to achieve this by seeking to widen and diversify the company's commercial activity. However, development opportunities for utilising the well-equipped facilities of the Wood and Steel Department were limited. Nevertheless, in the late 1960s the department had adjusted to producing a wider variety of cabinets and specialised in make-up desks as printing companies switched from hot-metal composition to paper and film make-up. However, the change was transitory. In the wider field of printing, the technology which brought in photo-composition was relatively short-lived. Computer-aided composition of both hot-metal systems and filmsetting systems finally gave way to the fully computerised digital image; the production organisation of which had little need of bespoke high quality furnishing. To utilise the resources of the Wood and Steel Department, the company realised that it must target a very different market if it was to continue.

A particularly successful long term contract which had been made during the war with a firm of scientific instrument makers, Thomas Ashworth and Company Limited of Burnley for the supply of wooden Moisture-Tester instrument carrying cases, continued. In contrast, a programme aimed at manufacturing high quality office furniture and hi-fi speaker cabinets was implemented. There also appeared to be a growing market for cabinets and drawers specifically designed for museums and similar curatorial uses. This development was beginning to attract a number of significant orders but unfortunately the project was launched at a time when public funding was suffering severe budgetary cuts and as a result never quite came up to expectations. The company also ventured into the realm of high-quality wood and glass partitioning for offices in the van of fashion for open-plan office-practice. It was a successful venture for several years until other companies entered the field with less expensive systems, then the orders steadily slipped away.

The casting of type continued and the market for supplies of type in a number of independent Commonwealth countries continued. Spicers International, which subsequently became part of the Reed Group, were agents for Stephenson, Blake products and there was, for a period a steady trade—particularly with Nigeria, Venezuela and Colombia. Unfortunately, as the work of the Crown Agents organisation came to an end, the transfer of credit from a number of these overseas customers ceased and the company lost money. The main foundry complex in Upper Allen Street was now much under-utilised, many of the stock rooms, workshops and offices were empty. The buildings were incurring considerable costs in the guise of business rates payable to the Sheffield City Council. A bid was made for rate abatement in view of the shrinking utilisation of the Upper Allen Street premises, but this failed. The company next sought to have the premises listed as Grade II historic buildings. This too failed. Faced with increasingly punitive business rates, the directors decided the only expedient left was to demolish the office block and factory accommodation which had been developed in the mid-nineteenth and early twentieth centuries which lay across Marsden Lane. The result was a successful easement in the amount of rates payable.

As the later developments in the Wood and Steel Department had led to the successful manufacture of film-make-up desks and light boxes, it was considered that an attempt should be made to enter the lithographic plate, chemicals, film and sundries market, particularly as many of the company's customers were moving into offset-litho printing. Unfortunately,

NOW AVAILABLE FROM SB SHEFFIELD ENGLAND

Caslon Old Face

ABCDEFGHIJKLMNOPQRSTUVWXYZ&
abcdefghijklmnopqrstuvwxyzfifflfffifflct QUQu
1234567890£$,.:;-!?'

Caslon Old Face Italic

AABBCCDDEFGGHIJKKLMMN
NOPPQRRSTTUUVVWXYYZ & QUQu
abcdefghhijkklmnopqrstuvvwwxyz fifflffifflct
1234567890£$,.:;-!?'

Caslon Old Face (roman & italic) is cast in the following sizes:
10, 12, 14, 18, 24, 36, 48, 60, 72 point

18 pt Bologna, also cast in 14 & 24 pt
ABCDEFGHIJKabcdefghijklmnopq

18 OLD FACE OPEN !
ALSO CAST IN 24, 30

MOLÉ FOLIATE, CAST IN 3 SIZES: 48, 60, and 72 pt

ABCDEFG

Please write or phone for fount price list of these and 70 other faces to:
STEPHENSON BLAKE
Sheaf Works, Maltravers St., Sheffield, S4 7YL
Telephone 0742-738531
London Office: 50 Farringdon St. EC4A 4BB (01-353 4427)

Stephenson Blake Border 420c

Fig 44 Stephenson Blake specimen sheet, 1980.
The London office was at this time located in Farringdon Street

this venture met with an early problem; Stephenson, Blake, on grounds of economy, did not feel able to offer twice daily delivery services which the established suppliers were offering. Nevertheless, the idea was pursued. Unfortunately, within weeks, the supplier of pre-sensitized litho plates had a production failure which resulted in a supply of defective plates. This quickly caused a loss of credibility on the part of the supplier and of Stephenson, Blake, and the company decided not to pursue that particular avenue further.

Meanwhile, the remnants of the foundry's engineering facility which had become the Engineering Products Department, still had valuable equipment available and, as part of a consortia contract, successfully marketed its expertise and facilities in precision engineering and produced dies and moulds for the manufacture of Rolls Royce Olympus engines which power the British Airways Concorde aircraft. A number of similar contracts followed but the orders remained essentially short-term and it became questionable whether the pursuit of this type of work was worth maintaining.

However, in the midst of this decline, the regular orders for type which came from the Fleet Street newspapers continued. There were certain sections of daily and evening newspapers where moveable type had enormous advantages over line-composed slug composition, particularly in stock market and other financial listings. These were constantly changing—not just daily but even between editions. The facility of being able to alter a single element of a market price by lifting just a single type and replacing it with another of identical set, was much quicker than by resetting the entire slug. For the better part of a century, Stephenson, Blake had worked closely with the three London evening papers and the National dailies by supplying type for their financial pages. One of the particular attractions of founders' type lay in the hardness of the metal, which was required to maintain an even typographical surface when placed side by side with newly cast slug composition. Each of the London news offices tended to have their own particular fount requirement which Stephenson, Blake had long accommodated. The *Daily Telegraph* listing was typeset in the pre-point system size of Ruby, 5.5 point or 13 lines to the inch; The *Lloyds Listing* was set in 6 point Lloyds—a face specifically cut for their listing. The *Evening Standard* listing was typeset in 5 point. The *London Stock Exchange* list was printed by direct letterpess on a Cossor Press by Couchman and Company. This listing was set in 6 point and cast in a typeface design known as Couchman. The re-setting of the *Stock Exchange Listing* was a continuous process which took about eighteen months to complete. In 1970, Couchmans, the printers complained that the type supplied was breaking down too rapidly and criticised Stephenson, Blake for allegedly lowering the quality of the type metal. The problem was solved. Thereafter, the Couchman type was cast in Mazak, the especially hard zinc alloyed type.

The pre-press composition of the *Financial Times* was undertaken in hot metal—with listings in typefounders' type until as late as 1984. Its listings were typeset in Emerald 14, a type size of 6.5 point—11 lines per inch, and cast from matrices which had been acquired from the London typefounder, Stevens Shanks in the late 1920s. The supplying of these particularly small sizes of type to the national newspapers even into the 1980s, throws an interesting light on the production situation: the use of handsetting was a practice which favoured the continued employment of hand compositors in the Fleet Street environment. In the latter years the metal-composed pages were never used for production but remained, because of trade union pressure, as back-up for the computer-originated pre-press plate-making process. Fortunately, these very regular orders for type provided a most lucrative market for the foundry and, in its later period, kept the operation financially viable.

Despite efforts to find trading solutions and new markets, it was impossible to change the unalterable and unpalatable fact: Stephenson, Blake and Company Limited was losing money and immediate steps had to be taken to reduce costs. Since the 1920s, the Stephenson and the Blake families had investment interests in a number of companies, one of which was the long-established Thomas Turton and Sons Limited at Sheaf Works, Sheffield, a company which, by coincidence had, a hundred years previously, belonged to Blake antecedents. The company was unique. It was the first integrated steel works in Europe: melting, refining, forging and converting steel on one site. Prior to their deaths, Sir H. K. Stephenson had been the Chairman of Thomas Turton and Company Limited, and R.G. Blake, a director. There was a considerable share-holding and diversified investment amongst the two families. Although Stephenson, Blake and Company Limited, the type-founders, represented the base of the families' financial interest, the wholly owned subsidiary Thomas Turton and Sons Limited was no longer a minor profit making subsidiary, but a highly profitable expanding business which had outgrown the parent company. With the deaths of the two senior directors, in 1947, Sir Francis Stephenson and James Blake succeeded to their directorships on the Board of Thomas Turton and Sons Limited.

As a means of rationalising the situation, the directors of both boards—Stephenson Blake's and Thomas Turton's—decided to form a holding company; Stephenson, Blake (Holdings) Limited. This expedient worked particularly well as it gave the Thomas Turton management much more operational freedom than it had formerly.

Fig 45 Thomas James Blake and Ernest Crapper, caster supervisor, 1995

However, the longer term problems relating to Stephenson, Blake and
Company Limited were a cause for concern. By the mid-1970s, the company
was losing sales and costs were rising. With the prospect of an uncertain
future, the organisational relationship between the parent company and the
subsidiary had to be resolved. There was now some dissension amongst the
members of the Board of Stephenson Blake (Holdings) Limited. Naturally
enough, this was rooted in an inability to find long-term solutions to the
rapidly changing technology and the typefoundry's ever shrinking order
books. It was agreed that because of the closeness of the directors and family
ties, an independent Chairman of the Board of Directors should be
appointed. As a result, a much respected local industrialist, Dr. Stephen

Bartolemé, CBE, the former Chairman of Spear and Jackson Limited, was invited to serve. He continued in this role until his retirement in 1985.

The trading state of the Stephenson, Blake and Company Limited within the Stephenson Blake (Holdings) Group had become critically non-profitable. A rigorous cost-cutting plan was implemented. It was decided to centralise the administration of the typefoundry within the Head Office of Stephenson, Blake (Holdings) Limited, at Sheaf Works, in Maltravers Street, Sheffield where Thomas Turton and Company Limited was situated. By October, 1975, it was recognised that the London office, even after it had been relocated to Graphic House, was no longer an economic proposition. In the face of such changed circumstances, the Rush Filmsetting consortia was wound-up and the Stephenson, Blake Graphic Equipment Division's activities were brought to a close. The office and warehouse, Stephenson Blake's London presence, was closed after 110 years. A number of the staff had served the company all their working lives and they either took their leave into retirement or moved on to other ventures.[1]

The rapidly reducing market now led to the disposal of the Farnworth Engineering Company Limited and it was decided that the operations of the Wood and Steel Department would have to be drastically reduced and relocated at the rear of the Upper Allen Street site. Following its transfer, the premises on the corner of Upper Allen Street and Jericho Street were disposed of to Richardson and Company Limited, a well-known firm of cutlery manufacturers, which was rapidly developing an international reputation for the manufacture of its patented, award winning laser-knives. Finally, it was agreed that the management cost of Stephenson, Blake and Company Limited having two joint managing directors could no longer be justified. As a result, James Barbour Blake and Henry Upton Stephenson relinquished their positions, but remained as non-executive directors on the Board of Thomas Turton and Sons Limited.

Meanwhile, the business of Thomas Turton and Sons Limited remained good. The firm's key products; special high speed steels, coiled and laminated springs, heavy-duty cutting implements, were in high demand and profitable. However, even at Sheaf Works, there still remained the problem of the exceptionally high business rate imposed by the then extreme left-wing Labour-controlled, Sheffield City Council. The company, in sympathy with a number of other manufacturing companies, decided it could no longer face the costs of remaining located in the City of Sheffield. In 1968, the company had purchased 12 acres of land from Chesterfield Corporation. Subsequently, a new factory was built and the works of Thomas Turton and Sons Limited and later, the Head Office of Stephenson Blake (Holdings) Limited, were relocated on the site which now formed

Fig 46 Stephenson Blake, the Casting Department, 1990s

part of the Broombank Industrial Estate, Chesterfield, Derbyshire—some six miles south of the Sheffield City boundary.

The problem of the foundry, located still in the original site in Upper Allen Street, though much reduced in operation and in geographical size, remained. The directors considered removing the whole of the operation to Chesterfield, but space was at a premium at the new premises and it was questionable whether the cost of moving the stocks of punches, matrices and type, as well as reinstalling the machinery, would be economically worthwhile. The cost of relocating the long-serving workpeople too posed difficulties.

As the 1990s approached, the foundry, in Upper Allen Street, was left to its own devices, the directors adopting a policy of accepting the typefounding operation benignly—providing it covered its costs. At this time, Thomas James Blake, the younger son of James Barbour Blake, assumed direction of the activities in the foundry in Upper Allen Street. In the preceding decade he had been closely involved with the management of Rush Filmsetting Limited and on its demise, had joined Photoscript, a company which was offering computerised type design and typesetting services and related facilities.

Unfortunately, this venture, like the traditional typefoundry, fell victim to the rapidly changing digital-imaging scene for, in the space of little more than a decade, the unthinkable, the unimaginable, had happened with incomparable speed. Even the developers of the mechanical photo-composition systems who had for some time been endeavouring, not too successfully, to apply computer controlled systems to their machines, were completely overcome by computer manufacturers who now made possible the creation of computer-generated, digitised typographical images.

The seemingly unbelievable and ridiculous forecast made in the 1960s by the American sociologist, Marshal McLuhan had come to pass.[2] The end of the Gutenberg Galaxy was in sight.

An observer of the rapidly changing scene recalls: *We witnessed, in the period 1955 to 1975, the introduction of offset printing into general printing companies. It had been coming for some time, usually through familiarity with that ill-regarded area 'small offset, in-office printing'. The traditional letterpress printers dropped their prejudice and began to change, but they were at pains to say that they would still be keeping their hot-metal composing systems and printing type for producing camera-ready copy. Then from about 1975 onwards, they began to get a shock as they compared the cost of renewing their Monotype installations or of replacing a Linotype or an Intertype. These machines were now costing from £20,000 upwards whilst a 'new fangled' Compugraphic typesetter could be bought for as little as £4,000. We had been expecting changes in typographic composition technology since the mid-1950s, when Penguin Books published their first paperback typeset by photo-composition, but the pace of change seemed slow and all but a few forward looking companies, simply ignored what they thought was nothing more than sophisticated technical hype. Anyway, we thought that when these new systems came into use that it would be the national press, the main provincial newspapers and the large book printers who would be leading the way. It did not turn out quite as we expected. From 1975 onwards, we would visit general printers, medium and small, who would, almost apologetically, tell us they had dispensed with their type and composing machinery and had installed Compugraphic equipment, and then later, Macintosh computers. In the space of fifteen years, 1975-90, the face of the British printing industry changed. Finally, the national newspapers, whom we thought would be the leaders of the technological revolution, were literally dragged to Wapping and the Isle of Dogs—in readiness for the 21st century.*[3]

Now, not only for Stephenson, Blake, but also for their formidable hundred-year-old adversaries, the Monotype Corporation, the Linotype Company and Intertype Limited, the writing was on the wall: hot-metal

Consort

ABCDEFGHIJ
abcdefghijklmn
KLMNOPQRSTU
opqrstuvwxyzœœ
VWXYZ&1234567890
abcdefghijklmnopqrst

Consort bold

ABCDEFGHJ
abcdefghijkm
KLMNOPQRST
nopqrstuvwxyz
UVWXYZ&12345678
abcdefgfifffiffiffl ,.;-!?''

Consort italic

ABCDEabcdefg
FGHIJKLhijklmno

Consort light

ABCDEFGHIJK
abcdefghijklmno
&1234567890£$

Fig 47 The Consort Series

Robert Besley first issued this design as Clarendon in 1845. It was reissued by Stephenson, Blake in 1905, following the acquisition of the Sir Charles Reed foundry. The face was revived and renamed Consort in 1956. A number of design variations and sizes were added to the series comprising Bold, Light, Condensed and Italic versions, in sizes 6-point to 36-point.

composition and typefounding was all but dead. For the unique family business of Stephenson, Blake and Company Limited, which had lasted through five generations there could be little room for sentiment. A business is only worth that which a purchaser is willing to pay for it. The Blake and Stephenson families well knew that, as they themselves had acquired their rivals' businesses. After almost two hundred years it was, for the majority of the Stephensons and the Blakes, time to quit. The families' interests and investments had over many years been spread and diversified and most of the succeeding members of the families had moved into other activities far removed from typefounding.

The historic collection of punches, matrices, machines, specimen books and archives, posed a disposal problem. Many organisations in Britain and internationally sought to acquire various sections. However, it was felt that a piecemeal break-up would destroy the value of the entity of a collection which is quite unique. There was a real threat that the collection might be sold to an overseas buyer and steps were taken to block its possible export. Whilst it was hoped that the collection might be donated or loaned to the City of Sheffield and the University of Sheffield for historical research and as a museum and library development, it was also understood that the shareholders expected some reward for the many years in which the holding company had borne the typefoundry's trading losses. Finally, the Stephenson, Blake Collection was acquired for the London Type Museum. However, the acquiring of such collections and the maintenance of them are two different issues and much greater financial input needs to be made before the archives of the Stephenson, Blake Collection are available for scholarly and public use.

Meanwhile, the buildings comprising the Caslon Letter Foundry situated at No. 199 Upper Allen Street, Sheffield remain. In their heyday, they accommodated and provided work for almost 600 people. Dramatic technological change has finally brought to an end over five hundred years of typographical letter founding. Within the gaunt and almost empty buildings the punchcutters' studio, the justifying shop, the typefoundry and the warehouses are there; remains of the past, gathering dust and seemingly waiting for the tolling of the foundry bell, which still stands high on the wall of John Stephenson's house, as if to summon to work the ghosts of craftsmen past. Thus ends the Gutenberg galaxy—not with a bang but with a whimper![4]

Fig 48 The bell on the wall of the foundry house.
1819–2002

Stephenson Blake Resurgent

I N the millennium year 2000, Stephenson Blake (Holdings) Limited sold the steel and engineering company, Thomas Turton and Sons Limited to Brunner and Lay, an American owned, but locally operating company, Padley and Venables Limited, of Dronfield, Derbyshire.

On the sale of Thomas Turton and Sons Limited and the drawing to a close of Stephenson Blake (Holdings) Limited, Thomas James Blake, the younger son of James Barbour Blake, reviewed the remaining activities of the business and resolved to re-launch the company in the millennium year, 2000. He acquired the registered name, the goodwill, and the plant and machinery relevant to the firm's current business and the historic foundry premises in Upper Allen Street.

The production of printers' brass rule was a manufacturing activity in which the company excelled. Although printing by letterpress is no longer a major printing process, there had developed a new and growing market in the supplying of brass rule and associated materials for use in the soft plastics industry where it is used in high-frequency, soft plastic, welding operations. Associated with the plastics market has been the call to produce decorative and graphic brass-dies. To facilitate this, Stephenson, Blake have invested in two computer-aided, precision die-cutting machines which are now working to capacity serving a specialised but growing clientele.

The casting of Mazak, zinc-alloyed type continues and is undertaken to meet the needs of customers requiring hard type for hot foil blocking and case-bound print-finishing production.

The wood manufacturing department continues to undertake commissions in high quality, bespoke cabinet-making. The company has specialist skills available relating to the design and making of curatorial specimen drawers and exhibition cabinets and has recently been successful in winning a long term contract to supply the Natural History Museum in London.

The business of Stephenson Blake and Company Limited continues into the 21st century under the direction of Tom Blake—a member of the fifth generation of typefounders.

Fig 49 The Foundry Gate,
199 Upper Allen Street, Sheffield, 2002

Appendix I

References

Chapter 1   A Historical Scenario: Sheffield Township, 1800

[1] There was cutlery making in the town as early as the fourteenth century. This is related in the *Canterbury Tales* by Geoffrey Chaucer. *The Reeves Tale: a miller* . . . a Sheffield thwytel boar he in his hose [1386]. (a Sheffield knife).

[2] A number of punches bear the mark *Huntsman*—having been punchcut in crucible steel produced by Benjamin Huntsman in his iron foundry in Attercliffe, Sheffield.

[3] *The nicker peckers,* Field, E., *A Brief History of File Manufacture,* English Steel Corporation Review, No. 4, 1967, pps. 20-23

[4] Hallamshire was an area within the southerly boundary of the West Riding of Yorkshire. It was, until the Norman Conquest, a Saxon settlement belonging to the all-powerful Earls of Northumbria. The Charter of 1624 which empowered the Cutlers' Company of Hallamshire, defined the geographical boundary which included Sheffield, Rotherham and southerly parts of the West Riding.

Chapter 2   The Caslons and the London Letter Founders of the Eighteenth Century

[1] Updike, Daniel Berkeley, *Printing Types*, Volume I, Harvard University Press, Third edition, 1962, p. 92

[2] Reed Talbot Baines, *A History of the Old English Letter Foundries,* revised by A. F. Johnson, Faber and Faber, New edition, 1952, p. 107

[3] Johnson Ball, *William Caslon, 1693-1766,* The Round Wood Press, 1973, p. 412

[4] Reed T. B. & Johnson, A. F. op. cit. p. 331

Chapter 3   Printers, Typefounders and the Sanspareil Matrix

[1] Berry, W. Turner & Johnson, A. F., *Specimens of Printing Types, 1665-1830,* Oxford University Press, 1935, p 321

[2] Mosley, James, *British type specimens before 1831*, Oxford Bibliographical Society, Occasional publication No.14, 1984. Two specimens, questionably dated 1808, comprise: one fount 'Sanspareil eight-lines Pica, the other Sanspareil fifteen-lines Pica. Cited Mosley, entry 82/83 p. 30, Berry and Johnson, location of both specimens in New York Typothetae not known, p. 27 and Reed-Johnson, op. cit. p 32

[3] Mosley op. cit. p. 43 and Berry and Johnson op. cit. p. 71. Slater, Bacon Specimen Book, 1809, Located in Columbia University Library, New York.

[4] Reed and Johnson, op. cit. p. 321.

[5] Mosley op. cit. p. 24. This Bower, Bacon and Bower Specimen Book, 1810, is now located in the Stephenson, Blake Collection in the London Type Museum.

[6] Flatware is a term relating to knives, forks, spoons and similar cutlery. In contrast is Hollow-ware which is the name given to vessels made from Assayed silver, Sheffield Plate and Electroplated silver-ware.

[7] John Garnet, the father of William Henry Garnett, appears in the earliest official Census, 1841 and in the Baptism Register as <u>Garnet</u>.

[8] Hansard, Thomas C., *Typographia,* 1825, p. 355.

[9] A reference to the earlier business name not the demise of Caslon III who died in Stoke-on-Trent in 1869 at the age of 88.

Chapter 4   Partnerships and Associations

[1] Colloquial language of South Yorkshire : *If one ever does anything for nothing, then one always does it for one's self.*

[2] A cutling shop is a local term used for a workshop where knives and similar sharp-bladed instruments are made. (knives, razors, chisels etc.)

[3] Blake, William Greaves, *A South Yorkshire Family of Typefounders,* Hallamshire Press, Sheffield, 1999, p. 29.

[4] ibid. p. 30.

Chapter 5   Blake, Garnett and Company of Sheffield , 1819-29

[1] Hansard T. C. op. cit. p. 355.

[2] Blake, Garnett and Company, *A Specimen of Printing Types, &c.,* 1819

[3] A traditional term relating to instant payment for goods bought. In English market towns there was often a particular point in a market place, indicated by a stone, known as 'the nail', where such transactions took place.

[4] Blake, W. G., op. cit. p. 30.

[5] *Sheffield Independent and Commercial Register,* 12th December, 1819, p.1.

[6] Hansard, initially incorrectly reported the sale of the William Caslon foundry, and said that it had been purchased by Bower, Bacon and Bower of Sheffield.

[7] *Specimen of Printing Types,* Blake and Stephenson, 1831, T. C. Hansard's copy, Stephenson Blake Collection.

Chapter 6   A Passing Partnership, 1830-1840

[1] Partnership agreement between James Blake and John Stephenson, 25th September 1830.

[2] Blake, W. G. op. cit. p. 31.

[3] Obituary, *Sheffield Mercury*, June 1831.

[4] Musson, A. E., *The Typographical Association*, Oxford University Press, 1954, p.89.

[5] Moxon, Joseph, *Mechanick Exercises, 1683-4,* Edited Davis & Carter, Oxford University Press, 2nd Edition, 1962 p.167.

[6]Chapter 7   Fashionable types

[1] Mosley, James, *British type specimens before 1831,* Oxford Bibliographical Society, 1984.

[2] Berry and Johnson, op. cit.

[3] Reed, T. B. op. cit. p. 309.

[4] Savage, William, *A Dictionary of the Art of Printing,* London, 1841, p. 801.

[5] Stower, Caleb, *The Printers Grammar*, London, 1808, p. 531.

[6] Blades, William, *Early Type Specimen Books of England,* London, 1875, pps. 21-22.

[7] Updike, D. B. op. cit., Volume II, p.196

[8] This is supposition. There is no definite evidence to substantiate this.

[9] Berry and Johnson, *Encyclopedia of Type Faces*, Blandford, London, p. 231.

[10] Gray, Nicolette, *Nineteenth Century Ornamental Types*, Faber and Faber, 1938, p. 23

[11] Updike, D. B., op. cit., Vol II, page 197.

Chapter 8   The Changing Scene 1840-1870

[1] *White's Directory of Sheffield, 1833*

Chapter 9   Mutual Friends and Competitors

[1] Printers' Register quotation

[2] McRae, John Findlay, *Two Centuries of Typefounding,* H. W. Caslon and Company Limited, 1920, p.75

[3] ibid. p. 77

[4] SB archive letter, Henry Stephenson to Henry Caslon, November, 1872

Chapter 10   Techniques and Technicalities

[1] Reed, T. B. and Johnson A. F., op. cit., p. 331

Chapter 11   Types: Gentlemen and Players

[1] SB archive letter, Elisha Pechey to Henry Stephenson, 21 March, 1887

[2] SB archive letter, Elisha Pechey to Henry Stephenson, 29 December, 1894

[3] SB archive letter, Henry Stephenson to Elisha Pechey, 19 May, 1895

[4] Betjeman, John, *Sunday in Broomhill*

[5] Sir Henry Stephenson and R. G. Blake were both Directors of the Sheffield Gas Company Limited

Chapter 12   Owners in Waiting

[1] Blake, W. G. op. cit. pps. 77-84

Chapter 13   Making the Point

[1] Legros, L. A. and Grant, J. C., *Typographical Printing Surfaces,* Longmans, Green, 1916, p.60 cites McKellar, Smiths and Jordan Company as setting the dimensions of the American Point & Pica.

[2] Expressing the actual size of the Printers' point, both in America and Britain, was not easy. There is a small differential between the standard American inch and the Imperial inch. This is further complicated as the division of an inch into 72nds produces a recurring decimal.

[3] *Caxton Magazine,* No. 22, April 1904, *Coming to the Point,* a report on the Lecture delivered by H. K. Stephenson, at the Regent Street Polytechnic, London. In their pursuit of excellence, Stephenson, Blake at the time, were seemingly unable to contemplate and take advantage of the developments which were taking place at the Mergenthaler Linotype Company which was successfully mass-producing line composition matrices by the use of the Waldo-Benton machine.

[4] *Caxton Magazine,* ibid.

[5] *Caxton Magazine,* ibid., Editor's comments

[6] SB archive letter, Elisha Pechey to Sir Henry Stephenson advising that Emile Bertaut, under contract intended to have his assistant cut the punch outlines on the Waldo-Benton machine.

[7] *Reply to the Caxton Magazine,* H. K. Stephenson's response to the critical report in the *Caxton Magazine* issued as a 4-page inset in the *British Printer.*

[8] ibid.

[9] SB Leaflet, *Truth or Fiction*, 4-page, 8vo leaflet sent out to customers with every order, January, 1905.

Chapter 14   The Broken Reed

[1] *Specimen of Modern Printing Types by Edmund Fry,* Printing Historical Society, 1986, p.8.

[2] SB archive letter, Sir Henry Stephenson to Eliot Reed, January 1897.

[3] The examples of Irish types are reproduced by courtesy of Dr. Dermot McGuinne, the author of *Irish Type Design*, see bibliography.

Chapter 15   Social Nuances

[1] *Autobiography of T. W. Smith*, privately published by H.W. Caslon and Company Limited, 1910?, p.8.

[2] ibid, p.10

[3] ibid, p.13

Chapter 16   Punch Cutters and Engravers

[1] After the 1750s, punchcutters were working directly on punch blanks which were made from crucible steel produced at the foundry of Benjamin Huntsman in Attercliffe, Sheffield.

[2] SB archive memo from Henry Stephenson to foundry overseer, August 1869

[3] From the 1860s, Stephenson, Blake's apprentices received training (and education) at the Sheffield School of Art, later the Sheffield College of Art. This instruction continued until the late 1960s. Apprentices and trainees in punchcutting, justifying and matrix making were afforded a unique course of instruction which included Drawing, Graphic Design, Practical engraving instruction in the School of Silversmithing and experience in printing techniques in the School of Printing

[4] SB archive document, William Oliver's contract dated 25 May 1872

[5] SB archive letter from Sir Henry Stephenson to William Kirkwood in Frankfurt, October 1895

[6] Several years after returning to Germany, William Kirkwood forsook punch cutting and became involved in the production of decorative leather goods. However, his patriotism was sorely tried during two World Wars. As the defeat of Germany came in 1945, he committed suicide

Chapter 17   Types of Influence

[1] *The Fleuron,* Volume 5, 1926, p. 131

[2] *The influence of the Kelmscott Press, The Times Literary Supplement*, No. 505, 28 September 1911, pps. 345-6

[3] ibid

[4] SB archive type specimen leaflet, *Old Style Book Letter,* issued 1911

[5] *British Printer*, 1916, p. 228. There is an excellent account of the activities of Legros and Grant by L. W. Wallis, Journal of the Printing Historical Society, No. 28, 1999, pps. 5-40

Chapter 18   The Call to Arms

[1] SB archive letter, R. G. Blake to Colonel H. K. Stephenson serving with the B.E.F., 28 September 1914

[2] SB archive letter, R. G. Blake to Sydney Caslon, 16 August 1916

[3] SB archive letter, R. G. Blake to Alan Richard, 27 August 1916

Chapter 19   Ambiguous and Ambitious Strategies

[1] SB archive letter, R. G. Blake to Sydney Caslon, May 1919.

[2] ibid, July 1919.

[3] *Two Centuries of Typefounding,* H. W. Caslon and Company Limited, 1920.

[4] SB archive letter, R. G. Blake to R. B. Fishenden, 21 June 1921.

[5] SB archive letter, R. G. Blake to R. B. Fishenden, 20 February 1923.

[6] Northend, William, ARCA, a note on the history of the family company from Northend family papers.

[7] SB archive letter, Frederick Warde, Princeton University to R. G. Blake, November 1924.

[8] SB archive, a personal letter from R. G. Blake to friend. This acclamation needs to be viewed with some reservation. There is every indication that Stephenson, Blake sent a copy of *Printing Types* to the Editor of *The Times Literary Supplement*. The principals nursed bitter memories of what they considered to be direct criticism of the company by the TLS on the 28 September 1911, and were determined to be seen to be typefounders *par excellence.*

[9] Whilst the *British Printer* cited 'firms', this was quite erroneous. J. W. Northend Limited was the only firm involved in the printing and finishing of *Printing Types*.

[10] *The British and Colonial Printer*, April 1924.

[11] *British Printer,* September 1924.

[12] *The British and Colonial Printer,* September 1924.

[13] Millington, Roy, *A History of J. W. Northend Limited,* a centenary history, Sheffield, 1989.

[14] SB archive letter, H. F. B. Stephenson to R. B. Fishenden.

Chapter 20   Humane Resource Management

[1] SB archive letters, references 1 to 9. These extracts are quotations from the Director's Letter Book.

Chapter 21   Cat and Mouse

[1] SB archive letter, R. G. Blake's letter to Harold Caslon following-up negotiations which had taken place over dinner, 31 October 1927.

[2] SB archive letter, R. G. Blake's letter to Daniel Caslon, 9 December 1930.

[3] SB archive letter, R. G. Blake's letter to Daniel Caslon, 16 October 1933.

Chapter 22   The Changing Face of Type

[1] *The Imprint,* No. 1, The Curwen Press, reprinted for the Wynkyn de Worde Society, 1972, p. 5.

[2] White, Reginald, *Stephenson Blake's Case History*, Circular, No .3, The Typographic Circle, 1994, pps.12-13.

Chapter 23   Dynastic Succession

[1] Many years after the death of R. G. Blake, a wall was removed in order to enlarge a particular work area. It proved to be a false wall. Behind it was a stock of Antimony and Tin ingots. Obviously, R. G., drawing on his experience of First World War metal shortages had hoarded a stock of refined metal in case of a dire shortage. Following his death, this had been overlooked and forgotten.

[2] The Ministry of Supply was singularly rigorous in applying the Order to requisition type metal for the war effort.

[3] SB archive letter, R. G. Blake to B. Lockhart, 26 September 1939.

[4] SB archive letter, R. G. Blake to B. Lockhart, 7 October 1939.

[5] SB archive letter, R. G. Blake to Ralph Caslon, 4 July 1945.

Chapter 24   Post-war Changes and Reorganisation

Chapter 25   The Ending of the Gutenberg Galaxy

[1] On the closure of Graphic House, the following item appeared under the heading of from 'Our own correspondent': *In the gloom of a damp October evening, the ghosts of many of London's now defunct type-founders gathered to beat the retreat as the last of The Ring closed its doors in the Metropolis. Among the many old bodies were Pica and Brevier from Blackfriars, Minion from Sir Charles Reed; Nonpariel and Diamond came from Stevens, Great Primer from Shanks and the venerable figure of Bourgeois from Caslon. Although not of London but with close association, came those two diminutive characters Ruby and Pearl from Miller and Richard. With due cere-mony, the name which had made such an Impact was removed from the wall by Chisel, wrapped in Saxon Black and on the slab serif of Skeleton Antique, conveyed to the tomb to join the host of matrices from which flowed the greatness of Stephenson, Blake.* Geoffrey Hulett, 1975.

[2] Reflections of the author after directing the North of England Regional operations of the Printing and Publishing Industry Training Board, 1969-82.

[3] McLuhan, Marshall, *The Gutenberg Galaxy: the making of typographic man,* Routledge and Kegan Paul, London, 1962.

[4] With apologies to T. S. Eliot (1888-1965). The ultimate line of his poem: *The Waste Land.*

Appendix II

General Index of Printing Types 1924, Specimen Book

The General Index of *Printing Types* issued by Stephenson, Blake in 1924. It has been included to show the incredible range of stock which the company offered at a time when the letterpress printing process still reigned supreme.

Abbey Text	490-492
Accents, Signs, Peculiars, &c	73,75
Albion	82
Aldine, Titling	85
Alexandra	523
Alexandrian Black	494
Algerian	522
Ancient Black	481-484
Antique No. 1	345
Antique No. 1 Skeleton	347
Antique No. 2 Skeleton	346
Antique No. 3	342, 344
Antique O.S. No. 2	114-115, 283-286
Arabian	521
Arrow Ornaments	573
Art Ornaments	651, 654-655, 662-664
Athenian	293-294
Athenian Condensed	293-294
Athenian Expanded	350
Augustan Black	495
Auriol	522
Auriol Borders	560
Auriol Ornaments	561

Auriol Outline	522
Baskerville Old Face	1-4,15,1162
Bewick Cuts	659
Black Letter	481-496
Black No. 3	488-489
Bold Britannic	423-426
Bold Grotesque	518
Bold Italic Grotesque	409
Bold Latin	332
Bold Latin Condensed	334-336
Bold Mercantile Italic	512
Bold Runic	518
Book and News Letter	1-80
Book and News Titlings	82-87
Booklet	118, 292-293
Booklet Italic	292-293
Borders, Ornaments, &c.	540-592
Braces	75
Brackets, Bold	581
Brass Dashes	591, 635
Brass Rules	631-642
Britannic	520
Britannic Bold	423-426

Britannic Italic	425-426	Crests	678
Card Pips	580	Crinkle Border	564
Cases of Brass Rule	631	Cube Rule, Brass	639
Cast Iron Furniture	624	Cymric Border	572
Catalogue Marks	592	Dashes	591, 635
Celtic Border	570	De Vinne	324-325, 328
Celtic Outline Border	571	De Vinne Condensed	327, 330
Chantrey	341	De Vinne Family in Display	323, 328-330
Chatsworth	311, 315-317, 321	De Vinne Italic	326, 329
Chatsworth Condensed	318,320	De Vinne Ornamented	519
Chatsworrth Expanded	312-314	De Vinne Ornamented Italic	519
Chatsworth Family in Display	320-322	Display Book Letter	97-118
Charlemagne	521	Display Letter	235-350, 505-523
Checks	667	Display Ornaments	579
Chess	666	Display Script	455
Chippendale	108-109, 263-265, 267-270	Draughts	666
Chippendale Initials	535	Ecclesiastical Ornaments	678
Chippendale Italic	266-268	Egyptian Border	557
Circles, Brass	641	Eighteenth Century	
City Arms	675	Flowers & Borderings	540-544
City of London Arms	674	Electra	510-511
Clarendon	348-349	Electros and Sundries	651-678
Clarendon, Extended	348-349	Elongated Sans Serifs	422
Clearface	106-107, 240-241, 244, 246	Elzevir, Titling	84
Clearface Italic	242-243, 245-246	Emblems	665-677
Clearface Bold	247-249, 252-254	Engadine	521
Clearface Bold Italic	250-254	Engravers Roman	308-310
Clearface Extra Bold	255-259	Estimates, Suggestions for	702
Clumps	623	Etrurian	522
Colonial Arms	676	Expanded	522
Combination Dashes	591	Expanded No. 2	522
Combination Flourishes	579	Extended Clarendon	348-349
Combination Vignettes	658	Fancy Brass Rules	637
Commercial Italic	462	Farmyard Electros	671
Condensed Antique No. 3	343-344	Figures, Specimens of	76-77, 601-616
Condensed Sans Serifs Italic	409	Five-Pointed Stars	580
Condensed Sans Serifs No. 1	422	Flanged Brass Rule	640
Condensed Sans Serifs No. 4	421	Flemish Expanded	520
Condensed Sans Serifs No. 5	406-407	Floral Ornament	576
Condensed Sans Serifs No. 7	308-401	Foreign Arms	676
Condensed Sans Serifs No. 8	412-413	Fractions	76
Condensed Sans Serifs No. 10	408	Freehand	462
Condensed Sans Serifs No. 37	415	Garland Ornament	545-547
Corners, Metal	589	Geneva Crosses	665
Corners, Rule	590	Georgian Old Face	5-8
County Arms	675	Georgian Old Face Italic	9

Graphic	522	Marigold Border	577
Grotesque, Bold	518	Masonic Signs	665
Grotesque, Bold Italic	409	Metal Furniture	623
Grotesque No. 3	416, 418	Metropole Condensed	340
Grotesque No. 4	417-418	Miscellaneous Borders	582-588
Grotesque No. 6	402-404	Miscellaneous Information	699
Grotesque No. 7	420	Missal Capitals	495
Grotesque No. 8	383-385, 388	Modern No. 16	34-38
Grotesque No. 8 Italic	386-387, 389	Modern No. 17	30-42
Grotesque No. 9	390-393	Modern No. 17 Italic	43
Grotesque No. 10	405	Modern No. 18	44-45
Grotesque No. 12	410-411	Modern No. 20	46-50, 175-178
Grotesque Old Style	517	Modern No. 20 Italic	54, 176-178
Grotesques and Sans Serifs	383-426	Modern No. 22	51-53
Grotesques, Sans Serifs in Display	419	Modern Roman Faces shown by	
Ground Borders	553-556	sizes	66-72
Hallamshire Old Style	112-113, 279-282	Multiform Border	577
Historical Record	vii-xiv	Newspaper Founts & Heading	
Hogarth	513	Types	78-80
Horses	670	Newspaper Headings	81
Imperial Script	451-454	Newspaper Titlings	82
Index	700-701	Old Face Open	154, 157, 159, 162
Indexes, Black and Shaded	668	Old Roman, Titling	87, 291
Initial Blanks, Mortised	539	Old Style Condensed	514
Initials	533-539	Old Style Engravings	659
Introduction	v-vi	Old Style Grotesque	517
Italian Old Style	116-117, 287-290	Old Style Head Pieces	660-661
Italian Old Style Italic	289-290	Old Style Initials	538
Labour Saving Brass Border Rules	636	Old Style No. 2	17-22
Latin	339	Old Style No. 2 Italic	32
Latin, Bold	332	Old Style No. 2a Italic	33
Latin Condensed, Bold	334-336	Old Style No. 3	23
Latin Elongated	337	Old Style No. 4	24-27
Latin Expanded	339	Old Style No. 5	10-12, 163-172
Latin Family in Display	333, 336, 338	Old Style No. 5 Italic	13, 166-174
Latin Old Style	519	Old Style No. 6	14-16, 170-171, 173-174
Latin, Shaded	516	Old Style Outlined	515
Latin, Wide	331	Old Style Roman Faces	55-65
Leader Rules, Brass	635	Old Style, Titling	87
Leaders	73	Olympian	521
Leads	622	Old Style Tail Pieces	661
Logotypes	75	Order of the Book	xvi
Loose Accents	73	Ornamental Dashes	591
Macaulay	523	Ornamented Initials No. 3	538
Manx Border	57	Our Ancestry	xv
Maple Border	564	Ovals, Brass	641

Palace Script	443-446	Saxon Black	485-487
Paragraphs Marks	581	Script No. 3	456-457
Parantheses, Bold	581	Scripts	443-462
Parisian Ronde	458-461	Seals	666
Peculiars, &c.	73-75	Shaded Latin	516
Pen Dashes	579	Shakespeare	520
Pen Print	523	Shapes, Brass	642
Peforating Rule, Brass	640	Ships	669
Persian Ornament	578	Signs, Peculiars, &c.	73-75
Phonetics	74	Simplex Border	550-552
Plaid Borders	568-569	Simplex Brass Rules	63
Plain Brass Rules	632-635	Skeleton Antique No. 1	347
Plain Dashes	591	Skeleton Antique No. 2	346
Pomona Ornaments, Series 1 & 2	663	Society Script	447-450
Prince of Wales Arms	674	Solid Squares	566-567
Queen Alexandra's Arms	674	Spacing Material	621-624
Queen Mary's Arms	674	Spartan	296, 304
Quotation Marks, Double	581	Spartan Bold	298
Quotations	622	Spartan Bold Condensed	299
Railroad Border	565	Spartan Bold Italic	300
Receipt Electros	667	Spartan Condensed	297
Recherché	509	Spartan Extra Bold	301
Reference Marks, Bold	581	Spartan Family in Display	295, 304-307
Renaissance Borders	548-549	Spartan Shaded	302-303
Romany	520	Sport Electros	665
Ronaldson Old Style	26-31	Spray Ornament	576
Royal Arms	672-676	Stars, Five-Pointed	580
Rule Corners	590	Stationery Sundries	666
Rules, Metal	75	Steel Furniture	621
Runic, Bold	518	Tablet Border	574
Runic Border	575	Text Initials	536
Runic Elongated	518	Time Tables	77
Runnymede	505-508	Titling Aldine	85
Saint George Initials	533	Titling Condensed No. 2	86
Sans Serifs and Grotesques	383-426	Titling Elzevir	84
Sans Serifs and Grots, in Display	419	Titling No. 2	82
Sans Serifs, Elongated	422	Titling No. 5	82
Sans Serifs Italic, Condensed	409	Titling No. 6	83
Sans Serifs No. 1, Condensed	422	Titling No. 7	84
Sans Serifs No. 4, Condensed	421	Titling No. 8	83
Sans Serifs No. 5, Condensed	406-407	Titling No. 9	82
Sans Serifs No. 7, Condensed	308-401	Titling No. 10	83
Sans Serifs No. 8, Condensed	412-413	Titling No. 11	82
Sans Serifs No. 10, Condensed	408	Titling Old Roman	87, 291
Sans Serifs No. 37 Condensed	415	Titling Old Style	87
Sans Serifs—see Grotesques		Total Rules	75

Town Arms	675
Trade Electros	652-653-669
Turbayne Initials	534
Typewriter No. 2, 12 Point	501
Typewriter No. 3, 12 Point	502
Typewriter No. 4, 12 Point Ribbonface	503
Typewriter, 10 Point	504
Verona	98-99, 135-142
Veronese	521
Violet Border	562-563
Washington Text	493
Wave Dashes	579
Waverley	521
Westminster Borders	558
Westminster Festoons	559
Westminster Initials	537
Westminster Light Face	276-278
Westminster Old Style	110-111, 271-275
Westminster Ornaments	559
Westminster Page Ornaments	656-657
Wide Latin	331
Wide Roman	522
Winchester Bold	200-203
Winchester Bold Condensed	204-207
Winchester Bold Shaded	208-210
Winchester Medium	191-194
Winchester Medium Italic	195-198
Winchester O.S.	100-101, 179-186, 199
Winchester O.S. Italic	182-186, 199
Winchester Wide	102-103-187-190
Windsor	228-230
Windsor Condensed	234-236
Windsor Elongated	237-238
Windsor Light Condensed	216-218
Windsor Medium	211, 219-223
Windsor Medium Italic	224-227
Windsor Outline	232-233
Wood Letter	691-698
Wood Ornaments	579

Appendix III

A Checklist of Stephenson, Blake Typefaces

Prior to the introduction of the point body system of measure, types were described by a named size (for example, brevier, bourgeois, minion, pica etc.). There was often no means of identifying a particular characteristic or classification of design by the description which appeared. Not all of the designs listed below were used and, in the main, the list relates to typefaces produced after 1880. The dates indicated are approximate. In some cases the preparation of a whole series took several years to complete. In the case of a number of founts, which were in preparation at the beginning of the first World War, these were not completed until the 1920s.

There are four principal sources for viewing Stephenson Blake type designs via type specimen books:

(a) James Mosley's *British type specimens before 1831* lists the location of British and American sources of the Blake and Garnett, and Blake and Stephenson specimen books, as well as the specimen books of the type founders who preceded them.

(b) The St. Bride Printing Library, Bride Lane, Fleet Street, London EC4Y 8EE. There is an extensive collection of post-1831 Stephenson Blake specimen books, including a well stocked collection of type specimen leaflets displaying various type families and series issued by Stephenson Blake during the period 1831 to 1990.

(c) The Stephenson Blake Collection (which includes a comprehensive collection of Caslon; Bower, Bacon and Bower; Blake and Garnett; Blake and Stephenson, and Stephenson Blake specimen books and leaflets) is now in the keeping of the London Type Museum, 100 Hackford Road, Stockwell, London, SW9 0QU. Currently access to these specimen books is limited due to the preparation of accommodation for the archives. The Type Museum also has many specimen books of foundries acquired by Stephenson, Blake and Company as well as foundries which pre-date it.

(d) *The Encyclopedia of Typefaces*, by Jaspert, Berry and Johnson, is a useful source of lettering and type design identification.

Abbey Text	1919	Purchased from U.S.
Adonis	1971	Designed for photocomposition by Andrea Cretton for the Typefoundry Amsterdam. Acquired by SB and cast in type.
Albion	1919	Created in 1910 for Monotype, acquired by SB.
Alexandra	1911	Acquired from Reed foundry.
Algerian	1908	SB created shaded Latin style.
Amanda Ronde	1939	Purchased design known as Undine Ronde.
Ancient Black	1904	Acquired via Reed foundry. Originally English No.2 from the stock of Wolf, London printer, 1582. Passed to John James foundry, bought by Fry and then passed to Sir Charles Reed foundry.
Athenian	1889	Punches cut at SB by William Kirkwood.
Antique Old Style No.2	1869	Purchased from Aubert Freres, Paris.
Antiques Nos. 1, 2, 3, 4	1904	SB Punches cut by William Kirkwood.
Arabian	1912	SB stylised sans serif.
Art and Craft	1914	Purchased from U.S.
Augustan Black	1905	Acquired from the Reed foundry purchse.
Auriol	1907	Purchased from Deberny and Peignot.
Baskerville Old Face	1906	Acquired from Reed foundry. Original cut at Fry's foundry about 1764. The larger sizes were used to complete the Georgian Old Face series. Most of the body sizes were the originals.
Basuto	1927	SB created.
Bell	1932	Searched out from the Sir Charles Reed stock at the request of Stanley Morison in 1926. Original cut by Richard Austin for Dr. Joseph Fry about 1790 and shown in the Fry and Steele specimen book of 1803.
Benedictine	1925	Reproduction rights purchased from Linotype Ltd.
Black No. 3	1880	Purchased from the Bauer Typefoundry, Frankfurt.
Bodoni	1927	Original SB version bought from a German typefounder. The issued version purchased from Linotype Ltd. and matrices prepared from a series of electrotypes. Bodoni also acquired from H. W. Caslon by purchase.
Bologna	1946	Petrarch from the American Type Founders. Based on the 15th century handwriting of Antonio Sinibaldi. Design modified and cut at SB.
Bold Latin	1885	Purchased from Deberny and Peignot.
Booklet Italic	1904	SB Designed by Elisha Pechey. Punches cut by William Kirkwood.
Britannic	1906	SB Derived from Rothbury *see Rothbury.*
Champlevé	1911	Purchased from Deberny Peignot See Naudin
Charlemagne	1886	SB created.
Caslon Old Face	1937	Acquired by SB as a result of purchase. SB had problems with the italic due to overhanging characters and kerning.

Charlemagne	1902	A stylised roman purchased by SB.
Chantry	1896	SB in-house condensed based on De Vinne
Chatsworth	1914	Designed and cut by SB. Begun in 1914 but not completed until 1921 due to war and staff shortages.
Cheltenham	1937	Acquired by purchase, H. W. Caslon Ltd.
Cochin	1937	Acquired by purchase, H. W. Caslon Ltd.
Chippendale	1915	SB designed in company. Work delayed due to war. Not completed until 1919. The matching series of Chippendale Initials designed by J. Naylor, the staff compositor in the London Office.
Chisel	1935	SB Created by Robert Harling. Punches cut by Karl Görner.
Clarendon	1906	Reissued by SB from originals acquired from Reed foundry purchase.
Clearface	1907	Purchased from American Type Founders. Punches cut by M. F. Benton at A.T.F.
Condensed Latin	1869	Purchased from Davies.
Condensed Sans No. 5	1879	Reissued, 1955
„ „ **No. 7**	1893	Reissued, 1955
„ „ **No. 8**	1913	Reissued, 1955
Consort	1956	Original Clarendon punch cut by Robert Besley of the Fann Street Foundry. Acquired as a result of purchase of Sir Charles Reed typefoundry. SB Consort Bold is the 1845 original design.
Copperplate Bold	1953	SB A bolder version of Youthline Script.
Coronation	1937	SB R. G. Blake contended that this was a version of Bodoni but he was challenged on this. Others said it had been plagiarised from the Corvinus design.
Couchman	1920	A six point, financial listing typeface acquired from Stevens Shanks.
De Vinne	1896	Purchased from the Central Typefoundry, U.S. Punches cut by Gustav Schroder.
Diamond Pendant	1912	Purchased from a German typefounder.
Display Script	1884	Purchased from Deberny and Peignot.
Dominus	1925	SB created
Doric 12	1870	SB reissue. The first example of a sans serif letter taken from the William Caslon IV 1816 specimen book.
Doric Italic	1892	Purchase of punches cut in Hamburg by H. John.
Echo	1956	SB Designed by Peter Bell.
Egyptian Expanded	1950	Purchased from Miller and Richard, Edinburgh.
Electra	1921	SB a light upright script based on Typefoundry Amsterdam's Ella cut by de Roos
Elongated Roman	1955	SB Victorian reissue
Elzivir titling	1908	SB reissue of an 1840s Modern

Emery	1935	SB purchased from the designer and punch cutter, Imre Reiner of Lugano Switzerland. SB tried to negotiate cost of development with Monotype Corporation. SB undertook extensive work rejustifying but finally abandoned the face.
Engadine	1890	A light pen letter. Punches of French origin.
Engravers Roman	1912	Purchased from the Inland Type Foundry, U.S.
Etrurian	1881	SB created.
Fancy Text	1871	Purchased from McKeller, Smith & Jordan, Philadelphia,
Farley	1907	Purchased from the Western Type Foundry, U.S.
Flemish Condensed	1905	Purchased from the Inland Type Foundry, U.S. Designed and punches cut by N. J. Werner.
Francesca Ronde	1948	SB created. Based on the handwriting of Lady Frances Stephenson.
Fry's Ornamented	1907	Acquired via the Reed foundry purchase. Original cut by Richard Austin for Dr. Joseph Fry in 1796.
Fry's Baskerville	1907	Acquired via the Reed foundry purchase. Originally Ornamented No. 2. Punches cut by Isaac Moore for Baskerville in 1768.
Ganton	1927	SB created series of titling and ranging figures.
Georgian	1909	SB a recreation of the original believed to have been cut by Joseph Fry around 1790. Allegedly Caslon's destroyed original Marr's Old Style. SB pressed its punch cutters and justifiers to speed production in order to beat issue of H. W. Caslon's Cheltenham.
Glenmoy	1931	SB designed heavy pen script.
Gondola Old Face	1921	SB designed.
Granby	1930	SB hybrid design using Monotype Gill Sans and Bauer Foundry's Futura. Like Gill had extended type family. The Ludlow Typograph Company, Chicago objected to Granby Shadow claiming that it was plagiarised from Umbra. R. G. Blake claimed it was derived from Tempo, which is a design close to Granby.
Graphic	1912	Purchased from the Bauer Type Foundry.
Grotesque	1955	A recut based on Thorowgood's 1832 version, acquired from the Reed Foundry purchase.
Grotesque No. 6	1880	SB originated.
Grotesque No. 7	1890	SB originated.
Grotesque No. 8	1920	SB Punches cut for SB by Prince.
Grotesque No. 9	1907	SB originated.
Guildford	1937	Purchased from H. W. Caslon's stock.
Hallamshire Old Style	1904	Originally the Avil series purchased from the Inland Type Foundry, U.S.
Hogarth	1904	Purchased.

Impact	1965	SB designed by Geoffrey Lee.
Imperial Script	1905	SB created medium weight script cut by Karl Görner.
Invitation Script	1949	SB created from merging Marina script capitals and Youthline lowercase.
Italian Old Style	1896	Purchased from American Type Founders. Punches cut by Jos. W. Phinney and originally named Jenson.
Italian Old Style	1906	Acquired from Reed's Foundry purchase.
Jubilee	1952	Designed by Eric Gill as Cunard and sold on to L. E. Deval, Elkin Matthews Limited.
June	1927	SB design.
Keyboard	1951	Redrawn by Robert Harling
Kennerley	1937	Purchased from the H. W. Caslon sale. Designed by Frederic Goudy.
Kensington Old Style	1919	Purchased from American Type Founders. Originally known as Cloister, designed by Maurice Benton.
Kingston	1924	SB created.
Klang	1955	Designed by Will Carter and purchased from Monotype.
Latin Antique	1880	SB Punches cut by Rochaix.
Latin Elongated	1879	SB Punches cut by Rochaix.
Lectura	1962	Designed by Dick Doojes for Typefoundry Amsterdam. Acquired by SB.
Lining Old Style No. 5	1909	SB series designed and punch cut from the original Caslon Old Face but with bolder strokes specifically to meet American Point Body measure.
London Script	1957	SB Pen letter designed by Imrie Reiner.
Long Imperial Script	1906	SB Script designed by Elisha Pechey. Punches cut by Karl Görner.
Macauley	1905	SB created stylised pen letter.
Madonna Ronde	1925	Purchased from the Bauer Typefoundry, Frankfort. Designed by Lucien Bernhard.
Marina Script	1936	SB designed
Mazarin	1926	Purchased from Deberny and Peignot, Paris. Designed by Robert Girard and engraved by M. Bourreau.
Mercury Script	1950	Purchased from Stevens, Shanks.
Metropole Condensed	1902	A condensed Latin
Missal	1880	SB designed
Moderne Italique	1904	Purchased. Designed and engraved by M. Tuleu.
Modern Caslon	1907	Purchased from the Western Type Foundry, U.S. A design almost the same as Plantin Old Style.
Modern No. 20	1828	Revived and recut from an earlier mid-ninetenth century version. Restyled from English No. 20 about 1910, with shortened descenders. Issued as modern No. 20 in 1955.

Molé Foliate	1960	SB redrawn by S. L. Hartz from a design by the Parisian typefounder Molé.
Monumental	1896	Purchased from McKeller , Smith and Jordan, U.S.
Naudin	1911	Purchased from Deberny and Peignot. Designed by George and Lucien Peignot both of whom were killed in First World War. Champlevé also purchased.
Norman	1878	Purchased from Phelps and Dalton, London.
Old face Open	1904	Acquired through amalgamation with Sir Charles Reed, Limited. Part of the Joseph Fry collection, dated 1788.
Old Roman	1937	Purchased from H. W. Caslon and sons. A Venetian Roman designed by T. W. Smith in 1895.
Old Roman SB	1878	Purchased from Beaudoire and Company, France.
Old Style No. 2	1878	SB Recreated from Old Style No.1.
Old Style No. 5	1912	SB Recreated Caslon Old Face but designed with short descenders.
Old Style No. 18	1884	Purchased from Ferguson, Glasgow.
Old Style Grotesque	1879	SB created.
Old Style Condensed	1876	Purchased from Phelps and Dalton, Boston, Mass.
Old Style Ornamented	1872	Purchased from Bruce and Company, New York.
Olympian	1906	SB stylised semibold pen letter.
Pabst Old Style	1904	Purchased from American Type Founders.
Palace Script	1923	SB created.
Parisian Ronde	1878	Purchased from Chappelle, Paris.
Pen Hand	1912	Purchased from the Bauer Typefoundry, Frankfort.
Perpetua	1930	SB Joint venture with the Monotype Corporation. Eric Gill designed and supervised the engraving of the matrices. SB version altered and slightly emboldened.
Plantin	1942	Rights acquired from Monotype Corporation Limited. It was designed and engraved by F. H. Pierpoint from a 16th century model. SB adapted it and Karl Görner cut the Plantin italic which was leaner than the Monotype version.
Playbill	1938	SB modified Victorian revival designed by Robert Harling.
Recherche	1919	A light pen letter acquired by purchase.
Renaissance	1922	Purchased from Deberny and Peignot.
Ribbonface Typewriter	1907	Purchased. Designed and cut in 1894 by George Weaver.
Roman No. 13	1910	Purchased from Bruce and Company, New York.
Romany	1967	Reissued from late-nineteenth century stock. Originally derived from Schelter and Giesecke's Romanisch.

Ronaldson	1905	Acquired on the purchase of the Sir Charles Reed typefoundry. This was one of the Reed foundry's best selling types and SB quickly modified the matrices and moulds in order to take advantage of its popularity.
Rothbury	1937	Acquired by H. W. Caslon in 1906 from the Inland Type Foundry. Designed by J. Matthews.
Runnymede	1908	Acquired from American Type Founders. Design based on Italian 15th century manuscript.
Roman Compressed No. 3	1937	H.W. Caslon fount. Substituted for Caslon No. 3.
Sans Serif Shaded	1948	SB Revival of a design engraved by Thorowgood and first shown in 1839.
Sans Serif Condensed	1885	SB Mid-19th century sans serif. Reissued 1952
Sans Serif No. 5	1881	SB created design.
Sans Serif Shaded	1948	SB revival. Original engraved by Thorowgood and first shown in 1839 as Sans Surryphs Shaded.
Saxon Black	1884	SB Created fount. Punches cut by Rochaix.
Scarab	1937	SB A version of Monotype Corporation's Rockwell.
Shaded Latin	1888	SB designed in house.
Shadow	1892	SB created from an 1834 Ionic design
Shakespeare	1890	SB brush letter
Society Script	1912	Acquired from Deberny and Peignot, Paris. Known as Calligraphique and, in the large sizes, as Ecriture Taille Douche.
Spartan	1912	Acquired from Western Typefoundry, US. A light Copperplate Gothic series acquired between 1909-12.
St. George	1914	Acquired from a foreign source. The series was prepared and launched at the Printing Trades Exhibition held in London in 1914.
Sylvan	1884	Acquired from Deberny and Peignot.
Tea Chest	1939	SB Design developed on the advice of Robert Harling.
Thorowgood	1953	SB Reissued design engraved by Robert Thorne, 1820-36. From Reed Foundry collection.
Thorne Shaded	1938	SB Taken from Robert Thorne's collection of 1820, part of the Reed foundry material. R. G. Blake searched for the pre-1890s versions at the request of Lund Humphries, of Bradford. The original Thorne matrices were defective so the series was recut by Karl Görner in the period 1938-48.
Times New Roman	1955	Series prepared from Stanley Morison's 1931 typeface design for *The Times* newspaper.
Typewriter	1907	Acquired from the American Type Founders.

Union Pearl	1700	Reivived in 1931 and cast to order. The earliest known decorated English typeface cut by the Grover foundry in 1700. Acquired by SB via the Sir Charles Reed amalgamation. Previously via Fry's and Fann Street Foundry.
Verona	1923	Acquired on advice of R. B. Fishenden from Leclede Type Foundry, St. Louis prior to its merger with Barnard Brothers and Spindler.
Veronese	1902	SB purchased. Eccentric style of Engraver's Roman.
Venezia	1927	Designed by George W. Jones and cut by Edward P. Prince for Jones as the Dolphin series. Jones had the matching italic designed by Frederic Goudy. Jones dissatisfied and sold the punches and matrices to SB for £200.
Vogue	1939	SB created.
Waring	1904	Acquired from American Type Founders.
Washington Text	1905	Acquired from Keystone Foundry, USA.
Waverley	1907	SB created medium weight brush letter.
Wedding Text	1934	Acquired from American Type Founders in the form of a fount of unrubbed letter.
Westminster Old Style	1907	Acquired from American Type Founders. Designed by T. M. Cleland in 1903 and known as Della Robbia.
Wide Latin	1883	SB created.
Winchester Old Style	1908	SB created. Based on Inland Type Foundry's Cheltenham. Engraved at SB by J. E. Uttley.
Windsor	1905	SB Designed by Elisha Pechey and engraved by William Kirkwood.
Youthline Script	1952	SB created.

Appendix IV

Glossary

Antiques
Blake and Garnett, and their successors described slab-serifed designs as Antiques. Other typefounders referred to the design as Egyptians.

Blacks
Original Black letter, also known as Gothic or Old English, had fallen from general use in Britain by the close of the eighteenth century. However, in the 1820s there was a revival and heavily emboldened versions began to appear, complementary in weight and design to the Fat Blacks.

Clarendon
A design issued by Robert Besley, 1845, in text or body sizes—generally—Brevier (8 point) to English (14 point). The character was essentially a slightly condensed miniaturised cutting of an Egyptian. It was subsequently copied by other typefounders and used for typographical emphasis in reference works.

Dissing (distribution)
The systematic returning of used type, letter by letter, to the appropriate boxes of a typecase.

Dressing
The breaking of the tang from the base of a cast letter left a burr. This had to be removed in order to ensure type height. The mechanical dressing of typefounders' letter was a relatively late innovation.

Dross

Lead and type metal alloys, when molten, produce dross—impurities which rise to the surface of casting machine metal pots. To effect clean type casting dross needed to be removed from the surface of the molten metal. Particular care was taken with its disposal as powdered dross was highly toxic and a known health hazard.

Electrotyping

Whilst Stephenson Blake punched and struck matrices in the traditional way—abjuring the 'growing' of matrices electronically, the company had electrotyping facilities from an early period. These facilities were used to mould and grow duplicates of woodcuts, wood and brass engravings, coats of arms and similar originals.

Family (type)

A collection of design variations derived from a common design. For example: Roman (primary design); Italic, Bold, semibold, extra-bold, condensed, extended, expanded, elephant, in line, out line, shadow, shaded, cameo, etcetera.

Fat Blacks

Bower, Bacon and Bower, Blake and Garnett, and Stephenson and Blake all produced Fat Blacks. The face was primarily offered in placard sizes and used for display setting. The design was mechanical rather than calligraphical. The stress on the design was vertical, the down stroke being unnaturally thickened, whilst the upstroke thinned to a hair line. The serif was, in the main, unbracketed and carried the same hairline weight as the upstrokes of the letter.

Fount (or font)

A set of letters of a single typesize comprising capitals [upper case], lower case, small capitals, figures, points (punctuation marks, ligatures, tied letters, diphthongs, accents and reference signs).

Jet-piece

The jet piece was the extended part of the tang. It was formed from the surplus of molten metal which accumulated as the mould channel filled.

Justifying

When a punch was struck into a copper blank to form the matrix, its shape was distorted. Justifying involved filing, grinding and burnishing. It was necessary to ensure that the image in the matrix was parallel with the face of the matrix. Equally; the depth of the strike and every other strike made to complete the fount had to be justified to exactly the same depth. The image also had to be set square with the body of the matrix to ensure the cast letter would be upright. The distortions in the side wall also had to be removed to ensure the matrix aligned and fitted exactly in the mould.

Laking (lakin)

A South Yorkshire term for absenting oneself from the factory or the coal mine on Mondays—usually following bouts of heavy weekend drinking. Piece workers were less of a problem but in factories and mines where discipline was maintained, employers' patience was often stretched to its limits. Sheffield's working class had a reputation for drunkenness and disorder dating back to the eighteenth century. Squalor, social depravation and drunkenness went hand in hand. The local pub or 'boozer' was a haven—it provided an escape from the realities of working class life. The Licensing Acts of the early twentieth century and the constraints placed on drinking and drinking hours during World War I did much to break the pernicious habit. Sir Henry K Stephenson was one of the founders of Earl Grey's Sheffield and District Public House Trust, a temperance charity.

Nick

The groove on the front of the shank of a letter in order to ensure the letter is correctly positioned during composition. The nick could be formed in the mould during casting or planed into the letter during the finishing. Typefounders frequently cut additional nicks by planing in order that certain founts or series might be readily identified.

Pin mark

A slight indentation in the side of the shank of a machine-cast type character where the mould ejection pin functioned. The pin mark invariably carried the initials or trade mark of the typefounder.

Point-bodied type

This is type cast on bodies which are measured in points from the front to the back of the letter. Common text or body letter ranged in sizes 6 point to 14 point. Display letter from 18 point to 72 point.

Point-lining

A system of establishing in points a regular dimension to the beard in order to effect the alignment of types from a different fount series or family and to enable the compositor to align accurately type of a larger or smaller size. Point-title lining was a term applied to an alphabet or fount comprising capital letter characters (upper case) only. Much was made in the early twentieth century specimens of the word 'Lining' which frequently prefaced the name of the type indicating that it had been cast on a point-size dimension body and the beard of the letters had been cast to a point-size alignment standard.

Point measure (Anglo-American)

The printers' point is a unit of measure first introduced by Pierre Fournier in 1737. The principle of measuring type in points related to the inch was finally adopted in the late nineteenth century, replacing the former type size names, the sizes of which were essentially arbitrary and differed in close dimension from typefoundry to typefoundry. American and British typefounders adopted the standard point of 0.0138 inch; America in 1886, Britain 1898.

Point-set

Of the three features of the Point system, this was the least practical. In theory, the letters of a particular size would be cast on fixed dimension bodies—subdivisions of the em of the size. Hence em quad of a 12 point letter would be 12 points. The lower letter 'm' would be 12 points wide, letters such as a, b, c, d, e, g, h, k, n o, p, q, v, x, y, z would be cast on a unit body 6 points wide, letters such as i, j, l, 4-points wide. The principle was that a compositor would have the skill to calculate the letters composed and apply point-unit spacing accordingly, thus (in theory) speeding up the justification of a composed line of type.

In many respects the promoting of Point-set revealed a complete lack of understanding on the part of the traditional typefounders. The Lanston Monotype Corporation's unit system completely superseded ideas of a Point-set. Monotype established a variable set-wise dimension for each particular type series. The set was determined by the x-height (common height of lower-case letters) and its relationship to the ascenders, descenders and height of the capital letters. The *set* of the em quad therefore was variable. Whilst the Point body may have been for example, 12 point, the set dimensions could vary from 11.75 points to 12.25 points.

The effecting of inter word spacing during the keyboarding and casting operations provided a range of spacing varying from 3 to 18 units wide. The unique Monotype unit spacing system made possible the mechanical typesetting of fine book work and commercial typography which technically outstripped line composing systems.

Polytyping
A process of making a duplicate image from an intaglio matrix. Woodcuts and wood- and brass-engraved, originals were duplicated by polytyping. The original was pressed into molten metal prior to solidification. This formed an intaglio image which was then used as a matrix. The image was dusted with graphite and a cast was made using an alloy with a high tin content and low molten temperature range. The process was also known as *dab casting*.

Rubbing
The finishing of cast types by hand to ensure burrs and unwanted particles of metal were removed, particularly round kerned letters. Large letter 2-lines pica and above (24 point) frequently required considerable hand finishing.

Sans Surryphs (sans serifs)
Early Blake and Stephenson spelling for sans serif founts.

Series
A range of type sizes comprising complete founts of a single typeface design (e.g. 6 point to 72 point).

Setters-up
Children or women labourers who assembled the cast letter into lines in preparation for the trimming of the base of the letters with a plane. Setters-up also worked in the warehouse in order to set up, assemble and pack founts of letter according to prescribed scales of fount make-up either in weight or frequency of letter usage.

Slug (slug composition)
The lines of cast composition (letter and words) produced by the Typograph, the Linotype and the Interype Composing machines.

Stereotyping
From the earliest days of the typefoundry, Stephenson Blake, in common with other typefounders, offered stock illustrations reproduced from wood cuts, wood engravings, or deeply cut engravings in brass. Before the introduction of electrotyping, these images for the stock illustrations were either replicated by stereotyping or dab-casting. The wet flong would be laid over the forme of type or over the woodcut/engraving and the flong would be pressed and gently beaten into the original image, with a stiff brush, pick-

ing up the detail. On completion of the stereo-moulding operation, the wet
flong had to be dried out before plates could be cast from the replicated
image. Carefully brush-beaten, wet flongs could produce some excellent
replicated images. With the development of the rotary newspaper presses,
dry flongs were developed to save time and obviate the drying-out period.
The image was created by mechanically pressing the flong on to the
imposed news pages. The dry flong was never quite able to pick up the fine
detail of the hand made flong. In the latter half of the nineteenth century,
the problems of creating a reasonable typographical printing surface led
newspapers to use type designs with the qualities of Ionics; characterised
by even letter strokes, unbracketed serifs, short ascenders and descenders,
and large x-heights.

Striking (strikes)
The indenting, striking by hammer blows, or pressure from a matrix fly-
press, of the punch into a copper blank to produce a matrix.

Sweating
In general, dab-cast duplicates, stereotypes and electrotypes had a thickness of about a pica (12 points) and needed to be mounted on a base which
brought them up to type height (post point system English standard 0.918
inch). This was done either by incorporating the duplicate plate by casting
a common lead base or by 'sweating' the duplicate plate on to a pre-cast
metal base using low temperature tin solder and flux.

Tang
The tang was formed in the foot of each letter from surplus metal poured
in the aperture of the mould. Following release from the mould the tang and
jet piece was broken off to form the feet of the type.

Tuscan
A typeface design particularised by swelling, waisting or decoration in the
mid-stem of an alphabet's letter, coupled with serifs formed from bifurcated or rolled terminals. The mid-Victorian designs ranged from highly
stylised and decorated forms to relatively plain, unadorned letters. Whilst
the first version appeared in Vincent Figgins' specimen book of 1815,
Tuscans did not really emerge until the mid-1820s.

Type Body Features

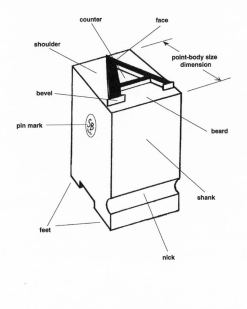

Profile of a hand-cast type

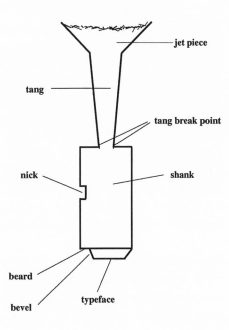

Type design terminology

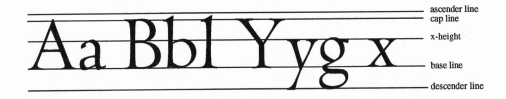

Type sizes (pre-Points system)

Approximate sizes in points

Minikin	3	Pica	12
Brilliant	3.5	English	14
Gem	4	Two-lines Brevier	16
Diamond	4.5	Great Primer	18
Pearl	5	Paragon	20
Ruby	5.5	Double Pica	22
Nonpareil	6	Two-lines Pica	24
Emerald	7	Two-lines English	28
Brevier	8	Two-lines Great Primer	36
Bourgeois	9	Two-lines Double Pica	44
Long Primer	10	Canon Four-lines Pica	48
Small Pica	11		

Wood-letter

Although both Stephenson Blake and Robert De Little cut wood-letter as small as 4-lines pica (48 point), the usual range of sizes began at 8-lines pica (96 point). Several kinds of wood was used; Pear, Apple and Maple being the preferred choices. In some instances Canary was used, whilst for very detailed or engraved letters Turkish Boxwood. In the 1930s trials were conducted using German made plastic but this proved to be both expensive and unstable.

Appendix V

Bibliography

Archer, Caroline, *The Kynoch Press*, Oak Knoll Press, Delaware, 2000 ISBN 0-7123-4706-6

Ball, Johnson, *William Caslon 1693-1766*, Roundwood Press, Kineton, 1973, SBN 900093-13-7

Berry, W.T. and Johnson, A.F., *Specimens of Printing Types, 1665-1830,* Oxford University Press, London, 1935

Blades, William, *Early type specimen books of England*, London, 1875

Circular, the Magazine of the Typographic Circle, Issue No. 3, Spring, London, 1994

Caslon, H. Daniel, *Typefounding and type design*, an address by H. Daniel Caslon, published privately by H. W. Caslon and Company Limited, London, 1932

Glaister, Geoffrey, *An Encyclopedia of the Book*, Oak Knoll Press, Delaware, 1996, ISBN 0-7123-0490-8

Gray, Nicolette, *Nineteenth Century Ornamented Typefaces,* Faber and Faber, London, 1976

Hanson, Thomas C., *Typographia: the art of printing,* London, 1825

Hey, David, *A History of Sheffield,* Carnegie Publishing, Lancaster, 1998, ISBN: 1-85936-045-9

Hey, David, *Historic Hallamshire*, Landmark Publishing, Derbyshire, 2002, ISBN 1-84306-049-3

Howe, Ellic, *The Typecasters, Monotype Recorder* Volume 39, No. 1, Monotype Corporation Limited,Summer, 1957

Jaspert, W. P., Berry, W. T. and Johnson, A. F., *Encyclopedia of Type Faces,* London, 1990, ISBN 1-84188-139-2

Johnson, Alister, *Alphabets to order*, Oak Knoll Press, British Library, 2000, ISBN 1-58456-009-6 (USA)

Johnson, A.F., *Type Designs, their history and development,* Grafton, London, 2nd Edition, 1959

Lane, John A., *The origins of Union Pearl* (Matrix 12)

Legros, L. A. and Grant, J. C., *Typographical Printing Surfaces,* Longmans Green, London, 1916

McGuinne, Dermot, *Irish Type Design*, Irish Academic Press, Dublin, 1992. ISBN 0-7165-2463-5

McLuhan, Marshall, *The Gutenberg Gallaxy,* Routledge and Kegan Paul, London, 1967

McRae, John Findlay, *Two Centuries of Typefounding*, H. W. Caslon and Company Limited, London, 1920

Millington, Roy, *A History of J. W. Northend Limited, Sheffield*, 1989, ISBN 0-901100-24-2

Mosley, James, *British type specimen before 1831*, Oxford Bibliographical Society, Paper No. 14, Oxford, 1984, ISBN 09-01-420-11-5

Mosley, James, *Memories of an Apprentice Typefounder* (Matrix 21), London, 2000

Mores, E., Rowe, *A dissertation upon English typographical Founders and Foundries* (1788), Oxford University Press, London, 1961.

Moxon, Joseph, *Mechanick Exercises on the whole Art of Printing,* (1683) Edited Davis and Carter, Oxford University Press, London, second edition, 1962

Reed, Talbot, B., *History of the Old English Letter Foundries,* Faber and Faber, London, 1952

Savage, William, *A dictionary of the art of printing*, London, 1841

Stower, Caleb, *The Printers' Grammar, London,* 1808

Smith, T. W., *The autobiography of Thomas White Smith*, H. W. Caslon and Company Limited, published privately circa, 1904

Stephenson, Lt. Col. Sir Henry K., *Printing: some account of its invention... and later developments in England.* Published privately by Stephenson Blake and Company Limited, Sheffield, 1941

Twyman, Michael, *Printing 1770-1970*, Oak Knoll Press, British Library, University of Reading, 1998, ISBN 0-7123-4596-5 (BL)

Updike, Daniel Berkeley, *Printing Types,* Oak Knoll Press and British Library, London, 2001, ISBN 0-7123-4734-8

OLD STYLE TAIL PIECES

Fig 50 Tail Pieces from the *SB Types* Specimen Book, 1952

Appendix VI

The Ancestry of English Typefounding

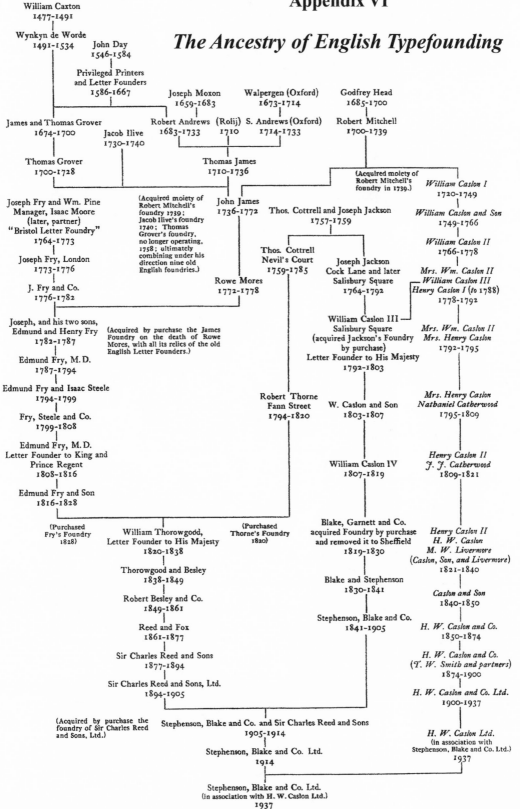

William Caxton
1477-1491

Wynkyn de Worde
1491-1534

John Day
1546-1584

Privileged Printers
and Letter Founders
1586-1667

Joseph Moxon
1659-1683

Walpergen (Oxford)
1673-1714

Godfrey Head
1685-1700

James and Thomas Grover
1674-1700

Jacob Ilive
1730-1740

Robert Andrews (Rolij)
1683-1733   1710

S. Andrews (Oxford)
1714-1733

Robert Mitchell
1700-1739

Thomas Grover
1700-1728

Thomas James
1710-1736

(Acquired moiety of
Robert Mitchell's
foundry in 1739.)

William Caslon I
1720-1749

Joseph Fry and Wm. Pine
Manager, Isaac Moore
(later, partner)
"Bristol Letter Foundry"
1764-1773

(Acquired moiety of
Robert Mitchell's
foundry 1739;
Jacob Ilive's foundry
1740; Thomas
Grover's foundry,
no longer operating,
1758; ultimately
combining under his
direction nine old
English foundries.)

John James
1736-1772

Thos. Cottrell and Joseph Jackson
1757-1759

William Caslon and Son
1749-1766

Joseph Fry, London
1773-1776

Thos. Cottrell
Nevil's Court
1759-1785

Joseph Jackson
Cock Lane and later
Salisbury Square
1764-1792

William Caslon II
1766-1778

J. Fry and Co.
1776-1782

Rowe Mores
1772-1778

Mrs. Wm. Caslon II
William Caslon III
Henry Caslon I (to 1788)
1778-1792

Joseph, and his two sons,
Edmund and Henry Fry
1782-1787

(Acquired by purchase the James
Foundry on the death of Rowe
Mores, with all its relics of the old
English Letter Founders.)

William Caslon III
Salisbury Square
(acquired Jackson's Foundry
by purchase)
Letter Founder to His Majesty
1792-1803

Mrs. Wm. Caslon II
Mrs. Henry Caslon
1792-1795

Edmund Fry, M.D.
1787-1794

Edmund Fry and Isaac Steele
1794-1799

Robert Thorne
Fann Street
1794-1820

W. Caslon and Son
1803-1807

Mrs. Henry Caslon
Nathaniel Catherwood
1795-1809

Fry, Steele and Co.
1799-1808

Edmund Fry, M.D.
Letter Founder to King and
Prince Regent
1808-1816

William Caslon IV
1807-1819

Henry Caslon II
J. J. Catherwood
1809-1821

Edmund Fry and Son
1816-1828

(Purchased
Fry's Foundry
1828)

William Thorowgodd,
Letter Founder to His Majesty
1820-1838

(Purchased
Thorne's Foundry
1820)

Blake, Garnett and Co.
acquired Foundry by purchase
and removed it to Sheffield
1819-1830

Henry Caslon II
H. W. Caslon
M. W. Livermore
(Caslon, Son, and Livermore)
1821-1840

Thorowgood and Besley
1838-1849

Blake and Stephenson
1830-1841

Caslon and Son
1840-1850

Robert Besley and Co.
1849-1861

Stephenson, Blake and Co.
1841-1905

H. W. Caslon and Co.
1850-1874

Reed and Fox
1861-1877

Sir Charles Reed and Sons
1877-1894

H. W. Caslon and Co.
(T. W. Smith and partners)
1874-1900

Sir Charles Reed and Sons, Ltd.
1894-1905

H. W. Caslon and Co. Ltd.
1900-1937

(Acquired by purchase the
foundry of Sir Charles Reed
and Sons, Ltd.)

Stephenson, Blake and Co. and Sir Charles Reed and Sons
1905-1914

H. W. Caslon Ltd.
(in association with
Stephenson, Blake and Co. Ltd.)
1937

Stephenson, Blake and Co. Ltd.
1914

Stephenson, Blake and Co. Ltd.
(in association with H. W. Caslon Ltd.)
1937

INDEX

A

Alphabetical list of Printing Types, 219
Alphabetical check list of SB Typefaces, 225

B

Bacon, Clay, 14, 16, 19, 41
Bacon, Henry Andrew, 19-20, 41
Baskerville, John, 8
Benson, Joseph, 28
Benton, Lyn Boyd, 81-82
Benton, M. F., 134
Bertaut, Emile, 82, 128
Berte, Anthony Francis, 61
Besley, Robert, 104
Bessemer, Henry, 61
Boulsover, Thomas, 3, 17
Bower, William, 14, 16, 19
British and Colonial Printer, 90, 101
Bruce, David, 61

C

Catherwood, Nathaniel, 23
Caslon Typefoundry, 91
Chiswick Press, 78
Church, William, 61
Cotterell, Robert, 13
Cotterell, Thomas, 10, 12, 103
Crapper, Ernest, 202
Cutlers' Company, 3, 16, 142

D

De Little, Robert, 179-80
Dickinson, Ken, 176

E

Edmonds, Denys, 195

F

Figgins, James, 75
Figgins, Vincent, 11, 78
Firth, Mark, 86, 88
Fishenden, Robert Bertram, 148, 153-56, 170
Fournier, Pierre Simon, 6, 8
Fox, Benjamin, 104, 176
Fry, Joseph, 104

G

Garnett. William Henry, 17, 19, 23, 28, 32, 37-38, 41, 121
Giddins, William R., 91-92
Goodhue, Bertram, 132
Gorner, Karl, 129
Grah, Richard, 158
Grandison, William, 80-81, 125
Grandjean, Phillipe, 6
Greaves, William, 64

H

Hamilton Manufacturing Company, 91
Hansard, Thomas, 17-18, 28, 34
Hanson, E. B., 113, 148
Harling, Robert, 174
Harrison, Victor, 187
Hay, J. W., 117
Hetherington, William, 187
Hemingway, John, 123
Hogarth series, 114

Hughes, Thomas, 28
Huntsman, Benjamin, 2

I

Imprimerie Royale du Louvre,
    6, 8

J

Jackson, Joseph, 10-12
Jenson, Nicholas, 6
Jones, George W., 147, 172

K

Kelmscott Press, 134
Kirkwood, William, 127-28

L

Lady Willoughby's Diary, 78
Lee, Geoffrey, 176
Levenworth, William, 81, 93

M

McLaren, James, 81, 124
McRay, John Findley, 147
Meggitt, William W., 127, 129
Miller and Richard, 78-81, 140, 145, 168
Monotype Corporation Limited, 158
Moore, Isaac, 104
Morison, Stanley, 173

N

Names of SB Fonts, 219
Northend, J. W., 152, 154-55

O

Oliver, William, 123-25

P

Pivotal Caster, 61
Pechey, Elisha, 82-85, 88, 113
Phemister, Alexander P., 78-79

Powell, Arthur, 74
Printers' Register, 74, 90

R

Reed, Charles, 73, 103, 105, 120
Reed, Eliot, 105-107
Rochaix, M. Jean, 124-25
Romains du Roi, 6
Ross, James, 122

S

Sheffield Furnace-pump, 61
*Sheffield Independent and Commercial
    Register,* 28-29
Sheffield Plate, 3, 17
Slater, John, 14
Smith, Henry Bannister, 42, 67-68
Smith, Thomas White, 68, 70-72, 83, 98,
    118-19

T

Tarrant, Frederick, 125
Taylor and Watkinson, 99
The Imprint, 170
Thomas Turton and Sons, 144
Thompson, William, 38-39, 66
Thorne. Robert, 10, 15, 47, 49, 103, 174
Thorowgood, William, 104
Tice, Francis Hayes, 127
Typefounders' strike, 44-45

U

Updike, Daniel Berkeley, 132
Uttley, J. E., 134

V

Ventris, F. W., 94

W

Welch, Patrick, 80
Wells, Darius, 81, 93
Wright, James, 192